CRAZY JUNGLE LOVE

Murder, Madness, Money & Monkeys

CRAZY JUNGLE LOVE

Murder, Madness, Money & Monkeys

Based on a true story

by

Carol Blair Vaughn

Published by

The Costa Rica Star®

To my Father

Who taught me how to thrive in Latin America:

> ~ Learn the language
> ~ Learn the culture
> ~ Learn how to stay out of jail

Thank you, Papi!

Illustrated Map of Costa Rica

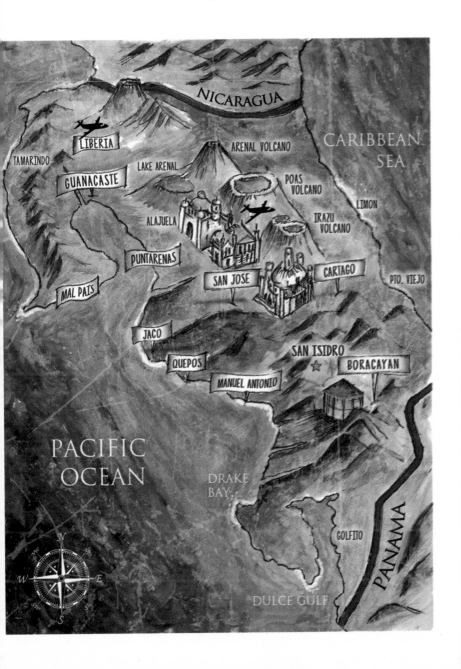

Gabriel García Márquez
1927-2014

Márquez was a Colombian novelist, journalist, short-story writer, and screenwriter, widely considered the most popular and perhaps best writer in the Spanish language since Cervantes. He was the winner of the 1982 Nobel Prize in Literature. Called Gabo or Gabito by his friends, Márquez was most famous for popularizing a literary style known as Magical Realism which uses magical elements and events in otherwise ordinary and realistic situations.

Márquez's best known books are *One Hundred Years of Solitude* (1967), *The Autumn of the Patriarch* (1975) and *Love in the Time of Cholera* (1985). Former President Bill Clinton is said to have called *One Hundred Years of Solitude* his favorite novel. In 2010 a Costa Rican film maker, Hilda Hidalgo, adapted Márquez's *Love and Other Demons* for an award-winning film by the same title.

Many of Márquez's works are set in the fictional village of Macondo, and most explore the themes of love and solitude.

A lesson Gabo is said to have learned from his own grandfather was also apt for the Bender death and drama:

"You can't imagine how much a dead man weighs."

Prison at El Buen Pastor

"The spirit of her invincible heart guided her through the shadows."

Gabriel García Márquez – *One Hundred Years of Solitude*

October 16, 2014

Ann Patton Bender sits outdoors at a communal picnic table in El Buen Pastor Women's Prison in San José, Costa Rica, Central America's verdant jewel. She's sitting alone, which doesn't bother her, because alone time in prison is rare. She enjoys the sunshine on her back, which warms her comfortingly—even the chest port that pumps medicine into her ailing heart seems less foreign in the sun. Ann has a lethal blood clot hovering just above her heart that medicine is hopefully helping to shrink. October is the height of the rainy season in Costa Rica, with daily downpours usually arriving later in the afternoon. Ann had paid her 150 colones (30 cents) wash fee, allowing her to bathe earlier that morning in a bucket of cold water, and bathing always made her feel better. This was one of the rare moments in prison when she felt warm, thanks to the powerful equatorial Costa Rican sunshine.

Ann looks down at the food in front of her. It's the same every day, always served in a blue plastic tray divided into three sections. One section is for beans, one for noodles, and the biggest one, of course, is for rice. Ann's tray holds only rice. Most prisoners in Costa Rica rely on family members to provide any good nutrition, since prison rations are meager, starchy, and not particularly healthy. Vegetables and meat are rare.

CRAZY JUNGLE LOVE

Later, looking back, this was an amazing contrast to the meals she and her husband John had shared, tucked in together at the long counter of the chef's kitchen in their 55,000-square-foot mansion in the south of Costa Rica, overlooking their own private jungle. *Those* were some wonderful meals, she reminisced. Ann yearned for both the comfortable surroundings she had known, and even more poignantly, for the man who had shared her life then as her lover, husband, and soul mate.

Ann smiles, thinking of how good her breakfast had been that morning. Two days a week, El Buen Pastor allows Ann's boyfriend, Greg Fischer, to bring her food from the outside. He had outdone himself today. He brought a nice chunk of cheddar cheese, sardines, cookies, several tins of nuts, and a large box of American breakfast cereal, which she would eat without milk throughout the day to keep up her energy and spirits. Oh, and some wonderful apples from San Gerardo de Dota. Apples are a rare treat in Costa Rica, and these were even locally grown! Ann would either eat the food herself, or trade it for cigarettes—her only remaining vice.

A prison buddy of Ann's approached and sat down. Her name was Sara, and she was looking for lunch company, as well as a tampon, as she had run out. Ann said she was sorry she couldn't help. Ann had endured an emergency hysterectomy following her nervous breakdown in 2001, which turned out to be a blessing in this place where good hygiene was challenging and supplies hard to come by. Ann and Sara had become friends during Ann's nine-month incarceration. Friends were key to survival in a Costa Rican prison.

Sara was forty-eight years old, to Ann's forty-four, and was serving a five-year, four-month sentence for selling crack cocaine and a one-year, eight-month sentence for attempting to bribe the arresting officer. Those sentences could not be served concurrently, and so she faced a term of seven years. Sara's sentence had been plea bargained down to this lesser number in court, *gracias a Dios* (thank God). Most of Ann's fellow prisoners were incarcerated for minor drug offenses, with major jail times assigned.

Sara's life story could not have been more different from Ann's. Sara had fled her family at age thirteen to escape sexual abuse at the hands of her uncle. Young, uneducated, and lacking in family support or opportunities, Sara soon became hooked on crack cocaine. She worked in the illicit sex business (prostitution is legal in Costa Rica, but only for of-age adults), and she eventually found herself arrested for selling small quantities of crack. In a desperate attempt to avoid jail, Sara tried to bribe the arresting officer with 2,010 colones, or $3.75. It was all she had.

CRAZY JUNGLE LOVE

Ann and Sara were about the same age, both smoked cigarettes, and both were childless. Sara looked after the less healthy and more fragile Ann, and Greg always made sure Sara was rewarded with gifts and treats at each of his visits. Ann was known to be very generous to the women who shared her *ámbito*, or cell block, but it's almost certain that none of her fellow prisoners knew that Ann and her husband had arrived in Costa Rica twelve years earlier with $600 million dollars—that would have surprised them a lot.

Ann Bender had been sentenced to twenty-two years in prison for the murder of her husband, John Felix Bender, in 2010. Ann always maintained that his death was a suicide, one which she had tried desperately to prevent. It was not his first attempt, she alleged. Costa Rica had tried her twice for the same crime, which wasn't unusual because unlike the United States, there is no prohibition against double jeopardy. Ann was acquitted in the first trial, but in the second trial Ann was charged with manslaughter, convicted, and was taken in handcuffs to Preventive Detention at El Buen Pastor Women's Prison.

Both Ann and her husband John had been diagnosed with bipolar disorder (manic depression), and had slowly been going wicked-crazy in their isolated, sprawling mansion known as Bender Dome. The property was located in the middle of their own 5,000-acre nature preserve, called Boracayán, in La Florida de Barú, Pérez Zeledón, Costa

Rica. They had created their dream life, in their dream home, until John Bender ended up dead of a single gunshot wound behind his right ear. Ann and John were the only two people present in the room on the night of John's death.

Ann had gone from her life married to a genius hedge fund manager worth $600 million, enjoying an isolated but extremely privileged lifestyle in one of the prettiest countries in the world, to sharing a living space with some of the worst of the worst female criminals. That scenario sounds like a recipe for a total disaster, yet Ann somehow seemed to hold her own among her fellow inmates, even managing to make friends and smile occasionally. Helpful to her survival, undoubtedly, was the fact that Ann spoke perfect Spanish and could communicate with both the prisoners and guards.

Life at El Buen Pastor (The Good Shepherd) was horrendous. Two British women who were incarcerated there in 2009 told their families, "Oh my God, they've brought us to the zoo." They reported no flushing toilets, no hot water, not enough wooden bunk beds for everyone, not enough mattresses, a scarcity of toilet paper, and worst of all, sometimes the food ran out and they would go to bed hungry. There was one public phone that inmates were allowed to use on Fridays for two minutes each. That phone could not make long distance calls, which Ann craved, to be able to speak with her family back in Michigan.

Amazingly, Ann Bender managed. The women around her took pity on her and helped her survive. Bipolar disorder is isolating and debilitating, but Ticas (female Costa Ricans; male Costa Ricans and mixed groups are called Ticos) are kind and nourishing women, and seemed to feel a kinship to Ann's tragedy. Every one of them had been duped by a man, robbed by a man, betrayed by a man, or let down by the legal system. Ann identified with them, and they rallied around her. As Christians, they believed in redemption and second chances. As a lapsed Jew, Ann surely drew strength from their convictions.

Perhaps Ann didn't share many details of her case with her cellmates, but anyone looking at the eighty-pound, sickly Ann Bender could certainly understand a possible motive of this frail woman. She was being injected with a dirty river water "cure" by her crazed husband, was suffering from Lyme disease and needed a cane to walk, was getting sicker and sicker both mentally and physically—wouldn't any woman lash out to try to save her own life? Wouldn't anyone try to end both of their suffering?

Of course, the alleged $7-20 million in loose jewels found in the Bender bedroom after John's death also seemed like a pretty good motive for murder. The morning after John's death, investigators found over 3,000 gems: diamonds, sapphires, rubies, opals, you name it. Some were found beautifully arranged presentation-style in customized display cases, while others were randomly tossed on counters; still others were stuffed willy-nilly in old backpacks on the floor. What was all this? Were the Benders jewel smugglers? Had they paid import duty on this collection? Where did they get all this loot? Who did it really belong to? Was it true, as Ann claimed, that the gems had been purchased as an investment during the global financial crisis of 2008-2009? The OIJ (Organismo de Investigación Judicial, Costa Rica's Judicial Investigation Police), similar to the American FBI but more powerful, who were tasked with investigating John's death had more than a reasonable number of doubts and hundreds of questions. Only Ann Bender, however, went to jail.

<<>>

Across Latin America, there has always been a disproportionate punishment for low-level, non-violent drug offenses. Seventy-five percent of Ann's fellow inmates were petty drug criminals. The punishment dispensed always seemed worse for women. Drug-trafficking organizations often took advantage of women's poverty and the need to provide for their families. Women were induced to carry illegal drugs, often across international borders, as *mulas de drogas,* or drug mules, with the moniker implying just how disrespected and vulnerable they would become, while the traffickers higher up the ladder reaped massive profits and escaped scot-free.

This was the story of Johanna, another of Ann's fellow prisoners, who was serving a six-year, six-month sentence for selling pot. Johanna had grown up in a household of drug dealers, but when Johanna's mother—the family's primary breadwinner—was busted for dealing, Johanna agreed to carry a suitcase of drugs to Europe. Instead, she was forced to swallow eighty-four latex-wrapped cocaine packets. She almost died, saving herself by telling officials what she had swallowed, at which point they hospitalized her. When she was released, she went right back to dealing drugs to support her family.

Johanna was a rebel at El Buen Pastor, and often ended up in "Las Tumbas," or "The Tombs," the equivalent of solitary confinement, located in a small, dark building at the very back of the compound. They say the rats there are the biggest on the property. Like ninety percent of the other women incarcerated at El Buen Pastor, Johanna had three children. Providing for those children could prove difficult, if not impossible, from prison. Drugs were common, available from both guards and inmates. Inmates outnumbered staff 511 to 180 in the Women's Prison. Inmates report constant thievery of everything from hair brushes, to toilet paper, to underwear, to drugs.

As shocking as El Buen Pastor Women's Prison may be to some, it is much less appalling than other Central American jails and prisons. *Agence France Presse* (AFP) said in 2015, "Costa Rica, a relatively well-off Central American nation, is far from being the worst example of prison overcrowding in Latin America." El Salvador's jails are 300 percent overcrowded, and Nicaragua's are 225 percent overcrowded. Costa Rica's prisons have a capacity for 9,000 prisoners, but are currently holding 14,000. There are three new prisons scheduled to open in Costa Rica in 2017. They will be called "Integral Care Units", and the one closest to Boracayán will have a capacity of 246 inmates.

Caroline Kennedy (the only remaining child of John F. Kennedy) visited El Buen Pastor Prison, not long after Ann was released, and chronicled her observations in July 2014 on her blog: *anywhereiwander.wordpress.com My Travels: Places I Have Been—People I Have Met.* Kennedy wrote of her experience at the jail,

"Every day El Buen Pastor witnesses its share of fights, most are petty feuds, the settling of scores, outbreaks of anger and frustration, but others are far more serious. There are some very tough women inside who manage to smuggle in knives and other weapons. They are constantly battling for favors from the guards or a position of power over the weaker inmates. Sometimes the prison officers break up the fights before they turn nasty, other times they are too intimidated to intervene, and many times they are forced to call in the police."

Kennedy also commented on the drug culture within the prison, "From cannabis to crack cocaine, everything, it seems, is available at Buen Pastor for the right price." All of the above are strictly prohibited within the Costa Rican prison system, per Executive Decree No. 25.883, governing the confiscation of drugs and the control of medications within the Costa Rican prison system. Problems of enforcement are certainly not unique to jails in Costa Rica; far from it.

The ratio of inmates to doctors at El Buen Pastor was 500 to 1, which made it extremely difficult for Ann to get the medical care she needed. Because there was no hot water, Ann found it very difficult to keep her heart medicine-dispensing chest port clean, and eventually it was removed. Boyfriend Greg Fischer, in an interview with *Inside Costa Rica*, complimented the kindness and care that the one physician on duty managed to give Ann. He said, "If I had to serve time in jail anywhere, I think I would choose Costa Rica. Folks here are compassionate and caring and generous, as much as they can be."

<<>>

El Buen Pastor (known in the streets as El Buen Pa') is located in an old convent that was condemned but then put back into service to alleviate overcrowding in other prisons. There is a large painted mural at the front gate depicting a lovely woman with high cheekbones, pouty full lips, and flowing hair; she is flanked by two birds, one blue and one red. The white face between a red bird and a blue bird reminds one of the Costa Rican flag—and the American flag as well.

There is a tall chain-link fence surrounding the compound, topped by razor wire. Armed guards watch near the entrance and from the turret at the top of the building. If you squint, you can see that some time ago this was a rather lovely property. The guards are jovial and friendly, although less so for visitors of Ann Bender. Ann's presence here has attracted international media attention, much of it critical of Costa Rica and its judicial system. The guards are suspicious of any mention of Ann's name, and don't allow anyone to go beyond the entrance area. The media coverage has clearly not been appreciated; Ticos are very proud people, especially regarding their legal system, and don't like to be shown in a negative light.

CRAZY JUNGLE LOVE

A writer for *Inside Costa Rica*, one of the online English-language newspapers in Costa Rica, tried to visit Ann in prison, but was turned away because there had been some unrest among the inmates, and guards felt it was unsafe for Ann to leave her ámbito. The writer left some artisanal chocolates for Ann which the heavily made-up and perfumed guard unwrapped, broke up with her pocket knife, then bunched them up with the wrapping paper and handed them off to another guard to take in to Ann. The writer never knew if Ann received the chocolates, or if she would ever be allowed another chance for an interview. The reception for the press at El Buen Pastor was not what one would call "warm."

The writer later learned that the incident which prevented her interview had been a rampage in the kitchen. It seems that the prisoners had unexpectedly been given fried chicken that day, rather than the usual inedible pieces of pork, or more commonly a meatless meal. When the prisoners discovered the treat, they basically rioted, stealing all the fried chicken to take back to their ámbito. When they reached their dorm, it was discovered that the chicken was tainted with bleach, probably from poor rinsing of the blue food trays. The inmates stampeded and were put in lockdown in their ámbito. Neither El Buen Pastor nor Costa Rica needed a story about that incident to get out in the press.

<<>>

The theme of Costa Rica having taken offense to nearly every part of Ann Bender's residency in this little country colored Ann's trials, convictions, sentencing, and incarceration. Press from around the world poured in to cover the story, then sent back scathing accounts of the trial, the justice system, and the alleged unfair treatment of a bipolar, grieving widow. The term "Ugly American" was never used in the local press, but folks sure used it in the streets.

Ugly American is the pejorative phrase used to describe what is perceived as arrogant, thoughtless, ignorant, and ethnocentric behavior of some American citizens abroad. The descriptor originated in the 1963 movie *The Ugly American*, starring Marlon Brando, about a group of Americans in Southeast Asia who exhibit a range of blundering, corrupt, and incompetent behaviors, often concentrating on impractical projects which serve their own ambitions, and ignore the needs of the local population. This was undoubtedly the impression the locals of Pérez Zeledón had of the eccentric Bender couple, living in their isolated mansion overlooking the jungle, and sitting on all that money and jewelry.

One television news reporter commented, "What would you expect to happen when two crazy Americans worth $600 million come to a developing country, throw their money around, alienate all their neighbors, kill each other, and then claim they didn't do it?" Many Ticos not only assumed Ann was absolutely guilty of murdering her husband, but were shocked at the gobs of money and man-hours being squandered on Ann's trials and conviction. They felt Ann's prosecution was an outrageous waste of public resources. Maybe it was. Ultimately, Ann was to be tried three times for John's murder.

<<>>

Ann finished her rice, and sat soaking up the sun, watching the buzzards cruise back and forth in search of a dropped or discarded morsel of food. She missed her animals from Bender Dome. Here there were rats the size of small cats who stalked around at night like they owned the place. There were raccoons that tap danced on the dormitory roof at night and woke Ann up. There were feral cats that came and went, and were adopted as pets by the prisoners who missed their own animals and children. Ann never managed to sleep very well at Buen Pastor. Bender Dome had no walls, just screens that were rolled down at night. There, wild animal visits were the norm, and a wonderful treat for Ann and John.

How she missed John today! His death was the beginning of a nightmare from which she thought she might never escape. She was sure she wouldn't last twenty-two years in this place. Mostly, she had to combat the waves of survivor's guilt that washed over her regularly. She just couldn't imagine what she could have done to save John's life. After all, she had also been very sick at the time of his death, and too weak really to win the scuffle over the 9mm Ruger John had used.

Still, not a day went by without Ann yearning for her handsome, powerful life partner, the Prince of Boracayán.

Boracayán—Bender Dome

"Crazy people are not crazy if one accepts their reasoning."

Gabriel García Márquez – *Love in the Time of Cholera*

Boracayán in Spanish means…well, nothing. The Benders made up the word because they thought it sounded like an exotic Central American plant. The happy lives they hoped to have at Boracayán were also invented and, unfortunately, the dream went sideways and John ended up dead on January 8, 2010, in their fourth floor bedroom, surrounded by 550 authentic and reproduction Tiffany lamps. The elevator to the bedroom level had been locked from within the bedroom, preventing anyone but Ann or John from entering or exiting.

Boracayán of Florida de Barú was purchased by the Benders in 1998 by buying out most of the tiny farms in the surrounding area. The purchase price was roughly $10 million, not that stunning a price for anyone worth $600 million, but a life-altering windfall for the neighbors who sold property to them. Word traveled fast that the Benders were buying up properties in Florida de Barú, and the traffic of people wanting to sell became so intense that John finally instructed locals to just stuff their deeds, surveys, and blueprints in his mailbox—he bought almost all of it. At the time of the purchase, folks in that area were still living in dilapidated farm houses with no electricity and poor road access, which became no road access during the rainy season. The farmers survived by raising unimpressive coffee crops and grazing skinny cattle.

The Benders chose that desolate part of Costa Rica precisely because it was remote and inaccessible—a bipolar disorder sufferer's dream. La Florida de Barú was the wild frontier in that era, and Costa Ricans commented about the property, "Not even a Tico would buy there!"

John said, "Perfect. This is home."

The total living space at Boracayán is about 120,000 square feet, including porches, the sculpture garden, a breathtaking view of a 600-foot waterfall, amazingly named Catarata Diamante, or Diamond Waterfall, an orchid and indigenous plant garden, and a reflecting pool stocked with tilapia. The compound has four separate houses, but the main house is the crown jewel. It has no external walls and no windows, only storm screens that roll down at night. The house self-cools from Pacific Ocean breezes during the day, and is moderately warm in the evenings. An amazing variety of wildlife wanders freely in and out at all hours, making the house a living statement of the famous Latin expression, *Mi casa es su casa* (My house is your house).

Nowadays the Bender Dome is looking fairly sad, since there are only two staff members left to look after things, and the jungle always seems to swallow properties faster than they can be maintained. The mansion stands dark and lonely, as if waiting for its masters to return.

Prior to the purchase of Boracayán, many Americans had already begun buying up Costa Rican real estate in a gringo land-grab, which furthered their reputation as greedy, self-interested northerners. A gringo is an often affectionate, but occasionally insulting term used to describe a foreigner in Costa Rica, usually an American, Canadian, or European. But the majority of those purchases were up north in the affluent Guanacaste area. In contrast, La Florida de Barú is in the southwestern portion of Costa Rica, 2,200 feet above the Pacific Ocean. This was virtually no-man's land in 1998.

This region is considered fairly dangerous, with many poisonous snakes, most famously the *terciopelo* (fer-de-lance, or velvet pit viper), and many other deadly species. The eyelash viper has been known to put a household pet down in seconds. There are warring monkey tribes, venomous spiders, stinging and biting bugs; and let's not forget the armed animal poachers hunting for their family's dinner.

This is what the Benders chose as home. This is where they founded the area's first animal rescue center, which they called Refugio de Vida Silvestre de Boracayán del Sur, or Wildlife Refuge of Boracayán of the South.

Contrast that scenario to that of celebrities like actor Mel Gibson who bought a 500-acre estate at Playa Barrigona (Big Belly Beach) in Nicoya, Guanacaste. Playa Barrigona was bought largely to get away from the paparazzi, but like the Benders, Gibson seemed to have brought his troubles with him. Currently back on the market again for $30 million, Gibson reportedly never visits because he is allegedly involved in a long-standing dispute with the municipality of Nicoya for blocking public access to the beach and violating maritime construction laws.

A visitor to Playa Barrigona commented about it, "So remote and jungley—no wonder Gibson went bonkers." This might have also been said about Boracayán.

<<>>

When Ann daydreamed about home during her months in prison, what she missed most were her animals. First and foremost was her ever-present companion and protector, a German shepherd named Millie. Millie kept her company when John was in his office working or in his custom gymnasium exercising. She accompanied Ann on her strolls around the grounds and made her feel secure, a feeling that Ann had craved since childhood, and finally felt at Boracayán with her handsome, beefy husband and a German shepherd at her side.

Also among Ann's favorites was Toth, her great black hawk who would eat tenderly from her hand. There was Lily, a three-toed sloth Ann had rescued and brought back to health. Lily was to be one of the first guests at Refugio de Vida Silvestre, and was amazingly tame—and of course—slothfully slow. A weekly bathroom break is normal sloth behavior in order to avoid leaving the trees more frequently and being attacked by predators. She learned to use the kitchen sink as her bathroom once a week.

Most amazing of the Bender pets was their jaguarundi, Leo, a seldom-seen weasel-like animal of the New World cat species. Jaguarundis have a long, slender body, short legs, rounded ears, and a small, flattened head. Before the time of the Spanish conquest of Central America, natives of Costa Rica kept jaguarundis as family pets. Now they are on their way to extinction, nearly eradicated by farmers trying to protect their chickens.

Ann was fascinated by Leo. Jaguarundis are very vocal cats with at least thirteen distinct calls recorded, including a purr, whistle, scream, chatter, yap, and a bird-like chirp.

The animals were very useful in keeping up the Benders' spirits. Unfortunately, any change in their pets' health resulted in a sympathetic change in the Benders' mental health also. When John's favorite bird, Wacker, was killed by a wild possum in the kitchen, John plunged into a deep depression. Ann felt this hastened John's suicide.

The Benders had to hire a team of armed rangers to chase off poachers who were accustomed to hunting birds and wild animals on the Bender property before it was Boracayán. There were peccaries (pigmy boars), and tepezcuintles (lowland pacas), both of which provide some of the best meat in that area. The birds were collectors' items: parrots, toucans, motmots, pecho amarillos, hawks, and other brightly colored wild jungle birds. During the day when the metal screens were up, the Benders often were visited by these creatures, and they always enjoyed watching the bird life from one of their balconies as the sun went down.

The Benders hired six full-time caretakers for the animals, and brought in veterinarians as needed. Their favorite vet was Dr. Adrián Solano of Corral del Sol Animal Hospital in Pérez Zeledón, the closest town to Boracayán. Dr. Adrian spoke perfect English, and was in fact educated at the renowned University of Guelph, Ontario Veterinary College, in Canada, and then at the University of California's Veterinary School, UC Davis campus; both are recognized as top-notch veterinary schools. "Dr. A" remembers the Benders as being a bit odd, but also as devoted animal lovers who spared no expense in their care and medical treatment. Dr. A especially remarked on Ann's gentle way with her pets and her ability to share their pain when they were injured. Ann knew all about physical and emotional pain.

Construction of Boracayán—including the moat and helipad—took four years and the labor of some 500 local workers, which made the Benders both hugely popular and also a target for malevolent neighbors. They became increasingly paranoid, which can only be partially attributed to their mental illness. Not everyone in La Florida de Barú liked the Benders, and they would soon discover that there were even more haters back home in the United States.

The Benders reforested the property extensively in an attempt to undo soil damage caused by years of coffee farming. They intended to make Boracayán into the region's only large-scale private haven for endangered, abandoned, or injured animals. Those animals were their tribe. John had also begun his new project as director of Exponential Biotherapies, Inc., a drug discovery and development company based in McLean, Virginia, which provided drugs to treat a range of inflammatory conditions from radiation sickness to avian flu disorders. He had plans to discover and experiment with lesser-known jungle plants that could be used to treat the refuge's animals—and hopefully, eventually, also lead to a cure for Ann.

CRAZY JUNGLE LOVE

Randi Kaye of *CNN News*, who did a special about the Benders in May, 2014, called *Inside the Mystery: Love & Death in Paradise*; described their situation: "It was supposed to be their lives, their future, but their lives took a terrible turn."

<<>>

The house itself is round, four stories high, with a view on a clear day of the Pacific Ocean to the west, Nicaragua to the north, and Panama to the south. Ann's light decorating touch is in evidence throughout. The real artistry, however, came from John's architectural design of open-plan living. We're talking *way* open, with no interior walls, not even around the bathroom. Whatever you could imagine might want to come visit, apparently did, from bats, to lizards, to frogs, to moths, to birds, to bugs of every description.

Ann and John loved to lie in bed in the early morning listening to the jungle waking up, and watching the fog roll in and over them while they lay in bed. It was like waking up in the clouds.

The master bedroom took up the entire fourth floor and was sparingly furnished with a giant bed—John's deathbed as it turned out—some snazzy built-in closet space, and of course the 550 Tiffany lamps that encircled the room, casting their magical multi-colored lighting over everything. Ann said that John had bought all the Tiffanys to "brighten her outlook on the world." Neighbors reported looking up at the house at night, and seeing it completely dark, except for the bejeweled crown of lights at the top—the jeweled crown of the Benders of Boracayán.

On the third floor was an office space with a giant custom-made desk and a state-of-the-art computer for John. In fact, almost all of the furniture at Boracayán had been specially constructed to accommodate John's enormous frame. Although John was technically retired (even at age forty-four), he continued to keep his hand in the stock market, especially when he saw the impending financial slide of 2008-2009, where he stood to lose a good portion of his millions. It was John's idea to transition from stocks and bonds to the collection of jewels. Jewels are easy to hide, easy to transport, and anyway, Ann loved them. John told his hedge fund manager and best friend, Pete DeLisi, that he was buying hard assets due to the global recession. He was using the jewels as currency. They owned about $7-20 million worth of jewels at the time of John's death. John stayed on top of the international financial scene, including the prices of jewels, via a massive satellite dish that they installed in the compound.

CRAZY JUNGLE LOVE

It was a charming, romantic life the Benders lived in Costa Rica. Said Ann, "We chose Costa Rica, and we were in LOVE."

Every evening, just before sunset, the Benders would go to the second floor of the Dome, which housed a chef's kitchen and an enormous dining area, and walk out onto the balcony to hear, smell, and enjoy the cacophony of the jungle, their Xanadu. They would wrap their arms around each other and stand gazing out over their estate until the sun set completely. Below them, their heavily armed security guards patrolled the perimeter, keeping them safe.

Some nights they could barely hear themselves think on the balcony, due to the sound of the blue cracker butterflies in the trees. There are nine species of cracker butterflies in Costa Rica, and some nights it sounded like they were all visiting at once. Crackers (*Hamadryas*) perch upside down in trees in the evening, and crack their wings to attract mates and ward off other males. They feed off tree sap, unlike most butterflies who feed off of nectar, and climb higher and higher in the trees as night approaches. The Benders were themselves exotic animals, and gravitated toward other animals of their tribe at Boracayán—until it all started to go to hell.

<<>>

In April 2001, John and Ann were traveling up the Quebradas Road in Pérez Zeledón toward the Biological Center (Centro Biológico de Quebradas) on a lovely afternoon. They were driving in their usual Ford F-350 and were on a mission to buy seed from Fudesemillas, a nonprofit seed company run by a lovely British lady named Rosemary Sylvester Bradley. Rosie was a microbiologist by trade, and sold the highest-quality seeds that the Benders had found anywhere near Pérez Zeledón. Boracayán deserved the very best.

Just as they were approaching the entrance to the swing bridge to Rosie's *quinta* (country house), a car came roaring up the dirt road and cut them off. The driver of the car jumped out, yelling "John Bender, you're coming with us!" All of the men in the car had guns.

Two men aimed guns at John's head, ordered him out of the truck, and marched him toward their vehicle. John was a large, muscular man, and began to resist, at which point shots were fired near his feet, so he complied with his abductors. By this time Ann had screamed in panic, bringing Rosie running across her bridge to see what was happening. Rosie insisted the men show identification, and it turned out that they were plainclothes police officers who arrested John and hauled him to the local police station where he was shown a summons. The cops said, "John Bender, you have been served."

CRAZY JUNGLE LOVE

The summons was related to an ugly legal battle Bender was involved in with his former business partner, Joel Silverman. Silverman had joined Bender in an offshore investment hedge fund known as Amber Arbitrage, which was based in the Cayman Islands. The agreement was that Silverman brought in investors, while Bender managed the portfolio and picked the investments. The two partners knew each other from an illicit backgammon ring, involving some serious gambling, in which they both participated, located on Long Island, New York. They had agreed to split the income from Amber 75% Bender, 25% Silverman. They had never put the deal in writing. Silverman was looking to get paid an additional $98 million he claimed he was owed.

Silverman received wages and performance bonuses between 1997 and 1999 totaling $1.7 million in accordance with their oral agreement. In 2000, Bender suffered a stroke, allegedly while on his honeymoon with Ann, and while recovering, made the decision to pull out of Amber Arbitrage, leave the United States, renounce his US citizenship, and move to Boracayán, which he had purchased in 1998. At that time Amber Arbitrage was valued at over $500 million. Love mixed with bipolar disorder often leads to impulsive, reckless decisions.

Silverman, already stressed out by a contentious divorce he was going through with his wife Linda, flipped out at Bender's plans, calling him a tax cheat and accusing him of hiding assets from both the IRS and Silverman himself. Both accusations may very well have been true. Silverman was beyond irate, and followed Bender all the way to Pérez Zeledón, hiring goons to scare the stuffing out of John and Ann to get revenge for his supposed financial loss.

The Benders were, in fact, terrified. Newcomers to Costa Rica, not yet proficient in Spanish, unarmed and unprotected, confused by the accusations, and worried about kidnappings in Central America, it took the rest of the night to process John out of the Pérez Zeledón police station, facilitated by Rosemary's kind help. Rosie noticed that the Benders presented passports from Grenada, rather than the US, and wondered what kind of trouble they were in back in the US. Grenada is an island country rumored among international visitors to protect shady and very wealthy characters and investors. Rosie had already heard that her seed-buying customers were very unpopular among their neighbors. Some folks were unhappy that they had not been hired to help build Boracayán, while others were pissed off that their favorite hunting ground was now off-limits to them. It made it harder for the locals to feed their families.

A security expert the next week told the Benders bluntly, "My advice is to get the hell out of here—now." They left immediately for Canada for three months, and when they returned, they hired some goons of their own, guards with paramilitary training who were armed with AK-47s. Millie the German shepherd now had backup, and Lily the sloth could use her toilet/sink unmolested. Ann could still not get over her fear and trepidation. Her mental health was deteriorating.

The Love Story

"That casual glance was the beginning of a cataclysm of love that had still not ended half a century later."

Gabriel García Márquez – *Love in the Time of Cholera*

CRAZY JUNGLE LOVE

The story of John and Ann Bender is at its very heart a love story.

If you've never been to Latin America, listened to Latin American music, or read Latin American literature, you probably have only a very vague notion of what love is like in Latin America. It's not a cheesy backdrop for an episode of *The Bachelorette* television show. There is real passion, even Shakespearean passion, which blossoms and thrives, including the accompanying heartbreak and tears.

Ann was born in Brazil; her father was an American banking executive, and her mother a Brazilian citizen. She became a naturalized US citizen as a youngster. She understood love. She was right there in the mix. People who are bipolar tend to be very passionate, "hot" folks. They burn too close to the sun sometimes. John was as hot as they come; he was on fire in his business, his investments, his physical appearance, and most of all, his adoration of Ann Patton Bender.

The Nobel prize-winning author Gabriel García Márquez described the Bender type of love exquisitely in his 1985 novel *Love in the Time of Cholera,* the story of a land where love was in the air like malaria and in the water like cholera—its infections inescapable. In Spanish, cholera can be both a disease and an impassioned madness. For the

Benders, it was both. The Bender love was operatic, quixotic, Dionysian, and a little sick.

Ann met John in March of 1998 at his Golden Mountain Farm in Charlottesville, Virginia, where he owned a sprawling 100-acre property with a lovely pond at its center. Ann was new to the area, and was introduced to John by a former girlfriend who had dated John earlier in his life.

Charlottesville, or "C'Ville" to locals, is a slowed-down kind of place, with a population of 48,000 and the proud home of University of Virginia. Thomas Jefferson was from Charlottesville. The Dave Matthews Band makes its home in Charlottesville; it's a laid-back, chilled-out environment.

John had purchased Golden Mountain Farm in 1996, telling his friends that he felt the need to live "somewhere green." It was both green and gorgeous, and the pond soothed his soul. You can watch a video of Golden Mountain Farm on YouTube at *"John Bender's Pond,"* with a dirge soundtrack in the background. Friends of John created the video in his memory after his death.

Ann, then twenty-eight years old, was a drop-dead gorgeous and exotic ingénue who vaguely resembled Audrey Hepburn: dark, delicate, elegant, and petite. Her father was an executive at Chase Manhattan Bank and had been working in Rio de Janeiro at the time of Ann's birth. Kenneth Patton III and his wife Gigi had one other child,

Ann's older brother Kenneth. The two siblings remain close and supportive, even today.

When John met Ann, she weighed a slight 105 pounds, tiny for her 5☐3☐ height. She was considered exotic by C'Villers, with her Brazilian past and refined demeanor. Ann had spent her youth in private schools, at private parties, on private beaches, and by age twenty-two, was contending with her own private hell of bipolar disorder. She had lived in Lisbon, London, and New York, finally earning a degree in Fine Arts from Ithaca College in upstate New York.

After graduation, Ann worked at Maryland Institute College of Art in Baltimore, an appropriate job for someone with her privileged background, but in a city that failed miserably in comparison with her previous sophisticated residences. In a snap, bipolar disorder-tinged decision, she decided to move to the more gentrified Charlottesville, where one of the first people she was introduced to was John Bender.

John Bender was a catch-and-a-half. Tall, powerfully built, handsome, educated, John was the complete package. He was destined to be the Cary Grant to partner Ann's Audrey Hepburn. He had worked briefly as a male model, and it was rumored that he had even once starred in a porno movie. He was exciting, rich, and from a powerful family. John was the older of two sons of Paul and Margie Bender of Philadelphia. Paul was a well-respected legal scholar who had worked for the Justice Department under the Clinton Administration. He retired from public service to teach law at Penn State University, John's alma mater.

John showed his mathematical genius at an early age, a genius that brought him phenomenal success in the stock market, the hedge fund arena, and in gambling—both legal and illegal. Atlantic City barred him from their casinos at one time for card counting. Only his most stupid or naïve friends would ever bet against him in any contest. John was a winner. He attended Penn State in the Physics Department, where he thought his only option upon graduation would be working for the Reagan administration arms build-up, helping to develop new ways to kill people.

Mercifully, that path was detoured abruptly on the day he visited a friend at the Philadelphia Stock Exchange. Here were people involved in high-energy options trading, making tons of money, and using skills John had in spades. He began buying options with his own money the very next day and winning—big time. Even his friends began asking him to buy winning options for them. By the time John met Ann, he was on the fast track to becoming a billionaire by age forty.

Here's how John and Ann's first encounter went. They were at a party, standing by the punch bowl chatting, when

John noticed that Ann's hands were shaking uncontrollably. He asked her if she needed a glass of water, thinking that might help whatever was causing the shaking. She answered, "Oh, I'm just on an enormous dose of lithium. I'm severely bipolar. So if I act strange, that's why."

Bingo! John admitted that he too suffered from bipolar disorder. They recognized each other immediately as soul mates. Ann's disorder manifested in long bouts of severe depression with few of the "up" moments, while John had the depressed times as well as amazingly energized, inspired, and productive times where he could work for twenty hours at a stretch. John also suffered from obsessive-compulsive disorder which tormented him, yet enabled him to be a beast on the Philadelphia Stock Exchange floor. John would wear medical scrubs when he was on the stock exchange floor, which other traders found off-putting and caused them to not take him seriously.

Meanwhile, he was mopping the floor with them.

<<>>

Although there has been much written on bipolar disorder disease, there has been very little written—or perhaps very little is known—about couples where both partners suffer from the same disorder. It is a difficult condition to manage. It must have been overwhelming to the newly minted couple and harder still for them as displaced people in a new land. The French have a term for this: *dépayesment*, which is the unsteady feeling you get when you are away from your home country. Yup, that was the feeling exactly.

Amy Reed, author of the book *Crazy* and a bipolar sufferer herself, described the feeling like this: "I feel like I'm a snow globe and someone shook me up, and now every little piece of me is falling back randomly, and nothing is ending up where it used to be."

The Benders were part of an exclusive club of folks suffering from this disorder, a club that includes Claude Van Damme, Dick Cavett, Patty Duke, Robin Williams, Vincent Van Gogh, Wolfgang Mozart, Sinead O'Connor, and Guanacaste's own Mel Gibson. The writer for *Outside Magazine* who wrote the most comprehensive article to date about the Bender saga, "Love and Madness in the Jungle," Ned Zeman, is himself bipolar, creating an immediate bond between Ann and the writer.

Bipolar disorder, or bipolar affective disorder as it is sometimes known, is a mental disorder marked by alternating periods of elation and depression. There are, for most people, manic or hypomanic episodes, as well as depressive episodes. It is an emotional roller coaster. The feeling is very similar to doing drugs, or falling head over heels in love.

When people are manic, their mood is high. They feel quicker, smarter, funnier, and livelier than everyone else. They have grandiose thoughts and plans. But when they are low, they take on the suffering of the whole world. They suffer sadness, anxiety, guilt, and hopelessness.

It is often extremely difficult for a bipolar disorder sufferer to maintain relationships. This disorder is often paired with eating disorders, substance abuse, obsessive-compulsive disorder, or suicidal tendencies, and it very often runs in families. John and Ann had bipolar disorder on both sides of their families. They were able to commiserate with each other about their difficult childhoods and teen years. They were truly perfectly matching bookends.

Ann's personal physician testified in court at her third trial for John's murder that Ann had continued using pharmaceutical assistance while she was in Costa Rica. There was no record of John taking any medications to help while he was in country. Folks who are bipolar are notorious for not taking their prescription drugs. Said author of *Genius by Birth, Bipolar by Design*, Stanley Victor Paskavich, "Saying I don't like my meds because they make me feel funny, is like cannibals saying they don't eat clowns because they taste funny." Bipolar disorder is no laughing matter, and the Benders were a partnership made for both passion and tragedy.

After an intense three-week courtship, John and Ann became engaged. Their families were supportive. Almost immediately, John revealed to Ann that he was saving money to buy an even better Shangri-la than Green Mountain Farm, and was deciding between Brazil and Costa Rica. Ann explained to John that she already knew Brazil, so it was decided that Costa Rica would be their eventual destination. Now the only bit of unfinished business was to find new homes for the dozens of stray cats John kept at Green Mountain Farm. John claimed he kept them all because, "They don't talk."

<<>>

Costa Rica has for many years landed in first place on the Happy Planet Index. This undoubtedly appealed to this couple of profoundly depressed individuals. Unfortunately, the title of Happiest Country in the World is somewhat deceiving, in that it does not indicate that the country is populated by wildly ecstatic citizens, whooping it up nightly and coasting through euphoric tropical days. Instead, happiness is determined by measuring a country's happiness in relationship to well-being, life expectancy, and social inequality, divided by its ecological footprint. The US ranks a sad 108th on this index.

A senior researcher at the New Economics Foundation explains,

> "The Happy Planet Index provides a compass to guide nations toward genuine progress, and shows that it is possible to live good lives without costing the Earth. We can learn much from smaller, often overlooked economies – making huge strides for their populations with limited resources. Too often governments prioritize accelerated economic growth above all other concerns. They lose sight of what truly matters – long, happy, sustainable lives for people around the world."

The romance that was launched in 1998 next to a punch bowl in rural western Virginia now relocated to the sleepy town of San Isidro de El General, in southern Costa Rica. This is the land of *pura vida* (pure life), and is known to be one of the most biodiverse countries in the world. Pura vida is more than an often-overused expression in Costa Rica; it's a state of being that goes a long way to defining this upbeat nation. It's a narrative for the country's laid-back approach to living. It's hello, how are ya', see you later, whatever, we're cool, and even thank you. Foreigners can almost function in Costa Rica by knowing just this one expression in Spanish.

Many Americans come to Costa Rica for "the three w's:" weather, weed, and women. But the Benders came with a higher purpose, and an epic love affair to fulfill.

Costa Rica is a country about the size of the US state of West Virginia, where people are well-educated, mostly Catholic, very attractive, and Spanish-speaking. They have not had an army since 1948, and are the oldest continuous democracy in Central America. They export coffee, pineapples, bananas, cacao, and sugar—much of this grown in the *Zona Sur* (Southern Zone), all around San Isidro de El General.

San Isidro (also known as Pérez to avoid confusion with other San Isidros in the country) is considered the epicenter of agricultural heartland. It was named after the Spanish patron saint of farmers, San Isidro del Labrador, and the cathedral that anchors the central park has a fresco on its façade depicting San Isidro toiling in the fields. Sadly, when the Pan-American Highway was built in the 1970s, linking the fancy northern parts of Costa Rica and its capital to the humbler southern towns and beaches, it bypassed Pérez, leaving it panting on the edges of the tourist trade and its potential economic boost to the town. This was the base camp for the Benders as they began to establish themselves in what was surely a kinder and gentler world than the one they had escaped. Pérez has a decidedly 1950s vibe—sort of Charlottesville with cilantro—and about the same population of 45,000.

In order to reach Pérez Zeledón, one has to drive up and over the Cerro de la Muerte (Hill of Death), along the Pan-American Highway, which experiences landslides, torrential rainstorms, and automobile accidents that sometimes stop traffic for hours. This is admittedly better than the ox-cart and horse trail that it replaced, but it's no US Route 95. By law, in the case of an accident, the coroner must arrive at an accident scene to pronounce a fatality, and that often takes quite some time. Even in the case of fender benders, vehicles must remain unmoved until the Traffic Police arrive and make their report. This tends to snarl traffic often. One Tica described how she met her husband on just such an occasion, while they were trapped on the mountain waiting for the coroner, and got to know each other on the side of the road, followed by a full-blown romance and marriage. This law was fortunately changed in 2016.

Cerro de la Muerte received its name back in pioneer days when early settlers had to struggle up and over the mountain on a steep, unpaved road; not everyone made it down to the valley alive. Every once in a while the fog lifts, giving people a view of the stunning Talamanca mountain range. All along the journey, you see wild orchids and bromeliads in the trees, massive prehistoric-looking ferns, small farms, and a landscape one American dubbed "Fifty Shades of Green." The journey from the San José takes about three hours by car or bus.

Pérez proper is a perfectly comfortable place in which to live, with a cathedral, central park, McDonald's, a sports arena (home of the Guerreros Del Sur, a successful soccer team), a weekly farmers' market, a library, three modern supermarkets, good access to medical care, a ridiculous number of gas stations, and three bus stations for ongoing travel or return to "Chepe," (the colloquial name for San José). The sidewalks are always in disrepair, which does not seem to deter Ticas from strutting around in frighteningly high heels. There are LOTS of shoe stores. Pérez has a bunch of moderately priced hotels and restaurants, a cultural center, and a couple of casinos. People are kind and friendly, but speak minimal English unless working in the service trades.

The Benders liked to stay at Hotel Zima (now a Best Western), on their way in or out of town, but eventually bought a small house to occupy in Pérez while Boracayán was being built. That house was later given to their head of security at Boracayán, forty-two-year-old Osvaldo Aguilar, so that he could bring his wife and children from San José and have them live in a nice neighborhood with good schools. Osvaldo still lives there when he is not at Bender Dome. He says he is very grateful that the Benders took care of him and his family with the gift of the house. He and thirty-one-year-old Marco Vargas are the only two remaining members of the thirty-seven person staff who maintained the nature reserve, and there's still plenty enough work for thirty-seven—work that now never seems to get finished. The jungle appears to be winning.

Osvaldo speaks fondly of doña Ana and her generosity. Don and doña are used often in Costa Rica to indicate respect for the person with whom you are speaking or to whom you are writing, and is usually used before their Christian name.

Osvaldo's mother died while he was at Boracayán, and Ann gave him paid time off and helped with the costs of the funeral. Everyone said Ann had a heart of gold. On the last day of her third trial, Ann gave Osvaldo and Marco $1,000 which they invested in a new car battery and a *chapeadora*, or weed wacker, that they used to beat back the jungle, and earn some money on the side when they could.

Osvaldo observed John and Ann daily riding around on their four-wheel-drive quads, and supervising the gardens, animal sanctuary, and property. He called Ann and John's relationship *puro amor* (nothing but love) and remarked on how affectionate and gentle they always were with each other. He was among the first to notice John's agoraphobic behavior and withdrawal from everyday activities at the Dome. He sensed trouble brewing. The other observer of the Bender behavior was Osvaldo Rojas, their majordomo who was in charge of the living space, cleaning, and grocery shopping. No one seemed to understand the gravity of what was going on with the couple, and how dangerous their relationship had become. Ann's psychiatrist described it as folie à deux (madness of two), a serious co-dependent condition.

John and Ann never attempted to become part of the social scene—modest as it was—of Pérez Zeledón. For English speakers in Pérez, there is an International Women's Club and a smaller brother club for men, both with monthly meetings; but most people entertain in their own homes. The Benders certainly had the best house in which to throw a party, yet never did. Osvaldo remembered only one party, which celebrated the completion of the house, with all those who helped and their spouses invited. After that, the Benders just hung out with each other. Neither of them drank, and neither of them enjoyed gossip or chit-chat. They were laser-focused on the nature reserve and its plants and animals. Most importantly, they were obsessed with each other. It was love—like cholera.

Costa Rica is a very family-oriented country, and Ticos are generally closest to their own families, with family activities dominating their leisure time. There are rodeos, dances at the Salón Comunal (the community center in Florida de Barú), church functions, religious and patriotic parades, graduations and weddings, and each town has a neighborhood bar or *soda* (café) where folks meet to eat and catch up. The Benders did none of that. They seemed to be content in each other's company, each buoying the partner experiencing the depressive phase of their disease, or tamping down the other's manic stage. Ann said the only time they both found themselves depressed at the same time was on the night of John's death.

One interest the Benders shared was a love of jewels. John had been fascinated by minerals and gemstones from a very early age, and after moving to Costa Rica, that fascination became almost an obsession. The couple became collectors, with a gorgeous assortment of jewels—precious and semi-precious—that they kept in their fourth-floor bedroom. The investigating officers who responded to John's death reported finding over 3,000 gems worth perhaps $15 million dollars, including diamonds, rubies, opals, sapphires, and more. They were found jammed into backpacks and suitcases, or just rolling loose on the countertops.

John had always said that in an effort to keep his assets untouched by the IRS and malicious lawsuits, he used the jewels as liquid assets, as his "bug-out bag," if the going got rough in Costa Rica. Naturally, the Costa Rican authorities suspected that instead, this was just a way for the Benders to beat sales tax, import tax, and other duties. The origin of the jewels was a mystery and cast tall shadows on the Benders' integrity. There were wild rumors that the Benders were flying prospective jewel clients into Boracayán, landing them on their helipad, and partying until several large deals had closed. There was suspicion among the locals that the Benders were nothing but high-class cheats. Some even thought they were *narcotraficantes* (drug traffickers), smuggling drugs and jewels through their mansion. The prosecutor at Ann's murder trial even suggested that Ann had killed her husband to get the jewels all for herself. These rumors were enflamed by the fact that the Benders were lone wolves, and no one knew them very well. People's imaginations ran wild.

Ann was very close to her family and stayed in touch via email. Naturally, Ann's parents were concerned about Ann being so far away, in a new marriage, and in a new environment. Ann was worried about them also, because her father had just been diagnosed with Alzheimer's disease. Despite his illness, Ann's father managed to attend all three of her trials, overcoming the family's concern that he would have one of his loud outbursts. Ann's brother, Kenneth Patton, was always available to her both day and night, and eventually quit his job at Macquarie Group Limited Global

Investment Bank to be able to help with her legal defense, manage the media, and assist with the *GoFundMe* site and *Please Free Ann Petition* (change.org) set up by Ann's high school friend Celine Bouchacourt, who was spearheading the drive from Switzerland. On the night of John's death, Ann's first phone call was to her brother Kenneth in Michigan.

Boracayán became the backdrop for the love affair of the decade in Costa Rica, but there were few observers of it and few witnesses to their *puro amor*. The workers came and went peacefully, never quite getting close to the Benders, and never invited inside the house. In fact Osvaldo Aguilar, head of security, said his first time inside the Dome after they moved in, was on the day of John's death, January 8, 2010.

Meanwhile, surrounding farmers and neighbors were getting more hostile and alienated. It is very un-Tico to not be uber-friendly and neighborly to the residents around you. That just was not the Benders' MO. They proposed fencing off parts of their land to prevent poachers and hunters from entering—but that also would prevent several farmers from getting to their fields and animals. Their request for the fence was turned down by the Municipality, but word of their intentions got out, and neighbors grew increasingly angry and resentful. In 2002 there was another hostile incident, late at night, involving guns and intruders.

Bender Dome by now had become a veritable Fort Knox, with its moat and armed guards patrolling on a strict schedule night and day. The guards were armed with AK-47s and handguns, and spoke to each other and to the main house via walkie-talkies. Ann was *never* without her walkie-talkie and the protection of her dog Millie. She seldom wandered far from the house. On a dark night in November of 2002, the guards repelled an intruder to the compound and exchanged gunfire, scaring him back into the night.

For the Benders, the shit had hit the fan. Ann was circling the drain emotionally, and John became frantic with worry and paranoia. On the advice of their head of security at the time, they decided to leave the country to try to regain their composure and peace of mind, and to allow more fortification of the Dome. They stayed in New Zealand for three and a half months before feeling strong enough to return to their Garden of Eden in Central America. Interestingly, New Zealand has quite a reputation for attracting doomsayers, especially among hedge fund managers, causing one manager to comment to *New Yorker Magazine*, "This is no longer about a handful of freaks worried about the world ending."

Were the Benders those freaks?

John brought Ann back with renewed determination to find a cure for her Lyme disease, help her control her bipolar disorder, and make the reserve a safe and successful operation. He seemed to have overlooked his own health and well-being in his passion and love for doña Ana. As could be expected, it didn't finish well for John, who was sicker than anyone—even Ann—imagined.

John's Death

"Every person is the owner of their own death."

Gabriel García Márquez – *Love in the Time of Cholera*

CRAZY JUNGLE LOVE

By the night of John Bender's death, he and Ann had rehearsed his final act more than you would rehearse the final act of a Broadway play for opening night. They would do macabre dry runs of his final moments. Ann claimed that the rehearsals calmed John down enough for them to go up to bed together and get some needed rest.

Ann described these evenings to Ned Zeman of *Outside Magazine* as follows, "Every day, during the last six weeks, we would sit down and he would take all the medications we had, and put them into piles and say, 'OK, when am I gonna start taking the pills'?"

John's paranoia had grown unmanageable and he had retreated to the point where he only spoke with Ann and his animals. Even his parents were being shut out, with John refusing to answer their concerned emails. Previously, they had emailed each other about a dozen times a month. He now had seventeen heavily armed guards patrolling Bender Dome, and for his personal protection he had acquired both legal Ruger pistols and illegal AK-47s.

It was one of the Rugers that ended John's life.

A few days before his death, John had emailed Ann while she was seeing her psychiatrist in San José, saying,

> "I'm losing my fucking mind right now.
> First sick again and now this shit. Today is a

total fucking nightmare and tomorrow will get worse. Just when I was feeling I could finally learn to be happy, now I get this and I want to be dead. I feel so fucking horrible. I want to kill everyone and then me...I deserve to die."

John was in a deeply depressive cycle—tragically at the same time that Ann was suffering one of her own.

The big debate at all three of her trials was if it had been Ann or John who had pulled the trigger of the gun that killed him. The community of Pérez Zeledón was almost unanimous in that it had been Ann, even though there seemed to be no motive for her to do so. She was portrayed as a gold digger, a black widow willing to kill John for his money. Forensic experts disagreed with each other on who killed John, at each trial.

On that fateful night, John and Ann completed "our evening thing," the tender moments on the balcony, enjoying the jungle's symphonic entertainment. They then moved inside for their usual bedtime ritual of two or three hours of playing John's favorite video game, *Fallout 3*, until John was ready for bed.

This is not a traditional lullaby game by any standards. Released in June of the year before John's death, *Fallout 3* features a protagonist known as the "Lone Wanderer," a non-player character (presumably played by Ann), and a dog named "Dogmeat," It has an "M" rating for mature adult themes, violence and depravity.

Fallout 3 takes place in the year 2277, 200 years after a just-ended nuclear holocaust. It is an action role-playing video game in which international conflicts between the United States and China have culminated in a Sino-American war. It is considered one of the greatest video games of all time; the Benders always liked the greatest everything.

Oddly enough, the soundtrack for the trailer for *Fallout 3,* which first attracted John to the game, was "I Don't Want To Set the World On Fire (I Just Want To Start a Flame in Your Heart)", a wonderful love song by the Ink Spots (1941).

The couple finished their evening rituals, locked the elevator off from the rest of the house; then John tenderly carried Ann up to the fourth floor bedroom. At this point she was having difficulties walking and was using a cane to help her hobble around; she weighed eighty-two pounds. John scooped her up and took her to the bedroom to tuck her in for the night.

John, ever the obsessive-compulsive, had to have his sleeping arrangements just so: nude, propped up by three carefully arranged pillows, wearing sound-deadening earplugs. The Tiffany lamps had been extinguished, and the screens dropped down to darken the room for sleep. Rituals and routines are of paramount importance to those suffering from obsessive-compulsive disorder.

Ann was just dozing off, in that half-in, half-out stage of pre-sleep, lying right next to John, when she thought she heard John say, "You don't know how it feels to wake up with your spouse half dead next to you." Ann opened her eyes, trying to wake up and focus on John's words. To her horror, what she saw was the unmistakable red dot of John's gun. John had brought his Ruger to bed with him and had it pointed at his head, which was propped up by pillows. Panicked, Ann rose to her knees to try to take the gun away from him. She told the CBS show *48 Hours*,

> "When I saw the gun I was stunned, and my immediate reaction was to get up on my knees and try to reach for it. The gun was loaded and cocked. I reached for the gun with both hands, and I was up on my knees. And I *did* put my hands on the gun. And the gun slipped through my hands. And it went off."

That exact recounting of the events that night is what the legal case against Ann Patton Bender hinged on. Folks on television, on the radio, in local bars, and at all gringo gatherings asked themselves the same questions.

~ Do guns ever really go off by themselves, or does someone have to pull the trigger?

~ Did Ann have any motive to kill off the man of her dreams?

~ Given the difference in their sizes and strengths, does the tussle over the gun make any sense?

~ How can you explain the fact that the single bullet that killed John entered the lower right back of his skull, headed at an upwards trajectory toward the left, and never exited?

~ Who else could have fired that rather large handgun on that rather dark night?

~ Why wasn't the gun ever fingerprinted?

~ How could the kill shot have been made by a left-handed person, which John was?

~ What would happen to all those jewels?

The list of inconsistencies and contradictions was nearly endless—actually enough to fill three separate murder trials over four years—including witnesses who changed their testimonies, as well as painfully unsophisticated local forensic analyses from around the 1970s. This case put Costa Rica on the map, and not in a good way. International press swarmed Pérez Zeledón like mayflies, sending live feeds back to Europe and the US, pulling the curtain back on the judicial system of this humble, peace-loving developing country. Only the taxi drivers from San José, who would bring the TV crews up and over the Cerro de La Muerte, seemed to be benefiting from this show. They were the source of most of the local gossip about John's death.

<<>>

After the gun went off, Ann went into overdrive. She ran around to John's side of the bed, just in time to hear the telltale death rattle from deep within his throat. John was gone. She turned on a light, found a walkie-talkie, and called down to the guard on duty, Moisés Calderón, for help.

At 12:15 a.m. Moisés was surprised by the gunshot upstairs. It had interrupted the jungle music, and before he could notify his supervisor, Osvaldo Aguilar, a crackly voice came over the walkie-talkie. Ann was frantically calling for help. It took at least five minutes before Moisés and Osvaldo, with Ann's assistance, could unlock the elevator, ascend to the fourth floor, and enter the tragic death scene. It was clearly too late to help John.

Osvaldo, now on the fourth floor for the first time ever, found doña Ana kneeling by her husband's side, stroking his lifeless hand. Once again, Osvaldo saw *puro amor*. Ann was trembling and crying, splattered in John's blood. Not far from her lay the Ruger on the floor: John's own 9mm Ruger P95. John had been killed by his own gun. There was no shell casing immediately in evidence.

Osvaldo made a cursory examination of the body to confirm that John was indeed dead, then turned his attention to Ann, his remaining boss. Ann's facial color was odd, and the skin on her forehead and cheeks was tight and waxen. She couldn't stop shaking. Osvaldo wasn't even sure that she could walk, but he knew he had to get her away from the horror of that bedroom. He gently helped Ann to her feet and escorted her to the elevator, and down to the second floor where there was a computer and a telephone.

While Osvaldo called the authorities to report the death, Ann managed to email the tragic news to her parents, and then she called her brother in Michigan, waking him in the middle of the night. Everyone was in shock and total disbelief. Ann's message to her family was succinct, "He finally did it." By that she meant that all the suicide rehearsals had finally culminated in this nightmare outcome; John had finally killed himself like he always said he would. Brother Kenneth was on the ground in Costa Rica forty-eight hours later, ready to help.

Ann took a tranquilizer, and tried to hold the edges of her fragile self together while she waited for the authorities to arrive.

This is where the stories of what actually happened on January 8, 2010, diverge wildly, depending on who you talk to and whether the conversation is on or off the record. No one tells the story of that night quite the same way. Gabriel García Márquez, in his book *One Hundred Years of Solitude,* calls this scenario "Macondo," a tiny settlement with almost no contact with the outside world, where the line between fantasy and reality is arbitrary, and one's interpretation of events depends entirely on one's cultural references. The Boracayán crime scene was 100% Macondo. Most of Ann's interactions with the authorities and the legal system in Pérez were straight out of Macondo. García said, "Macondo is not so much a place as a state of mind, which allows you to see what you want, and how you want to see it."

<<>>

The crime scene was described in court by the Costa Rican authorities as having been processed completely, normally, and by the book. Under Tico law, unless there is a death by natural causes, it is first assumed to be murder rather than suicide. Such was the case at John Bender's deathbed. The Fuerza Pública (local police), the OIJ, the Red Cross, and the coroner all flocked to the scene with their respective teams. It got real crowded.

Staff at Boracayán privately described the scene as one of total chaos. There were cops gawking at the house, leering at Ann, taking selfies in the bedroom on their cell phones, texting descriptions to their neighbors and friends of the never-before-seen luxurious living space, going through cupboards, playing with iPods, trying on sunglasses, fondling the jewels, and here and there helping themselves to a souvenir or two. According to the team of forensic scientists brought in by CBS' *48 Hours*, there seemed to have been very little effort at all to protect the crime scene. Everyone thought Ann was guilty.

Millie the dog was relegated to the first floor beside the sloth's cage. Neither of them understood the chaos that had descended on their peaceful home. Millie was an exquisitely well-trained service dog who obeyed Ann's every word and gesture, but this was all too much for her. Osvaldo was assigned crowd control, and had back-up from both Moisés and now their boss from Imperial Park Security, José Pizarro. Osvaldo tried to occasionally check in with Ann to comfort her.

The authorities questioned Ann briefly. She told them the same story she continued to tell everyone: John killed himself. She tried to prevent it, but was unsuccessful. They confiscated her clothing as evidence. They sealed both her and John's hands in evidence bags, which forensic experts later testified destroys evidence in the jungle heat. No one fingerprinted the gun, or took fingerprints until many hours after John's death, probably after the prints were compromised by the tropical conditions.

Ann was brought downstairs in different clothing, but with her hands bagged, to await transport to the police station. They then brought John down on a gurney to await the coroner's transport to the morgue. Ann was seen still crying and stroking John's hand awkwardly while they waited, both of them still wearing evidence bags. Authorities left the two of them waiting like that for over an hour.

Upstairs, the various teams continued to trample the crime scene, and eventually they found the spent shell casing. It was not very near the bed, behind it, but someone could very well have kicked it there in the melee. They had begun photographing the crime scene now that there was some daylight, creating what one forensic expert (not involved with the case) would describe as the "worst crime scene photos I've ever seen." Apparently, the light wasn't good enough to really clearly see minute details, such as blood spatter.

By mid-morning, Ann had been taken on the one-hour ride down to the police station in San Isidro de El General, the same one where she and John had gone after they were assaulted on the road to Rosemary's. Ann gave her witness statement to the authorities in a hesitating, soft voice. Again, she declared that John had taken his own life, and she had been unable to prevent it. Never had she felt so frightened and alone. Of the important people in her life, she never could have guessed who would be the next to bail on her, her trusted attorney Juan de Dios Álvarez.

She dialed Dr. Arturo Lizano-Vincent, her San José psychiatrist, and said, "My husband just shot himself. Please, can you admit me?"

<<>>

Dr. Lizano-Vincent was waiting for her at the renowned San José Hospital CIMA. CIMA is a very well-respected private hospital where nearly everyone speaks English. Many expats use CIMA for medical procedures that would cost them double (or more) in the US. They report that at CIMA, they are treated like celebrities—mostly in private rooms—and even the cafeteria food is first-rate. If you are coming to Costa Rica for medical tourism, especially plastic surgery, CIMA is the place to be. They get wonderful patient reviews. It's expensive compared to other local hospitals, even to use their parking lot.

Dr. Lizano-Vincent specializes in issues of addiction. His education was in psychiatry and neuropsychopharmacology, and he is one of Costa Rica's leading experts on depressive bipolar disorder. Ann was in the right hands and in the right facility. She was there for six full months, trying to regain her equilibrium and strength.

Dr. Lizano-Vincent testified at Ann's third trial that he was simply horrified at Ann's appearance when she arrived at CIMA. He found her almost unrecognizable: emaciated, covered in lesions, a "flat" affect, a locked stare into space, in short, one hot mess. He immediately put her on a morphine drip, strong antibiotics, anti-inflammatories, vitamins, and anticoagulants through a chest port.

Observers at that first trial asked each other, and themselves, was John trying to kill Ann? Was Ann trying to kill herself? Was she not justified in pulling the trigger to save herself from John's nightly "curative" injections of dirty river water and his craziness? Had Ann not barely escaped from *The Island of Dr. Moreau*? Shouldn't she be admired for saving her own life? Why had no one mentioned self-defense as a possible motive for her alleged actions? Even at the end of three trials, those questions still loomed large.

No one imagined that Ann would *ever* be tried for John's death, much less convicted and sent to prison; she was obviously way too sick to be charged.

Dr. Lizano-Vincent testified that his diagnosis of Ann was a rare disorder called folie à deux, more recently known as shared psychotic disorder. This is a psychiatric syndrome in which symptoms of delusional beliefs and hallucinations are transmitted from one individual to another. It presents when two individuals live in close proximity, are isolated, and have little interaction with others. Folie à deux, thy name is Bender Dome.

Shared psychotic syndrome usually occurs only in long-term relationships in which one person is dominant and the other is passive. Couples account for seventy percent of diagnosed cases, and it is most common when there are preexisting conditions such as depression, delusion, or paranoia.

The most famous instance of folie à deux was that of Margaret and Michael, a French married couple from the 19th century who believed that their house was being invaded by random people who scattered dust and lint all around their house. More egregiously, they walked around in the couple's shoes, grinding down the soles and heels until they fell apart.

Folie à deux sounds amusing and whimsical; there is even a Sonoma, California winery named after it. But the bottom line is that two people go insane together. They advance each other's mental illness and exacerbate the symptoms in each other.

Dr. Lizano-Vincent stated at trial, "We all go a little crazy for other people in our lives, do we not?" The disorder is often treated, as Dr. Lizano did with Ann, with anti-psychotic drugs, and it often disappears by itself with no meds at all, when the couple is no longer together.

Quoting the Ink Spots:

CRAZY JUNGLE LOVE

"I don't want to set the world on fire,

I just want to start a flame in your heart.

In my heart I have but one desire,

And that one is you, no other will do."

After six months under Dr. Lizano-Vincent's care, Ann was released and discovered that she had regained her health—but had lost all her money, property, and jewels.

Love Strikes Again

"I felt I was the one going to die, my sister said."

Gabriel García Márquez – *Chronicle of a Death Foretold*

CRAZY JUNGLE LOVE

Joke frequently told among gringos in Costa Rica:

Question: *How do you become a millionaire in Costa Rica?*

Answer: Arrive with $5 million and let the Ticos take it from there…

Many people think that Costa Rica is a third-world country. It's not. Costa Rica is a "developing" country, and even that term is going out of vogue. Many people think that Costa Rica is a banana republic. It is, but only because of exporting a lot of fabulous bananas, not because Ticos are backward or primitive people.

Ticos are well-educated, and there are many professionals graduating annually from good universities, both Costa Rican and abroad. It is estimated that there are some fifteen thousand lawyers working in Costa Rica today. It only stands to reason that some of them would be less than honest—if not kings of corruption.

John Bender, who was the decision maker in his marriage to Ann, made a typical gringo mistake in his attorney selection. The expat websites, message boards, and Yahoo and Google groups are filled with posts warning Americans of lawyers who take your money and then disappear. They caution against greedy and dishonest lawyers who find ways to swindle or double-cross you. Ticos will advise you to hire two lawyers: one to do the work, and the other to watch over his shoulder, *por las dudas* (to be safe), then cross yourself twice. You must perform careful due diligence before entering into any business transaction, especially when there is $600 million at stake. John was a gambler—start to finish—and with his attorney choice he bet the bank—and lost.

In Costa Rica, you need a lawyer for absolutely everything, from registering your car, to real estate deals, to employee disputes, to applying for legal residency. With a good lawyer, the world is your oyster. The Benders didn't really speak much Spanish in 1999, and they seemingly failed to understand that Costa Rican law is based on Napoleonic or Roman law, rather than common law like in the US. John never colored within the lines anyway, as demonstrated by his business deal with Joel Silverman with no written contract whatsoever. We saw how well that worked out.

The Benders' primary lawyer was a sixty-something Tico by the name of Juan de Dios Álvarez, a senior partner at Álvarez Aguilar Abogados Asociados. He specialized in real estate, trusts, estates, international law, finance, corporate, and business law. That pretty much hit all the Benders' needs. He had an office in San José, was a big burly guy like John Bender, and of course, spoke perfect English. *Tuanis* (cool)—as they say in Costa Rica—a perfect choice.

Many North Americans have been lulled into complacency when dealing with Ticos with good English-language skills. Although it usually indicates that they are well-educated, it does not always follow that they are honest. Many a couple seeking to adopt a Tico child, or an American looking for a Tica wife, or a single lady looking for romance, has been duped by an English-speaking Tico. Costa Ricans tend to be charming and engaging. Face it: it's always harder to identify a scam artist if they speak a foreign language. You miss the nuances, intonations, facial expressions, and body language which would tip you off that something was amiss when you are dealing with cross-cultural relationships.

Juan de Dios Álvarez helped Ann and John through the process of becoming first temporary, then permanent legal residents of Costa Rica. They applied, and were accepted, under the *inversionista* (investor) category, which is what wealthy people qualify for under Costa Rican immigration law. John applied as the primary, as he was able to prove his vast wealth and intention to invest in Costa Rica, while Ann applied as his dependent, who didn't need to show any proof of income to obtain residency. The other categories are *pensionado* (retirees), *rentista* (small investor), and *vínculo* (spouse or child of a Costa Rican citizen). Lots of Americans never bother with any of the above, thereby becoming "perpetual tourists" who are required to leave the country every ninety days to renew their visas. There are horror stories of immigration officials at the border refusing re-entry to some of these "border hoppers," and people have reported that they had to pay or bribe their way back into the country to obtain their new visa.

Costa Rican officials have declared as a national priority businesses related to tourism, forestry (like the Benders), or low-income housing. The Tico government must have been thrilled to have such wealthy investors interested in an ecologically sophisticated project which would be located in such an out of the way and underdeveloped part of the country. It was a win-win for the Southern Zone.

During that initial residency application process, the Benders signed an unlimited power of attorney with Juan de Dios Álvarez, enabling the Benders to exit and enter the country freely, while having the work on Boracayán and their residency paperwork continue forward uninterrupted, because Álvarez was fully empowered to make decisions in their absence. This is a much more common occurrence in Central America than in the US—and the Benders had grown to trust their lawyer completely. They were adjusting to a brand-new country and culture, and John was recovering from a mild stroke, while Ann continued to battle her Lyme disease and mental illness. They had enough on their plates. Alvarez had reportedly been an absolute nobody prior to being hired by John, operating out of a rundown corner office of a side street in San José.

Suddenly he was a star managing one of the biggest trusts in Costa Rica, all thanks to John Bender.

Says Garland Baker, a naturalized citizen who has resided and offered legal advice in Costa Rica since 1972,

> "A power of attorney is a blank check. Lawyers who might be having financial problems or just want money have been known to either sell property or negotiate a fat mortgage. They get the loan money, and the real owner has the obligation to pay off the mortgage."

Someone once said the definition of a Costa Rican attorney is, "One who defends your estate against an enemy, so he can appropriate it later for himself." It's a super-simple way to separate an unsuspecting gringo from his cash. The conflict of interest laws are seldom enforced.

It is difficult to recognize just exactly when Juan Álvarez realized that he was dealing with naïve and gullible gringos, perhaps the most gullible gringos to ever be swindled in Costa Rica. Most Americans chat with neighbors and friends about legal and real estate issues, or join the Association of Residents of Costa Rica (ARCR), who specialize in these issues; not the Benders. They were following their bliss, and no one was going to rain on their parade. They isolated themselves more and more each day.

They were also getting sicker each day, and probably not completely aware of it. One of their neighbors described their situation as "the blind leading the blind," in that they only relied on each other for advice. Other neighbors simply chalked it up to typical American arrogance. John disliked doctors, he rejected them and their care, and was hell-bent on finding a way to cure his beloved Ann, hopefully with plants and river water found right on their property.

Several of the Benders' neighbors opined off the record that they felt from the jump that Juan Álvarez was feathering his own nest, building his own Shangri-la, and would figure out a way to get the couple out of his way later. With any luck, they would probably self-destruct on their own, and Álvarez could swoop in and snatch the fortune and land rights right out from under them. It had happened many times before in Costa Rica—many times.

And so John and Ann placed $70 million dollars in a trust to be solely managed and supervised by Juan Álvarez. This protected them from American tax issues, Joel Silverman's collection efforts, and made them almost immune from any IOUs and debts they had left behind in the US. They felt that their money was now untouchable, and besides, John had already renounced his American citizenship.

Garland Baker, who helps newcomers in Costa Rica avoid just these kinds of pitfalls, admonishes newbies as follows,

> "Rule #1: Do not give money to lawyers to hold in trust. The truth is that some lawyers are crooks and solicit money from the clients for home or land purchases. If the lawyer keeps the money, the foreign client is faced with a lengthy and uncertain legal battle. At best, after a long court battle, the client turned victim will win a judgment that may or may not be collectible."

Like most foreign landowners in Costa Rica, the Benders created a *sociedad anónima*, a corporation into which they put their land, cars, houses, and $70 million. Álvarez advised them to do this, and by now they were relying solely on his wisdom. He also advised them to invest in jewelry and gemstones, assets which were portable and held their value. In the event of John's death, the reserve would be the first beneficiary to his fortune, Ann would be the second. Those plans were sadly lost in translation at the time of John's death. Ann's good friend from prep school, Celine Bouchacourt Martenot, described the situation thusly,

> "John and Ann's money was, and is, in a trust... The Costa Rican trustee, a lawyer named Juan de Dios Álvarez, stole from

them from day one. John's dying was the trustee's ticket to owning everything, the money, the jewels, the Refuge—he wanted Ann out of the way. And miraculously, got just what he wanted."

A less sympathetic blogger from Colorado who lived in San José described it this way,

"What a bunch of douche bags. They should've had their financial affairs established and put in force in the United States before ever going to Costa Rica. Her husband is to blame for not filing appropriate paperwork. Ann should have been the trustee, not some random Costa Rican man."

Sadly, the Bender case with an allegedly crooked lawyer is not very unusual in the history of foreigners in Central America. The Benders seemed to have failed in their due diligence in researching the background of Juan de Dios. They could have made very good use of a private investigator for this task. Cody Gear, a well-known PI in Costa Rica, commented on fraud in general in Costa Rica as follows in 2013:

"Fraud in Costa Rica, believe it or not, seems to be endless. Fraud, whether it be real estate, marriage, investment, or squatters, can cost you everything you have. The toll financially and emotionally from enduring such frauds goes without comment.

The local print and electronic news service in Costa Rica report frauds on a daily basis. The OIJ is understaffed and underfunded to deal with the amount of frauds that are reported to the agency. Additionally, if you are not a Costa Rican citizen, your case will be given a very low status and probably will never be investigated in time."

<<>>

Two fabulously popular stories about rich people being swindled in Costa Rica are the stories of "The Brothers," and "The Cubans." The Brothers was a humongous investment operation functioning from the late 1980s until 2002. They have since folded, but not before making off with what investigators claim was between $400 and $800 million, mostly from Americans and Canadians. The scam was a Ponzi scheme managed by brothers Luis Enrique and Osvaldo Villalobos. The minimum entry investment was $10,000. Interest rates were 3% a month, paid in cash, or 2.8% compounded. Some 6,300 individuals were involved in this scheme as investors, including a small number of Ticos. Luis Enrique was fond of quoting Bible scripture to his investors which seemed to persuade them that he and his scheme were copacetic.

In the end, Osvaldo Villalobos was sentenced to eighteen years in prison for fraud, but his brother Luis Enrique is still at large.

A competitor of The Brothers was Savings Unlimited (SU); unofficially known as "The Cubans." The founder of Savings Unlimited was a casino operator named Luis Milanés Tamayo, aka "The Cuban." An initial investment of only $5,000 was required to get in this game, and SU paid roughly the same dividends as The Brothers. Milanés would tour his investors through his casinos, explaining that they were seeing first-hand where the profits were being generated. Roughly 2,000 victims fell for this Ponzi scheme, including many Americans, Canadians, Europeans and a few Ticos.

The Cuban shuttered his business in 2002, but was on the lam for six years before being caught in El Salvador, traveling under another Tico's passport. He was sentenced in 2015, convicted of aggravated fraud. Although The Cuban had agreed to pay the plaintiffs back in full, it seems he has yet to refund roughly $500,000 of that debt.

Note to self: If it looks too good to be true, it's probably false, whether in Costa Rica or anywhere.

<<>>

Seemingly the only good guy (besides Oconitrillo) in this saga was the former accountant for Juan de Dios Álvarez, a fellow named Milton Jiménez. Jiménez claimed he had discovered that Álvarez was pilfering from Ann's estate. Scandalized, he quit Álvarez's law firm and began working for Team Ann. Jiménez declared that he was so distraught over Ann's financial ruin and distressing legal situation, that he opened Álvarez's books to Team Ann. In sworn legal depositions, Jiménez testified that Álvarez (allegedly) had bilked the Bender trust of millions of dollars, which he used to create an exclusive equestrian center, invested in grandiose real estate ventures, and underwrote an extravagant lifestyle for himself and his family. This was how Jiménez explained Álvarez's seemingly new-found wealth. Meanwhile, Ann had to rely on friends and family to be able to pay doctors and put food on her table.

Álvarez justified his actions by producing a post-nuptial agreement between John and Ann, in which Ann waived her rights to all John's property, which left Álvarez in charge of everything. This confusion might have taken years to sort out had this issue gone to court, and Álvarez was perhaps betting that Ann would not make it much longer. There had never been a pre-nuptial agreement drafted; Ann's understanding of the agreement was that the post-nuptial contract became null and void at the time of the inception of the trust.

After six months, Ann was released from the hospital. She had regained much of her strength, was able to walk better, had regained about fifteen pounds, had benefited nutritionally from CIMA's healthy gourmet cuisine, and had stabilized her bipolar disorder with the kind help of Dr. Lizano-Vincent and the CIMA psychiatric staff. She was feeling human again. Ann emerged into the bright sunshine and smiled at the comforting feel of it. She was going home. That's what John would want her to do. She took a taxi to meet her brother Kenneth at the apartment he had rented in Escazú, the posh suburb near CIMA. Kenneth had not been completely candid with Ann, in her weakened condition, about exactly what had happened to her beloved Boracayán.

Later that evening Kenneth broke the sad news to her. All of her furniture, appliances, electronics, computer, and jewels had been confiscated by the OIJ as evidence in the case against Ann as a jewel smuggler and a murderer. Most of the staff, who had remained there loyally for as long as they could without payment of any kind, were gone. Álvarez had failed to visit, or pay anyone, or keep up with property taxes. He had sent someone to remove the art from the sculpture garden and the indigenous petroglyphs. There were no Tiffany lamps to keep her company at night. Heck, the OIJ had even taken the television and microwave. The OIJ considered all of the Bender household effects to be evidence in the murder trial which followed.

During her hospital stay, Ann had remained in contact with her defense lawyers who had assured her that it was impossible under Costa Rican law for her to be charged with John's murder, due to what is called *inimputabilidad*, or her diminished mental capacity. Inimputabilidad is a legal term indicating that a person cannot comprehend the consequences of committing an illegal act, and should not be held accountable or responsible for the act committed. There was plenty of proof of her mental incapacity from her attending physicians at CIMA, who had Ann's medical records going back to even before John's death, some three-thousand pages of documentation. Her lawyers assured her that Costa Rica would never find a severely-ill, forty-three-year-old woman guilty of the crimes of which she was being accused.

Unfortunately, Ann's lawyers never, ever, claimed that she was innocent. Because Ann was a smart lady, that omission by her lawyers began to weigh heavily on her. She, of course, knew that she was innocent of killing her husband John Bender. Ann turned to John's most trusted advisor for advice: Juan de Dios Álvarez. Juan promised her that everything would work out fine, that she was not to worry for a minute, he would take care of everything, and Ann would remain a free person, able to finish the work on the reserve, and live out her golden years there surrounded by all her plants and animals.

Álvarez certainly seems to have *not* been able to take care of everything. On August 24, 2011, Ann was arrested and charged with first-degree murder for the killing of her husband John Felix Bender over a year earlier, on January 8, 2010.

<<>>

Things looked pretty bad for Ann and her financial future in Costa Rica. Juan Álvarez had removed her as a beneficiary of the Boracayán trust and canceled her credit and debit cards. Her jewels and most of her worldly possessions had been confiscated by the OIJ. She had lost her beloved John, the rock of her existence, her nature reserve was going to hell in a hand basket, and she was no longer surrounded by the wonderful beauty of the Southern Zone and her animals. The criminal court had seized her passport, and it was time for her dear brother to go back to Michigan to look after his own affairs. Wow.

This is where Ann's luck began to change and improve She met Gregory Fischer.

Ann had always liked beefy guys. Wrote Ned Zeman of *Outside Magazine* about Ann's attraction to John, "John was Ann's ideal specimen. He had massive shoulders and thighs the size of armadillos; his face, with its strong cheekbones and wide-set features, projected a quiet intensity that could play as aloofness or arrogance. Or both."

Amazingly, Ann had met another superhero for her life in the form of body builder and physical trainer: fellow American Gregory Fischer. Greg was originally from Deer Park, New York, and was in Costa Rica pursuing various business ideas as an entrepreneur, and continuing his career as a successful physical trainer of well-to-do Americans in San José. He was thirty-nine years old when they met. He had vivid blue eyes, a strong jaw, a white and wide smile, and shoulders that connoted strength and power. Ann had found herself another perfect package. Greg seemed to take to his role of Superman protecting the fragile Ann Bender virtually immediately. They became a couple. They moved in together. They bought a Chihuahua puppy to share and spoiled it rotten. Ann began to hope for a good future for herself after all.

As it turned out, Greg Fischer was probably the only reason that Ann survived her harrowing nine months in prison. The food was inedible, especially for someone as delicate as Ann, and Greg made sure Ann always had something nutritious to eat, with a little extra to trade or barter with guards or other prisoners. Ann's fellow prisoners were wowed by Greg's hunky build and handsome face; everyone seemed to like him—even the guards.

Greg was Ann's only conduit to the outside world, bringing her emails from her family, correspondence from her legal team, messages of support from some neighbors at Boracayán, and really, a reason to hope. He made sure she had soap, toilet paper, clean clothes, reading material, and any medicine that she was permitted from the outside world. There are no uniforms in Tico prisons; people wear their own clothes and those who have been incarcerated for numerous years begin to look quite raggedy.

When Greg showed up looking like Tarzan, smiling that electric smile of his, with adorable new photos of the Chihuahua puppy, the light came temporarily back into Ann's eyes. Greg, in turn, told *Inside Costa Rica*, "Ann is the love of my life," and he fought valiantly and ferociously to keep her healthy—and alive.

Despite his physical appearance, Greg was not just a dumb jock; far from it. Greg became the leader of the *Free Ann Campaign*, rallying her friends and family for the fight, and managing the social media aspect of her struggle. His motto on Facebook was, "Working every day to help save Ann Maxine Patton from the terrible injustice done her by the people she trusted most." He was Ann's new rock, and the recently enamored couple suffered greatly being apart while Ann served out her nine-month sentence.

Greg wrote on Ann's *GoFundMe* page which was endeavoring to raise money for her legal defense:

> "Nobody likes to be in a position of having to ask for charity, particularly from people you don't know, but drastic situations require sacrifices and humility, in my experience… You can make the difference for an innocent woman who has been maligned and mistreated for years … by the very people who had a legal and ethical responsibility to protect her interests. Instead, for the sake of greed, they have manipulated the judicial system and essentially committed Ann to a death sentence."

Was Greg referring to Juan de Dios Álvarez and his legal team?

A friend of Greg's named Rob Lasco described Greg like this: "He had the heart of a lion, the smarts of a scholar, a personality that never ended, and a very loving warm way about him."

In a world where some people are never lucky enough to fall in love once, Ann was fortunate enough to fall passionately in love twice.

This love wouldn't last, though. Greg Fischer would later be found dead in his bed in Escazú.

A national English-language newspaper in Costa Rica dubbed Ann's saga a "Tropical Gothic Tragedy," and they put her on their list of the "Six Top Crime Stories of 2014 in Costa Rica." *Outside Magazine* called her "Central America's Most Captivating Accused Murderess." The CBS television show *48 Hours* wanted to come document Ann's heartbreaking story. All of this attention served to alienate and annoy the Costa Rican judicial system, and her hardest battles in that arena still lay ahead of her.

The legal battle for Ann's freedom, jewels, and fortune was just getting started. This time she had to face the battle virtually all by herself.

First Trial

"Death has no sense of the ridiculous."

Gabriel García Márquez – *Love in the Time of Cholera*

Throughout Ann Bender's myriad legal challenges and emotional abandonments by boyfriends, lawyers, and husbands, she was plagued by an elusive and debilitating disease which made everything even more difficult: Lyme disease.

Ann probably contracted Lyme disease in Charlottesville, as it is almost unheard of in Costa Rica. Lyme disease is a bacterial infection spread by deer tick bites, and it is estimated that there are over 329,000 new cases each year in the US. The first stage of LD causes fever, fatigue, body aches, and headaches. A strong treatment with antibiotics can usually cure you at this stage, but it must be treated very quickly, and of course, it must be identified correctly, despite its common and confusing symptoms. LD is called "the great imitator" because its symptoms tend to mimic many other problems.

The bacterium which causes LD, *Borrelia burgdorferi*, was named after Willy Burgdorfer, PhD, who first identified it in 1982. The most frequent early symptom is an expanding circular skin rash called "erythema chronicum migrans," literally meaning chronic migrating redness. It is easily recognizable as a circular bull's-eye pattern of three to five centimeters in width, with a white core in the center. The bull's-eye appears in days or weeks after exposure and spreads from the center outward. Some people never get a bull's-eye rash, but have LD nonetheless. The rash is neither painful nor itchy, but it's a precursor of tougher times ahead. It seems quite likely that Ann, with all her other ailments and suffering, might have missed the symptoms entirely. She surely felt that a bull's-eye had been painted on her since birth.

Lyme disease has been around for thousands of years, but was isolated and only recently identified and named after Lyme, Connecticut—an epicenter of LD-infected deer ticks. A 5,300-year-old mummy, "Ötzi the Iceman," was famously found with the bacteria which cause Lyme disease, in 1991, by German hikers in the Eastern Alps. Ötzi was between 40 and 50 years old when he died. He had apparently lived a rough life, based on his scars and many knife wounds, and died with an arrow through his left shoulder, followed by being clubbed to death. The Iceman had 61 tattoos and many scientists surmise that these were made for medicinal purposes. The tattoos are all on or around joints, sights of chronic pain in Lyme disease sufferers. Ötzi the Iceman is one of the most incredible discoveries in scientific history, yielding fantastic information from his well-preserved body and the contents of his perfectly intact stomach.

Only recently, in 2012, was LD included as one of the top ten notifiable diseases by the US Centers for Disease Control and Prevention (CDC). There are many more years of research necessary to find an appropriate cure for this disease, especially in its later stages. Both John and Ann

Bender were crushed that even with all their money, and access to the best medical care in Costa Rica, they could not fix this problem for her.

Ann found herself in those later stages of Lyme disease at her first trial in January, 2013. The disease causes inflammation of the brain, nerves, heart, blood vessels, and joints. Short-term memory loss and loss of other thinking skills are not unusual. Motor function often becomes impaired, resulting in trouble standing or walking, especially without a cane, which Ann relied upon to walk. Chronic Lyme disease causes lingering symptoms in only one out of ten people. There is no definitive cure for those with late-stage Lyme disease.

This was Ann's condition as she struggled up the front walkway of the Tribunales de Justicia de Pérez Zeledón, the Courthouse, in January, 2013, for Trial #1 for the murder of her beloved husband, John Felix Bender. Little did she know that she would have to endure two more trials after this one. She was only forty-six years old.

<<>>

Here is legal activist Garland Baker's take on criminal courts in Costa Rica:

> "Expats take heed. Stay out of court, especially criminal court, unless there are no other options. The criminal court system in Costa Rica is a quagmire and a long drawn-out, horrific experience. It seems the only winners are the bad guys who know how to tweak the system to their favor by slowing down the process so cases expire, or by throwing up so much smoke, the judges are blinded from the facts."

Many American motorists who have been involved in automobile accidents while on vacation in Costa Rica discover, much to their horror, that they must stay in the country until the incident goes to court and is resolved. This could take years.

The Costa Rican judicial system, El Poder Judicial, tends to be difficult for many foreigners to fully understand. Since it is based on Napoleonic law rather than English law, there are some major differences in how justice is doled out, and how suspects (*imputados*) are treated. There are no juries; instead criminal cases are heard by a three-person tribunal, featuring one chief justice and two additional judges. Verdicts do not have to be unanimous—majority rules—

although all three verdicts in Ann's trials were one-hundred-percent unanimous. There is almost no bond system and the posting of a bond is a very rare occurrence. No one would have ever considered bonding out a flight risk like Ann.

The Costa Rican Civil Law model sees crime as an offense against the State, rather than against an individual. The State assumes the role of both investigator and arbiter. There are two levels of crimes in Costa Rica. The more serious are known as *delitos* (felonies) because they involve greater amounts of harm or threat. Delitos include crimes against life or family, sex crimes, property damage, human rights crimes, drug trafficking, and drug use. This was Ann Bender's frightening category.

People close to Ann's case concluded that Costa Rica proceeded almost as though she was guilty until proven innocent, rather than the reverse, as would have been the case under US law. They felt that the system most definitely favored the prosecutor (*fiscal*), who was allowed to rant during the trial on how rich the Benders were, how much the trial was costing this little country, how arrogant the Benders were, how filled with a sense of entitlement, and how uppity their friends, family, legal counsel, and press entourage appeared to be. That performance would probably not have been tolerated in a US courtroom.

CRAZY JUNGLE LOVE

Attempts by the reporter from *Inside Costa Rica*, who sought to obtain official transcripts from the three trials, were thwarted, due to the transcripts having already been sealed and archived in San José.

Costa Rican courts have a huge backlog of cases, and the government has neither the staff nor the financial means to resolve them. Unfortunately for Ann, they pulled out all the stops in their pursuit of her as a murderer. Ann was on the stand three years after John's death. Many of her fellow Americans wondered privately who stood to gain from the pursuit of Ann, and the answer to most was obvious. There were millions of dollars at stake, which her attorney, Álvarez, had allegedly appropriated as his own. Lawyers in Costa Rica seldom go after each other in court as a matter of professional courtesy. People wondered out loud if someone was being paid off. No one could figure out a possible motive for Ann to have killed her husband, yet three years after John's death, she was walking up the sidewalk to stand trial for Murder One. It would be very convenient for the other side if Ann were put in jail for a long, long time.

<<>>

A stroke of tremendous good luck for Ann was a random meeting in San José with a lawyer named Fabio Oconitrillo. Oconitrillo was a well-dressed, elegant, gentle man with impeccable manners and a total command of the English language, who had just quit the largest criminal defense firm in San José to start his own practice. The timing of this chance meeting could not have been more fortuitous; Ann began to have hope again.

According to *Outside Magazine*, Oconitrillo said to Ann at their first meeting in his offices, "I just have to ask you one question. Did you at any point confess to shooting John?" After hearing Ann's response, Oconitrillo told her to plead not guilty, and they would immediately begin to prepare an aggressive defense.

Oconitrillo had his first great client, and Ann had another guardian angel.

On the other side of the courtroom was prosecutor Luis Oses, a tough, street-smart, pit bull attorney who would slouch in his chair, squinting at Ann with his close-set eyes, looking like he had slept the night before in the rumpled clothes he was wearing to court. The contrast between Oses and Oconitrillo could not have been more pronounced: Oconitrillo with his neatly assembled notes in color-coded and labeled binders versus Oses, whose clothes and papers alike looked like an unmade bed. Oconitrillo had a lovely paralegal at his side, also very well put-together and attentive. Oses was by himself. The stage was almost set for class warfare between the aristocratic Team Ann and the "Peasant Prosecutor" operating without his muzzle.

<<>>

Team Ann had come from San José, up and over the Cerro de la Muerte, the night before to check into Hotel Zima before dusk. Zima has a nice outdoor dining area and bar overlooking the swimming pool, secluded from prying eyes and the press. It was beginning to look to Ann like the mention of her name in the press just incited jealousy and anger—which was better to avoid.

Ann's entourage included her brother Ken Patton, their grandmother and Ann's namesake, Ann Esworthy, her old friend Celine Bouchacourt, and the mysterious hunky Greg Fischer. Also present were two of John's friends, Pete DeLisi, a fellow hedge fund guy, and the US family lawyer Brad Glassman, since deceased. It was a strong support team, both emotionally and intellectually. John's distinguished parents from Philadelphia were unable to attend, but sent court statements which unequivocally supported Ann's testimony.

The Pérez courthouse is right on the Pan-American Highway, in a 1950s-looking blue and white building with window air conditioners hanging out of the side walls, three courtrooms, a snack shop, and wooden benches lining the open entrance hall where people sit while awaiting their hearings. Ann's trial was held in the largest courtroom, which featured a hanging mural showing a bare-breasted Lady Justice standing over an unfortunate supplicant at her feet. The image is repeated as a fresco on the front of the building, facing the road.

There was security guarding the building, and one has to pass through an archway similar to what is found at an airport, although if it was a metal detector, it was not working properly. Guards go through your handbag and briefcase. They are armed. In Costa Rica it is usually mandatory that police officers have a high school diploma, but in the Southern Zone there are fewer candidates from which to choose, so officers may not be very well-educated. Costa Rica abolished its army in 1948, so there aren't a lot of ex-soldier security guys around; it's mostly "mall cops" guarding government buildings.

Team Ann came caravanning up to the front entrance, where there were two private guards, paid for by Ann, awaiting to help usher them safely into the courthouse. One guard remained near Ann in the courtroom, the other just outside the doors. This might seem excessive, were it not for the fact that even a reporter for the English-language newspaper *Inside Costa Rica* who was covering the trial had received death threats on their home telephone. Team Ann was taking no chances, and the other side was taking no prisoners. It wasn't exactly clear who the other side really was in this court case.

The trial was conducted completely in Spanish and lasted from January 14 to January 21, 2013. Just six courtroom days. The chief judge was José Luis Delgado, who led the other two judges with bravado and efficient competence—the other judges barely uttered a word and seemed just along for the ride. They sat at a long table at the front of the room, each with his own microphone, and would disappear during breaks through a door behind them. A sound technician fussed over them constantly, adjusting sound levels on everyone's microphone, and making sure the height was correct for each witness. The witnesses sat in a wooden box facing the judges with their backs toward everyone else. Oses and Oconitrillo sat on either side of the witness box, each at their own table, Oses by himself, Oconitrillo with Ann, his paralegal, and the translator hired by the court to assist, should the now very bilingual Ann need any help.

The courtroom was air-conditioned, which meant Ann was probably always cold. The onlookers learned quickly to bring sweaters, and one translator even wore leg warmers and fingerless gloves.

The courtroom floor is sloped, with wide platform steps descending to the trial area. Never was there a more perfect trip hazard (Costa Rica is a country full of trip hazards), and each day someone at the trial would take a tumble while coming or going. The walls are painted green, a color matching Ann's face on days when she did not feel well. It was always difficult for Ann to enter or exit and she needed assistance from her brother or good friend Celine to navigate the steps.

Costa Rican law allows criminal defendants to address the courtroom, and certainly everyone wanted to hear what Ann had to say. She spoke for seventy-five minutes, sometimes using the interpreter, and gave a full history of her loving and passionate marriage to John, their purchase of Boracayán, John's suffering with bipolar disorder, and his constant desire to kill himself. She was very convincing, and during the breaks, people who did not know her said she was a sympathetic witness, and even a tragically sad widow. People felt empathy for her.

On cross-examination, Oses appeared slightly bored, and Ann responded to his questions with one-word answers only. The trial was already losing steam. Finally, Chief Judge

Delgado himself interjected, asking Ann, "Did John himself give you any reason why he wanted to commit suicide?"

Ann responded, "He told me he was not a good person—that he had failed to cure me. He told me he was tired of living a very hard life with everything he was facing. And he also told me he was scared that he could harm somebody, and he was sure I would be safer without him." Onlookers said among themselves, "Hello, self-defense," but Ann's defense team stuck like glue to a suicide defense.

Meanwhile, Ann's American entourage sat stoically in the audience, standing witness on her behalf, no one understanding one word of the proceedings in Spanish, but all united in support of their poor, falsely accused friend and relative. That first night, Ann threw a party for the team at an outdoor restaurant in San Isidro. People were trying to keep their optimism in check, because it seemed to everyone that the prosecution's case was pathetically weak.

Watching Ann, it became clear that she had a new love interest in Greg Fischer. He was right at her side steadying her, making sure she ate, making sure she was warm enough, and affectionately protecting her from people who tried to get too close. He was an exceedingly likable guy and clearly smitten with Ann. Said Ned Zeman, who was at both the trial and the party, covering the events for *Outside Magazine*,

"I was struck by the realization that the friend was actually the boyfriend. During all the time I'd spent with Ann, hashing over the deepest intimacies of her life, she'd never mentioned anything about a relationship. Instead, she described her life as being almost always alone."

<<>>

The trial continued for four more days, with the understanding that a verdict would be rendered on Friday, *si Dios quiere* (God willing). Several experts were brought in to testify for the Prosecution—the two most memorable and damaging to the Defense: Luis Aguilar, an investigator for one of Costa Rica's top forensic units, and Dr. Gretchen Flores, a renowned Tica pathologist.

Giant, grisly death scene photographs were projected onto a video screen, with much more fussing by the audio-visual technician, and were left up throughout both Aguilar's and Flores' testimonies. It was almost too much for those in the courtroom. Ann could not bring herself to look, members of her family appeared ready to faint, everyone was squirming in their seats and looking as though they might throw up. The reporter for *Inside Costa Rica* remembered thinking, "That pitiful woman has to relive the worst day of her life every day and now has to re-experience it in living color. How will she possibly make it through this ordeal?"

Here is what the photos showed:

> On the left side of John and Ann's tousled bed lay John Bender—nude, bloodied, and in a semi-curled position, as though he was asleep, earplugs in place. His head was twisted to the left, toward the mattress, revealing the fatal wound in the back right side of his head. There was no apparent exit wound. His left hand and wrist dangled off the left side of the bed, a small river of blood cascaded down, staining the mattress, finishing in a small pool on the floor. Next to the pool of blood was John's Ruger. The bullet casing was shown behind the bed.

To most people, the choreography of that death scene made no sense at all—none. The obvious questions were:

> ~Why would someone about to kill themselves put in earplugs before going to bed?

~Why out of all those 5,000 acres of land did John choose the few inches right next to Ann to kill himself? An expert from the television show *48 Hours*, not connected to this case, stated that it is exceedingly rare for someone to kill themselves in the presence of a loved one.

~How did a left-handed person take that shot?

~Why did the body look so peaceful—no signs of a struggle?

~How did the gun and bullet casing end up in those positions?

The whole scene was puzzling and confusing. More Macondo.

The two experts called by the prosecutor were adamant that the blood spatter pattern on and around John's body was inconsistent with suicide. Both argued that there was no evidence of the struggle with the gun as Ann had described. Dr. Flores testified that John could not have made that shot from his lying down position, and then end up with his right hand down at his side. Death was instantaneous, and there would have been no more movement of the body thereafter. It was scientifically impossible.

Spoiler alert: Several people would change their testimonies at subsequent trials.

The defense argued eloquently that John was clearly suicidal. His friend Pete DeLisi testified, describing three different occasions when John had confessed his attraction to suicide. Ann produced John's email where he described the same theme. She also recounted a time when she had thwarted John's attempt to throw himself off the open elevator of their house, only two months before his death.

DeLisi testified, "Both I and my family knew his condition. And we knew it was just a matter of time until this moment would come."

Oconitrillo did a masterful job of proving John's ability to fire guns with either hand, and in fact he did always practice shooting using both hands. John wore his Ruger always on his right hip, and photos were produced illustrating that fact.

Finally, there was extensive evidence that the crime scene was compromised in the hour between John's death and the arrival of the authorities. Oses claimed Ann had lots of time to wash her hands and move the murder weapon. Others claimed authorities themselves had lots of time to scatter evidence and help themselves to souvenirs. Oconitrillo pointed out that gunpowder residue anywhere on Ann was logical—she had been asleep at John's side.

Oconitrillo summarized the case as follows:

> "There is not a single piece of criminalistic evidence from which we can conclude, one-hundred percent, that my client committed homicide. You don't kill your husband because you are feeling bad one day. There is no motivation, and with no motivation, there is no homicide... Were they eccentric? Yes. It's not a crime. Were they millionaires? Not a crime, either. They lived in a four-story castle? Again, not a crime."

Oses stated:

> "The version of events given by Ms. Ann is false... And the elements of the crime scene prove that John Felix Bender did not shoot himself. Considering that she ended the life of her husband in what the penal code defines as a cruel manner, we ask for twenty-five years in prison."

The onlookers gasped audibly and were shushed by head judge Delgado.

The final word that Friday came from Ann herself, by now looking very diminished and sleep-deprived. She trembled noticeably as she tried to gather herself enough to address the Court.

She said, "I'm innocent. I did not kill John. Since this trial began, on Monday, this is the first time in three years that I feel I have rights. It's been three years of hell. And I feel listened to and protected by the justice system. And I would like to thank you."

At this point, Judge Delgado declared that the verdict would be read to the court on Monday.

<<>>

Monday arrived, revealing a packed courthouse, spectators lining the lobby and spilling out onto the street. TV cameras from around the world were shooting close-ups of Ann's sad and exhausted face. This was absolutely the best *telenovela* (soap opera) ever experienced in Costa Rica!

Court officials seemed to be less interested in the outcome: Oses didn't even show up, and Judge Delgado allowed another judge to make the announcement, which was delayed two hours.

Francisco Sánchez read the fateful verdict:

"Based on the evidence presented, we have unanimously decided the defendant is acquitted."

The stunned and elated Team Ann caravan packed up quickly to return as soon as possible to San José. Meanwhile, Luis Oses filed an appeal for a retrial, while the separate lawsuit against Ann as a jewel smuggler, tax scofflaw, and money launderer continued its slow, lumbering progress through the courts.

Here's looking at Trial #2.

A New Love

"Love is the only thing that interests me."

Gabriel García Márquez – *Love in the Time of Cholera*

In Ann's mind, her legal problems were close to being resolved. She would continue the struggle to get her property and land back from Juan de Dios Álvarez, her jewels back from the OIJ, and fight the ridiculous money-laundering and racketeering charges unjustly levied against her. The way her recent trial had gone gave her confidence that all would turn out okay. It would be a struggle, but she had an excellent lawyer, and was living in a kind and fair country that would protect her rights. Costa Rica had confiscated her passport (they probably considered her a flight risk), but after the ordeal of her trial and reliving the horror of John's death, she was ready to tuck into her new normal—and take time to regroup personally. She had already refocused herself on her new man: Gregory David Fischer.

Ann threw herself into her new relationship with fervor. Greg was now forty years old, slightly younger than Ann, and was from Deer Park, New York. He had studied at the state university, SUNY, in New Paltz, New York, and was devoted to physical health and body-building, much as John had been. Ann certainly had a "type." Greg was a personal trainer and entrepreneur who had moved to Costa Rica after living in Florida and Arizona. He was also in a 12-step recovery program, which made him compassionate about Ann's drug regime for her bipolar disorder and Lyme disease. Friends described Greg as kind and nurturing, exactly what Ann needed to help put herself back together after her wrenching tragedy.

The couple lived together in an apartment in Escazú, an upscale suburb of San José, with their "guao-guao," the affectionate name in Costa Rica for a puppy. This puppy was at Greg's side in November, 2014, when Greg was found dead in his bed in Escazú.

No autopsy was performed; as by law in Costa Rica, an autopsy is not required unless foul play is suspected, which in this case it was not. Ann was in jail at the time, so could not be blamed for his death.

Conspiracy theories as to why Ann's boyfriend had died so young, and apparently healthy, ran wild throughout the expat community. Officially, the coroner declared that Greg had died of either a heart attack or an asthma attack. The more romantic folks in both the American expat and Tico communities felt otherwise. One week before Thanksgiving, 2014, they said, Greg had died alone— obviously of a broken heart. A former private detective from California began posting theories as to what might really have befallen Greg, involving strange foods and magic potions available in Costa Rica's witchcraft capital, Escazú, but nothing ever came of these theories.

Greg and Ann had only fourteen months to enjoy their newfound love before Ann would once again be brought to trial, this time with an exceedingly different and horrifying outcome.

It must have been quite an adjustment for Ann to go from twelve years living in the back of the beyond, in the jungle of the Southern Zone, surrounded by wild animals and hostile neighbors, to living in a sophisticated and worldly ambiance like Escazú. She grew her hair very long. She bought new clothes. She and Greg went out to eat in some of the amazing restaurants in their neighborhood. They were never party people, but they did take advantage of the art galleries, the National Theater, and the gourmet food markets within walking distance of their apartment. Ann didn't drive, but Greg took her to doctor's appointments, and anywhere else she fancied. They were very happy together.

Poor, neglected Boracayán in Florida de Barú stood empty, virtually abandoned by its owners. In fact, no one was quite sure at this point who the real owners were, or who should be paying for its maintenance. The OIJ had all the furniture growing mold and mildew in a storage locker somewhere. The jewel collection, which Ann estimated was worth $15 million, had been reduced, according to the OIJ, to $7.2 million. Ann could not even bring herself to go back to visit Bender Dome. A former employee of Ann's informed her that John's extensive gym equipment was being used in the Costa Rica president's mansion. She felt quite naked without her jewels and pets, and would often long for the gorgeous sunsets and wildlife symphony seen and heard from the balcony at Boracayán, the made-up name of a made-up, unfulfilled dream.

<<>>

Greg and Ann chose to live in Escazú, close to CIMA Hospital, whose doctors and staff had helped Ann put herself back together after John's death. Escazú is considered to be one of the trendiest, chic, and upscale suburbs of San José. Lots of Americans live there, and lots of tourists call it the Beverly Hills of Costa Rica.

It is actually a very old colonial town, discovered by Spanish explorer Juan de Cavallón, in 1561. The Indigenous already living there must have been thrilled that they had been "discovered" at last. The name Escazú originates from the word "itskatzú," meaning "a rock to rest on" in the language of the indigenous Huetar tribe. A traumatized, recovering Ann Bender most definitely needed a rock to rest on at this point in her life.

Interestingly, beginning in the 1600s, the Escazú area was renowned for its *brujas* and *curanderas*, or witches and witch doctors, healers who used folk remedies to cure people. In fact, folks from all around Costa Rica would come to Escazú for consultations and treatments from these witches. Brujas were generally widows, abandoned wives, or single women who earned their living by selling natural medicines made of roots, herbs, leaves, and animal parts. These pilgrims believed that the brujas had very special powers and magical skills which offered protection from hexes—especially the dreaded "Evil Eye."

In 1821 (the year of Costa Rica's independence from Spain), the local Escazú government passed a law that prohibited brujas from practicing their magic. Public outcry was so strong that the law was amended to allow brujas to practice their sorcery—provided that they did not incorporate Christian religious symbols, especially crosses. Several famous witches from that era are still discussed in hushed tones today. Two of the most infamous were Norlico Ratón, described as an ancient man with small eyes who sneezed all the time, who would sell you powders to sprinkle in the coffee of someone you wished to transform, and Ña Matea, said to be able to remove the curse of the Evil Eye using potions made of bugs, mostly scorpions and cockroaches.

This probably did not sound so off-the-wall to someone who had allowed her husband to inject her with river water as a cure. Ann had felt for several years that she might have a hex on her. High time it was lifted.

Brujería, or witchcraft, is still practiced today in Escazú, and there is a church in nearby San José called Iglesia de la Oración Fuerte al Espíritu Santo (Church of Strong Prayers to the Holy Spirit), where it is rumored that you can be cured of everything from hallucinations to bad luck to unemployment to nervousness. Ann might have needed all of those cures.

Escazú also boasts a huge English-speaking expat community, many living in luxurious private homes or gated condo complexes. There are many fine hotels and upscale B&Bs. The prestigious private K-12 bilingual Country Day School is located there. There are two country clubs from which to choose. Real estate prices are known to be the highest in the country in Escazú.

There are many gringo-targeted chain restaurants and car dealerships, as well as spas, gyms, and one of Central America's largest and most modern shopping malls, Multiplaza. There was much in Escazú to help Ann feel human and grounded again in this world. She could even revisit her arts and culture interests at the Jade Museum, National Museum, and Costa Rica Art Museum. In March, there was the *Día del Boyero*, a celebration of oxcarts and their drivers, with dozens of *boyeros,* or oxcart drivers, from all around the country forming a colorful and s-l-o-w parade of folkloric beauty.

All things seemed possible again to Ann Bender, and she had a loyal and valiant companion at her side in Greg Fischer. Her health began to really improve, as did her spirits. She finally felt ready to take on some of the dozens of requests for interviews she had received from the American media to describe her mind-boggling experiences living in Costa Rica. Television and print media came calling in droves.

<<>>

The first major television interview Ann granted was in May, 2014, with Emmy-award winning investigative reporter Randi Kaye of CNN's *Anderson Cooper 360*. Randi Kaye and her crew spent a fat week in Costa Rica touring Boracayán, interviewing Ann, her family, her doctors, and other people close to the family and close to the lawsuit. The program, titled *Inside the Mystery: Love and Death in Paradise*, aired on May 27, 2014.

Stunningly, eight days before the show aired, Ann was convicted of Murder One at her second trial for John's murder, and sentenced to twenty-two years in prison. She was hospitalized for six months in the Psychiatric Hospital before they took her to Buen Pastor Prison to serve out her sentence. They had reduced her sentence from twenty-five to twenty-two years, in deference to her health issues. Both Randi Kaye and the American expat community were stunned at this turn of events.

Everyone who had heard of this case was curious and dazzled by the Benders' wealth, their fairy-tale marriage, their escape from the US, their mental illness and paranoia, and their bizarre lifestyle in the jungles of Costa Rica. Americans often feel as though they have one foot on a banana peel in Costa Rica: one slip and you can lose it all. They had seen it happen to many fellow expats who had come to *Ticolandia* full of hope and enthusiasm, and ended up with close to nothing. Folks wanted to understand this cautionary tale so as to avoid landing in the same predicament, on the same banana peel. CNN helped to enlighten them.

Through on- and off-screen conversations with Ann and others, Randi Kaye was able to shed light on much of what had gone wrong with the Benders and their dreams. She was not, however, able to answer the question everyone always asked: "Was John's death suicide, murder, or a horrible accident?"

Ann admitted that she had known that she was "different" since her pre-teens, around ten to twelve years old. That sensation was a precursor to her adult diagnosis of bipolar disorder. That disorder helped explain Ann's snap decision to move to Charlottesville, her moving in with John after just two weeks together, and her acceptance of John's marriage proposal shortly thereafter. People watching the CNN show commented that there didn't seem to be a full deck of cards between the two of them.

John's associate from the Philadelphia Stock Exchange, Pete DeLisi, described John to Kaye as follows: "I think he was a tortured genius. There were times when his depression would last for a period of weeks." His statements certainly reinforced Ann's testimony about John's state of mind at the time of his death.

John Bender's mother, Margie Bender, described the couple's love as being "love at first sight," and described how the lovers felt that their romance had been written in the stars. She said, "There was the feeling that they were at the same place, that they had exactly the same goals and the same values."

Kaye was able to get further information on Ann's suffering due to her Lyme disease. Ann told Kaye, "So that's why I walk with the cane. I have permanent nerve damage in my hands and in my feet. The infection passed the blood barriers, so it's in my spinal cord and it's in my brain."

CNN was able to obtain interviews with others, including their closest neighbor at Boracayán, an American tree farmer named Paul Meyer, who seemed to be one of the few people the Benders knew well. Meyer described his first meeting with Ann,

> "I remember Ann very well from the first encounter. Beautiful woman, hair up in a ponytail, white tank top, tanned, two-way radio on her hip. OK. I'm living next to Lara Croft, Tomb Raider, and an investing legend."

Kaye interviewed Ann's psychiatrist (with Ann's permission), Dr. Arturo Lizano-Vincent, and that conversation went like this:

> Dr.: "I thought that they must have both been psychotic."
>
> Kaye: "And in that case, they feed off each other's manic moments?"
>
> Dr.: "Yeah."
>
> Kaye: "Shared craziness…"
>
> Dr.: "Shared craziness, yeah."

Ann: "I know that there's definitely something to the concept of the two of us having gone mad together."

Edgar Ramírez, a lawyer for the prosecution who would appear largely responsible for Ann's conviction in Trial #2, described his theory on what was happening between the Benders, characterizing the issues from a stereotypical Latin male's point of view. He described the couple's trouble as follows:

"They were having problems because Ann was frequently taking trips out of the country to buy precious stones and jewels."

For Ramírez, the whole case centered around Ann lusting after all the jewels, and being willing to bump her husband off to get them. There was, of course, never any proof of that accusation. Ramírez even called Ann a "cold-blooded killer."

Ann's defense team seemed to have failed to convey the extent and urgency of the couple's mental illness. Ann wrote in an email to John's parents, "For the first time in eleven years, we find ourselves in the unfortunate position of both being depressed at the same time." Two days later, John was dead. There seemed to be absolutely no connection to the jewels. John had simply gone around the bend. Said Kaye, "They had hoped to escape here in the clouds of the jungle. The isolation instead would lead to a descent into madness." Pete DeLisi later told *48 Hours*, "John and Ann had problems that no amount of money could fix."

Ann told Kaye, "Had I been in my right mind, I would have behaved differently."

Ann's physician, Hugo Villegas, described her physical condition at the time she was admitted to the hospital after John's death, "I found her shockingly frail and thin, only weighing sixty-six pounds, severely malnourished with pockets of pus and abscesses on her skin." Those were the result of John's secret river sauce he was injecting her with, and the reason the reporter for *Inside Costa Rica* suggested self-defense as a possible motive.

Ann describes how the police would not leave her alone while in the hospital. They would barge into the room, fully armed, just to make sure she was still there. The term Keystone Kops comes to mind when Ann speaks of these officers. Certainly, the police were taking advantage of the situation to get a front-row seat to the freak show of the decade; they had never seen anything like this before in their lives. Renowned legal consultant Steven Ferris explained that it was not at all unusual in Costa Rica for hospitalized prisoners to escape during their hospitalization.

Some have even left, then returned without detection. Hence the frequent bed checks of Ann.

Ann describes her ongoing battle with Juan de Dios Álvarez to recover her property, and the money from the trust. Ann has sued Álvarez for fraud, and estimates he owes about $20 million to the trust. Costa Rica has removed him as a trustee for failure to execute his fiduciary duties properly. Álvarez declined to speak with CNN, saying he was following the advice of his lawyer.

John had written in one of his final emails to Ann before his death, "I am a total fucking loser for ever getting involved with that total scumbag."

Kaye ends the interview by asking Ann (this was before the conviction for murder in Trial #2), "What do you want to do with the rest of your life? Where do you go from here?"

Ann answers, "I know what John wanted me to do with the refuge. And a lot of that will depend on the resources that are left. He wanted me to start helping people with mental illnesses and to create an aspect of the refuge that would allow for retreats for people with mental illnesses."

Kaye asked, "What do you want for you?"

Ann answered, "I want peace for John because I know he's not at peace."

Kaye closes by saying, "John Bender's ashes are in an urn near what Ann says was his favorite view looking out from the refuge. A refuge she's trying to save, a paradise that will never be the same."

<<>>

Even before CNN aired Randi Kaye's *Love & Death in Paradise, Outside Magazine's* Ned Zeman had published a comprehensive article on the Bender affair titled *Love and Madness in the Jungle,* in June, 2013. Zeman was a consultant with CNN. The article had marvelous photos of the Bender Dome and also had the advantage of having been written by a member of the club: Ned Zeman also suffers from bipolar disorder and "gets" it.

This is the introductory paragraph to Zeman's article:

> "A brilliant American financier and his exotic wife build a lavish mansion in the jungles of Costa Rica, set up a wildlife preserve, and appear to slowly, steadily lose their minds. A spiral of handguns, angry locals, armed guards, uncut diamonds, abduction plots, and a bedroom blazing with

550 Tiffany lamps ends with a body and a compelling mystery: Did John Felix Bender die by his own hand? Or did Ann Bender kill him to escape their crumbling dream?"

Everyone was sensationalizing the Bender saga, which needed no sensationalism at all. It was already over the top.

The local Tico press covered this case extensively. *The Tico Times* wrote about Ann four times and interviewed both her and her family. Another local paper, *A.M. Costa Rica*, published three articles about the investigation and the trials. *Inside Costa Rica* (now *The Costa Rica Star*) always tried to hit the news first, and wrote six articles about the Benders. They felt the impact on the expat community was strong enough to have a reporter in the courtroom. *The New York Daily News* was all over the story, as well as the *Daily Mail (UK)*, who sent reporters to cover the last trial. A fringe newsletter called *Laconics Round Table* picked up on the Jewish connection of the Benders, Zeman, and the investigative reporters from *48 Hours*, and wrote an anti-Semitic rant about the case. Ann sure knew how to get ink!

More people probably became aware of the Bender saga through the *48 Hours* show which was aired twice, titled *Paradise Lost: Investigating the Death of John Bender*, with correspondent Susan Spencer, which won awards for its number of viewers. This *Special* will be addressed in future chapters. It is quite likely that CBS's intervention with forensics specialists was the only thing that kept Ann out of jail after her third trial.

One of the most outspoken "experts" on the case was a self-described "Deception and Credibility" expert named Renee Ellory, who consults with corporations and law enforcement to help them determine the honesty and integrity of their employees and associates. She wrote about Ann extensively on her blog, analyzing every facial expression and mannerism of Ann Bender—something questionable at best given Ann's constant morphine treatment and other pharmaceuticals she was taking—and Ellory came to the following conclusion:

> "I don't think Ann killed John for money, but I do think he was very determined and headstrong, and he was taking her down in his spiraling depression with him. And Ann knew it and didn't know how to get away from him, or perhaps she didn't want to give up their 'dream' of the sanctuary. I think she knew she was going to die with him if something didn't change and John wasn't open to do anything. I suspect Ann didn't know how to get away because he'd seek her out, too, and around him she knew she wasn't as strong as he was. She was the

weaker of the two. I suspect Ann couldn't take it anymore and felt this was her only way out. She wanted to survive and this is what she had to do to survive."

The hardest part may well have been surviving the next two trials.

A Short Second Trial

"His examination revealed that he had no fever, no pain anywhere, and that his only concrete feeling was an urgent desire to die. All that was needed was shrewd questioning ... to conclude once again that the symptoms of love were the same as those of cholera."

Gabriel García Márquez – *Love in the Time of Cholera*

The English-speaking press were not the only media to cover Ann's trials with curiosity and rapt attention. Costa Rica has a vibrant media scene that includes nine major newspapers, busy FM radio stations, private and public TV channels, and cable TV in most households. The case was also followed closely in Costa Rica's neighbor to the south, Panama, which also has a large expat community, as well as in other Central American countries. This was a soap opera, that no one could seem to get enough of. It had everything: murder, madness, money, and monkeys. Perfect.

The members of the Bender family were laser-focused on Ann and her health, as well as her complex and puzzling legal cases. The world around them, however, continued to turn, and the Benders were only marginally aware of what was going on elsewhere in Costa Rica.

Between John Bender's death in 2010 and Ann's second trial and conviction for first-degree murder in 2014, Costa Rica was under the leadership of its first female president: Laura Chinchilla. The press in Costa Rica were initially consumed with the anticipation of having such an amazing event in this tiny democratic country, and then equally consumed with the crashing disappointment of how awful she turned out to be. A 2013 opinion poll released a survey which placed Chinchilla as the historically worst president ever in Latin America. Ouch. The Benders could not vote, but had petitioned President Chinchilla for help with Ann's case, and received a formulaic response of "No."

In 2012, Canadian Paul Watson, the infamous founder of the Sea Shepherd Conservation Society, was detained in Germany on an extradition request by Costa Rica, allegedly for an earlier altercation with a boat that was shark-finning in Guatemalan waters. Watson was famous in Costa Rica for being known as an eco-terrorist. He skipped bail and no longer hangs out anywhere near Tico waters. Lots of press coverage.

Coffee leaf rust knocked a half-million people out of work in 2013 by devastating coffee plantations all across Central America, including Costa Rica. The financial losses were incalculable. Despite this terrible blight, Costa Rica's GDP growth averaged 4.5 percent between 2000 and 2013, compared to the global average growth of 3.8 percent for the same period.

Costa Rica became the only tropical country in the world to have reversed the scourge of deforestation nearly one hundred percent. John Bender would have been elated with that news, as reforestation of Boracayán and the surrounding area had been a primary goal of the Benders.

President Obama came to Costa Rica for two days in May, 2013, on his way to Mexico to discuss drug trafficking and organized crime with Central and South American leaders.

Probably the most newsworthy and closely followed story between 2010 and 2014 was another soap opera involving a fellow American millionaire who was also accused of murder, but in a neighboring expat hot spot, Belize. Belize is the only country in Central America whose official language is English, as it was a former British colony— British Honduras. Belize borders Mexico and Guatemala, and is the least populated Central American country. With English being the spoken language, and noting the scarcity of residents, Belize is considered a great country in which to "disappear," and there are many Americans who do just that. The millionaire about whom the press went gaga was none other than John McAfee, the creator of McAfee anti-virus software. McAfee came to Belize with $100 million, but ended up with just a couple million when he departed in 2012. Plus, he was an accused murderer, like Ann.

John McAfee arrived in Belize in 2008, at the age of sixty-two. Like John Bender, McAfee was a mathematical genius. He used his great intellect to create the wildly popular McAfee anti-virus software, and helped to pioneer the instant messaging revolution. After taking his company public, he pulled up stakes, moved to Belize, and wanted to try something. Like Bender, a heart attack was the precipitating event for this radical move. McAfee reportedly made $100 million on the sale of his software company. That much money can sure buy a whole lot of "different" in an impoverished country like Belize.

McAfee embarked upon what he called a "social engineering project" in Belize, a bizarre arrangement whereby he lived with seven young women at once and "studied" them. His "core of seven" was a teenage groupie tribe of "misfits, runaways, and troublemakers," by his own description on his blog, *John McAfee Was Here*. He assembled this tribe of outcasts with the help of the owner of Lover's Bar in Belize, who was following McAfee's description of physical requirements for the girls. These young ladies were never referred to as prostitutes, although they were paid to live with him.

McAfee stated that he chose girls for their "level of intelligence, education, cultural refinement, family connections, age, looks, experience, etc." Photos revealed a group of rough-around-the-edges brown and black girls, lounging around his pool and house, looking fairly stoned. Some of them were armed. Neighbors called them his "johntourage." In 2012, McAfee was arrested for unlicensed drug manufacturing and possession of unlicensed weapons. He was released with no charges.

In 2008, McAfee himself looked like he had been playing in his mom's hair dye: tufts of poorly frosted blond hair stuck out of his head, and he had two white stripes in his beard. He was tanned, very physically fit, and covered in tattoos. Like Bender, McAfee's paranoia had led him to be fully armed at all times. He had armed guards patrolling his house and challenging passersby, and a pack of eleven nasty dogs who would roam the property at night to prevent intruders. The dogs, it seems, were his undoing.

McAfee's closest neighbor on the Island of Ambergris Caye in Belize, Greg Faull, a fifty-two-year-old Florida builder, was found dead of a single gunshot wound to the back of his head, in his home in November, 2012. The death was allegedly the result of a dispute between Faull and McAfee over the eleven ferocious dogs let loose at night. The dogs snarled at everyone who walked the beach in the evening, and prevented residents from exiting and entering their cars and homes. We are not talking about chihuahuas and shih tzus here.

The officers investigating Faull's murder described McAfee's lifestyle as follows, "...his lifestyle involved drug-filled sex games, unhinged conspiracy theories, armed guards, and a large dose of paranoia." Belizean former Prime Minister Dean Borrows called McAfee "extremely paranoid—even bonkers."

In November, 2012, the Belizean police began an investigation of McAfee as a person of interest in the murder of Gregory Faull. The police raided McAfee's property that same year, causing McAfee to abruptly flee to Guatemala—without his harem. He claimed he had eluded the police by burying himself in the sand and lying there for hours with a newspaper placed loosely over his face so he could breathe. He was eventually deported back to the US from Guatemala, and Belize auctioned off all his assets. This was followed by the mysterious and complete destruction of his house by fire. As so often happens to Americans in Central America, it doesn't usually pay to go up against the authorities—or your neighbors.

McAfee, like Bender, had also become interested in cultivating plants for medicinal use on his land on Ambergris Caye. He claimed he was very close to perfecting an amazing all-natural antibiotic. Unfortunately, much of his scientific research on this subject was destroyed in the house fire.

In between stays in Guatemala, McAfee escaped to Miami for some R&R, and while eating at a diner there, he met his future wife, the former call girl Janice Dyson. McAfee describes their meeting on his blog:

> "After I got out of Guatemala, I was resting in Miami, and a woman came into a diner and offered to blow me for $100... I was exhausted, and told her, no thanks, but if you'd like to cuddle, I'll compensate you."

They proceeded to have a whirlwind romance on the run, after McAfee told Janice's pimp to take a hike, or get sent home in a body bag.

McAfee moved with Janice to Lexington, Tennessee, where he found work as a security expert for *Fox News* via Skype, and sometimes showed up at hacker conferences if he felt that the security was good enough to keep him safe. He had become a huge target for hackers, so he had others buy his computer equipment for him under their own names. He would change his IP address several times a day. He ran a cyber-security company called Future Tense Central out of his home. McAfee refused to discuss how much money he has left from the $100 million sale of McAfee, and in 2015 was arrested for driving erratically; he claimed he was high on Xanax at the time.

In 2016, McAfee sought the Libertarian Party nomination for President of the United States, but was beat out by Gary Johnson of New Mexico. Quoting a reporter for *Inside Costa Rica* about John McAfee's and John Bender's lives, "You really could not make this shit up."

Besides both being mathematical geniuses, they seemed to also possess a remarkable libido. Investigation into a correlation between high IQ and high libido reveals that scientists have dubbed these individuals "sapiosexuals."

Counsel and Heal Magazine stated:

> "Scientists have found numerous characteristics that set brilliant geniuses apart from ordinary Joes. Besides a high score on a

math test, studies have linked certain personalities and traits to high intelligence:

Trait #1: You have a high sex drive.

Trait #2: You use drugs."

McAfee now claims a former cocaine baron, "Boston" George Jung, newly released from the slammer, is writing McAfee's formal biography, titled *No Domain*. No date has been set yet for its release. A new movie is being developed about John McAfee's life titled "King of the Jungle," which will star Johnny Depp as McAfee.

<<>>

Ann and Greg were only vaguely aware of what was happening elsewhere in the world during those two short years of their love affair. Their lives were filled with lawyer's appointments, press interviews, doctor's appointments, and cherished time together. Ann was profoundly in love again, but this affair was much healthier emotionally than her previous relationships. She had stabilized, now that she was no longer on the submissive side of a folie à deux partnership.

They were so caught up in their own love affair they barely noticed major events happening around the world:

In millionaire's news, in 2010, Picasso's "Nude, Green Leaves and Bust" painting had sold at a Christie's auction for $106.5 million. It portrayed Picasso's love for his then-mistress, Marie-Therese Walter, a lover he painted with great frequency in that period of his life.

Thirty-three miners had been rescued after sixty-eight days trapped underground in a Chilean mine disaster; that was only one quarter of the time Ann would end up trapped at Buen Pastor Prison.

The "Don't Ask, Don't Tell" military policy in the United States was repealed.

Julian Assange (co-founder of WikiLeaks) was arrested in England, accused by two Swedes of sexual assault—more sapiosexual activity.

In 2011, Osama bin Laden was killed by US Special Forces, while surrounded by several of his wives.

The Space Shuttle Atlantis touched down, ending the US thirty-year space program.

In 2012, Barack Obama was reelected president of the United States.

The world kept turning…

Most importantly for Ann, there were new discoveries on the bipolar disorder front. It had been discovered in the 1990s that the drug lithium—the oldest and most successful mood-stabilizer for bipolar disorder—had "neuroprotective" effects, meaning that lithium was effective over longer periods of time. Vital research was being conducted in the early 2000s by Dr. Husseini Manji, MD, of the Brain and Behavior Research Foundation. Dr. Manji had proposed an interesting theory on what exactly goes wrong in folks with bipolar disorder, and his research was showing great promise for those sufferers:

> "We think that in bipolar disorder, one of the problems is that a very finely-tuned system, almost like a thermostat, is faulty. When a person is coming out of a depressive episode, the cellular thermostat should and does prevent mood from "overshooting" in the other direction. But in bipolar disorder, the thermostat inside the nerve cell is sluggish, it is not well-tuned, and so when you come out of your depression, you overshoot over to the manic side of the mood continuum."

Continued Manji,

> "We don't need to know everything about

> the brain to arrive at better treatments… I believe our recently gained knowledge is moving us close to some important improvements."

Light at the end of the tunnel! Such good news for Ann, and so sad that John would not benefit from these new scientific discoveries. In Costa Rica, one person a day attempts suicide, and Ann was constantly consumed with the guilt of not having been able to prevent John's.

In 2014, researchers from University of Michigan created the first stem cell model for bipolar disorder, which they hoped would uncover the origins of the condition and open the door to new treatments. There is no definitive cause for this disorder. In 2014, 5.7 million adults in the United States were affected by bipolar disorder. This is significant because Americans tend to keep better scientific records on these disorders than most countries. Recently, stem cell treatment has also been effective in the treatment of Lyme disease.

Also hopeful, were further studies on Lyme disease, particularly studies on why some people have persisting symptoms, even after having been treated with antibiotics. It was discovered that some bacteria causing Lyme disease died in the first day of antibiotic treatment, but a small group, dubbed "persister cells," managed to survive the antibiotic onslaught. Apparently, they survive by going into a dormant state, and can be reawakened once the antibiotic treatment is complete, and then begin to grow again. Experiments using pulsed doses to kill the bacteria (stopping and starting) to kill persister cells once and for all were successful. Johns Hopkins Research Hospital has been doing amazing work on curing Lyme disease. Even more hope for Ann's future well-being.

<<>>

Ann Patton Bender's second trial for the murder of her husband John Felix Bender began on Monday, May 19, 2014, in the same courtroom in Pérez Zeledón in which she had been acquitted just fourteen months earlier. Again, there is no ruling against double jeopardy under Costa Rican law. It was the beginning of rainy season, euphemistically called "the green season" by the Costa Rican Tourism Board, so as not to discourage the influx of tourist dollars, which comprise 12.5 percent of Costa Rica's GNP. The tourism industry brings in about $1.92 billion annually. It's big business, with lots of jobs involved, and government officials were quite concerned that Ann's trial might tarnish Costa Rica's image for foreign visitors.

The rainy season almost always offers bright, sunny mornings followed by rain after lunch. Ann was feeling buoyed by the support of her legal team, friends, and family as she slowly walked up the entrance ramp to the courthouse on a Monday morning, with the sun warming her shoulders. Greg Fischer walked closely at her side, lending love and support.

In the courtroom there was a new three-judge panel: Judges Adolpho Calderón Barrantes, Cristian Calvo, and Liner Zuñiga Herrera. This time the trial would wrap in only eight days, with prosecutor Edgar Ramírez wasting no time in leading the judges to his personal conclusion: Ann was guilty.

Ramírez opened the retrial by predicting, "We will demonstrate that there is convincing evidence, scientific proof that is irrefutable." He explained that this second trial was the outcome of an appellate court's decision to overturn Ann's original 2013 acquittal. The appeal was based on multiple "inconsistencies" from the first trial, the most egregious being:

1. Bender was found peacefully in a sleeping position, with no sign of the struggle Ann had described at the first trial.

2. No gunpowder residue was found on John's hands. (Ann had none either, but admitted to

having wiped her hands off on napkins which were found by the OIJ on the second floor of Bender Dome.)

Among the evidence judges cited in their guilty verdict at the second trial were:

1. Photos of blood patterns from the scene, which seemed to indicate the gun was fired from some distance away from John's body.
2. A torn pillow, which indicated the gun was not fired at point blank range as there was no gunpowder on it.
3. The gun was found too far from the body to have been a suicide.
4. The trajectory of the bullet seemed improbable for a person firing the gun himself.

Chief Judge Calderón declared:

> "Beyond the fact that there was no blood on the Defendant [Ann], beyond the fact that the pistol was found in another place, beyond the tampering of the crime scene, the only reasonable explanation, considering the body's position and the evidence found on the body, is that the bullet wound is homicide, because there is no way the victim could have done it."

It should be noted that the prosecution was never able to establish a viable motive for the alleged murder.

Said the local press about Trial #2, "Doubts about Patton's guilt remain. Prosecutors still haven't identified a motive for the killing, and after Bender's death, Patton discovered that his fortune had been taken from her (Ann) by the lawyers controlling his trust."

Said Jack Schwager, a close friend and admirer of John's who attended the second trial and wrote about it online at: *The Death of John Bender and a Miscarriage of Justice:*

> "This retrial and changed verdict seems very much tied into corruption and a theft of the assets in a trust John and Ann established, which includes the reserve and the funds to run it. John's parents strongly support Ann, which says everything."

In Trial #2, two of the prosecution's witnesses radically changed their testimonies from Trial #1. Firstly, in 2013, the forensics expert stated that suicide was possible; at Trial #2 he said it was absolutely impossible.

Secondly, at Trial #1, one of Bender's employees stated that Ann was frail, weak, and unhealthy at the time of John's death. At Trial #2, he swore that Ann was strong and healthy, and that the couple had fought on the day of John's death. Two complete reversals, both under oath.

It was revealed by the defense that a "ballistics expert" was paid directly by Juan de Dios Álvarez to testify against Ann, resulting in Álvarez being able to collect $14 million from John's life insurance policy.

Schwager stated, "We are concerned the missing trust money will be used to ensure Ann never leaves prison alive."

Trial #2 concluded on May 28, 2014. She was found guilty on all counts and sentenced to twenty-two years in prison, reduced from the twenty-five years suggested by the prosecution.

Ann was immediately remanded to a psychiatric hospital's suicide ward, where she was held under guard until they deemed her healthy enough to be moved into Buen Pastor Prison.

Fraud, Corruption, and Injustice

"It was as if God had decided to put to the test every capacity for surprise and was keeping the inhabitants of Macondo in a permanent alteration between excitement and disappointment, doubt and revelation, to such an extreme that no one knew for certain where the limits of reality lay."

Gabriel García Márquez – *One Hundred Years of Solitude*

CRAZY JUNGLE LOVE

In 2000, John and Ann Bender came to paradise as newlyweds with an ambitious dream and a thirst for adventure—and $600 million. In 2014, all that was left was a widow in a psychiatric hospital on her way to prison after being convicted of the premeditated murder of her husband. Oh, and she was, to use the vernacular, *desplatada*, financially busted, barely able to scrounge together enough money for the prison pay phone.

How does THAT happen???

To Americans, Canadians, and Europeans, it's probably hard to understand how such a horrendous situation could occur. To folks living in Costa Rica who are accustomed to the Tico justice system, law enforcement, lawyer corruption, etc.—this is not that unusual. It diminishes Costa Rica in the eyes of foreign investors and visitors. Stories abound of unsuspecting gringos who have come to Costa Rica with stars in their eyes and fists full of dollars, and either spent decades in litigation, or walked away in disgust with nothing. And that is very sad for the many honest folks in Tico paradise who treat gringos fairly and kindly.

The Tico Times wrote in 2012 on the topic of land fraud,

> "For all of the country's abundant charms, things can get pretty ugly in Costa Rica—especially when buying property. For foreigners caught in land swindles and

fraudulent property schemes, the dream of owning their own little slice of Tiquicia can become a nightmare of drawn-out legal wrangling in Costa Rican courts. It also doesn't take much to steal property here— corrupt lawyers and notaries can create false property transfers and turn your land over to another individual."

Welcome to the world of Ann Bender in 2014.

Explains Attorney Roger Peterson of *CostaRicaLaw.com*, "To get your property back, depending on the complexity of the case, can run you $20,000, $25,000, or $35,000." Ann's case was as complex as they come, and she was as broke as they come.

The World Bank ranks 181 countries based on how well they protect foreign investors. In 2008, Costa Rica ranked 164th for protecting foreign investments, flirting with Iran, Senegal, and Haiti at the bottom of the list. The Benders could have accessed that information on their computers. They didn't. Costa Rica has moved up considerably on the list since 2008, but it was too late for the Benders.

There are many examples of Americans and other foreigners whose investments have turned into nightmares, even for those who should definitely have known better.

Forbes Magazine's Jesse Bogan wrote in 2008 of the case of American Robert Sprague who invested in Escazú:

> "Robert Sprague aged 65, retired six years ago from a job as a Latin America senior analyst at the US military's Southern Command in Miami. In 1982 he bought 2.5 acres of rolling pasture in Escazú, a San José suburb. Since then, Sprague says, he has kept up on the property tax (0.25% of recorded value) and visited often. To keep off intruders, he lets a family live on his land in a wood shack. 'Being an intel guy, you are always leery of something,' he says. Then, all of a sudden, a little rat slips through the back door and shorts out the whole system."

Forbes continues the story, "As Escazú became an incorporated, ritzy locale for foreigners and embassy residences, real estate values soared. When Sprague readied to sell in February, he discovered the property had already been 'sold.' The land registry pointed to a document in which he had supposedly signed over power of attorney authorizing the sale—and a receipt claiming he had been paid $300,000 for the land. Sprague says the documents are fake and his signature is forged. His civil and criminal suits are pending."

Another example of having to defend one's investment in Costa Rica comes from the case of a young Texan named Edward Sides who bought a convenience store in Herradura in 1996, right after graduating college. Herradura is a coastal town on the Pacific Ocean, 2.5 miles north of the popular beach city of Jacó, and known globally as the fishing capital of Costa Rica. Many big-league fishermen fly or sail into Herradura, bringing with them buckets of American dollars. Sides purchased the land and a house from a squatter, but went the extra mile to find the legal owner and obtain the title, after paying her $5,000. His biggest challenge, however, was still ahead, as he grappled with some fifty other squatters living on the property in structures ranging from cardboard shacks to nice homes with swimming pools. Sides confronted the squatters, showing them their eviction notices from the court in Puntarenas.

Sides ended up having to bus in 350 police officers to back him up. It wasn't enough. He hired a private security company of seventy, and built a hefty metal barricade around his property. Next he brought in bulldozers to tear down the illegal homes. The squatters turned violent and rushed the guards with rocks and Molotov cocktails. Several folks were injured.

Sides figures the property is probably worth $2.5 million, but only if someone is daring (or maybe poorly informed) enough to buy it. All of Costa Rica is "buyer beware."

As proof that no individuals or companies in Costa Rica are immune from land grabs and legal shenanigans, let's call the next example "Bamboozled." In 2001, six hundred squatters took over a 2,000-acre bamboo farm owned by Standard Fruit Company, a wholly owned subsidiary of privately held Dole Food. Dole is pretty big and pretty powerful: sales in 2007 were $7 billion. Standard Fruit jumped in immediately to protect their land, beginning a long eviction waltz with the squatters, with some ending up being evicted four and even five times.

Fed up, Standard Fruit hired a former Costa Rica supreme court judge whose specialty was agrarian law. The case dragged on for seven years. Standard Fruit reportedly spent $5 million defending land that was worth $10 million. But in the end, Standard Fruit won. Obviously, not everyone has the patience and deep pockets to wage that kind of battle.

Finally, a case with many similarities to the Bender fiasco was that of a French couple, Fabianne Ferande and Marc Bauer. The couple fell head over heels in love with Costa Rica and set their sights on opening a hotel in La Fortuna de San Carlos. "Fortuna," for short, is considered the gateway to magnificent Arenal Volcano, and connects the Arenal area with the Monteverde cloud forests. Both of these areas are among Costa Rica's most popular tourist destinations. Ferande and Bauer wanted to employ locals, safeguard the environment, and live out their lives in peace. Unfortunately, they also fell victim to an unscrupulous lawyer, and lost $475,000 in the process.

This story begins in 2009, the year in which the French couple entered into a five-year lease arrangement for the hotel. Two years later, much to their delight, the hotel came up for sale at auction. The couple was represented at the sale by a Tico attorney who had been recommended to them by their own French Embassy. They had been willing to pay up to $550,000 for the property, but their lawyer told them they only needed to offer $364,825; which they did. The lawyer told them there was no need to attend the auction, which would probably just confuse them and that he would represent them and handle all of the details. No worries.

The couple transferred all the money into the lawyer's account, and sat back waiting to take possession of their new hotel. Sadly, the sale fell through due to the original hotel owner backing out at the last minute. The French couple at this point had transferred $395,000 into the lawyer's account—for the purchase and legal fees. How to get the money back?

The couple confronted the lawyer directly, and managed to get back $100,000. With the help of their embassy and a new lawyer, they are hopeful that they can recover the rest. Long time expat residents have two words for them: Good luck.

Another foreigner who lost his shirt in real estate in Costa Rica battling against the entrenched Costa Rican power structure, according to an English-language news site.

> "There are two kinds of property theft. One is where someone moves illegally onto the land of another and tries to gain possession by staying there (squatters). The second is white collar fraud, involving lawyers and notaries creating false paperwork that transfers the title of property to another. Sadly, even fellow expats get caught up in stealing property and other assets from each other because they believe they will not get caught by the law. The number of expats attempting to swindle other expats should not be underestimated, and also tends to be way under reported."

<<>>

Team Ann was stunned and amazed by the horrible results of Ann's Trial #2.. After the trial, the team was spread out geographically, but united in their warrior spirit to continue defending Ann and support her in any way possible. No one had the funds it would take to mount the defense that would be necessary to secure Ann's freedom. They were sick with worry that she would not survive her incarceration.

Team Ann now consisted of:

> ~Ken Patton, Ann's brother, and his new fiancée Kathy Turetzky
>
> ~Pete DeLisi, John's mentor in the hedge fund business
>
> ~Gregory Fischer, Ann's new love and guardian angel
>
> ~Fabio Oconitrillo, Ann's lawyer, who was now working, by necessity, pro bono
>
> ~Ann's 97-year-old grandmother, after whom Ann was named

~Ann's two parents

~Celine Bouchacourt Martenot, Ann's high school friend

~Jack Schwager, John's supporter and colleague

~Paul Meyer, the Benders' neighbor from Boracayán

This group got together and decided to create a *GoFundMe* page to try to raise funds for Ann's defense, as well as a petition, *Free Ann Bender*, which they circulated to as many outlets as they could, including Facebook and Twitter. None of the Team Ann members were public relations professionals; they were operating solely on love for Ann, and total panic that she would die in jail. They feared both natural and nefarious causes. They had every reason to be concerned. The following is the petition they circulated, written by Kathy Turetzky, on *change.org*, and an update to the petition posted September 1, 2014:

Petición para el Presidente de Costa Rica

Please free Ann Bender (Ann Maxine Patton) from prison.

On May 27, 2014, a Costa Rican court unfairly convicted Ann Bender (Ann Maxine Patton), a U.S. citizen, to a 22-year prison sentence. She was convicted of murdering her husband, John Bender, when he in fact committed suicide in bed next to her on the night of January 8, 2010. There is documented history of suicidal ideation on John Bender's part including an e-mail introduced into evidence dated just a month before stating that, "I feel so fucking horrible I want to kill everyone and then me... I deserve to die." There is also testimony from friends and family that he suffered from a bipolar disorder in addition to numerous other mental health issues.

Ann also suffers from a number of physical and mental ailments and is likely to struggle being in detention due to the level of treatment she requires. The overwhelming stress of years of wrongful litigation, compounded by the grief of having to re-live the most terrible tragedy (watching your spouse of twelve years commit suicide) is something I hope none of you will ever have to face

Ann Patton's civil rights in Costa Rica have been grossly violated. In addition to being unfairly convicted of murder, she has also been defrauded and manipulated by a trustee whose very duty as a fiduciary was to protect her interests. Instead, he took advantage of his position of trust and the tragedy of John's suicide to steal millions of dollars, all the while not abiding by the trust decree in which Ann is a beneficiary. Ann has not received a penny from the trust in over two years and has relied on the support of friends and family, but they have nothing left to give. Nobody expected this, and certainly not to continue for almost five years.

This 22-year prison sentence was decided in a SECOND trial for the same charge. During the first trial in January, 2013 she was UNANIMOUSLY acquitted by a panel of three judges. Costa Rica does not have a legal ban on double jeopardy, and although it is considered an option to have a second trial on appeal, it rarely happens. This case is entirely about money, and nothing to do with justice. Not a single person is asking for justice for John Bender's death, not even his own parents who strongly opposed the Prosecution of Ann. How often is there a murder case where even the family of the victim supports the accused?

All of Ann Patton's wealth has been taken from her in Costa Rica. She has no funds to defend herself from this gross violation of her civil rights and needs financial support. An appeal has been filed against this unfair conviction. However, it is clear that based on her medical history, Ann's odds of surviving a 22-year prison sentence are very limited.

Also, Donations are needed to help fund Ann's legal Defense and save her life.

Any amount is appreciated and will help save the life of a woman who has given so much to this country and its people.

CRAZY JUNGLE LOVE

POSTED BY

CELINE BOUCHACOURT MARTENOT

Many of you have been moved by Ann's story and have asked me for details and how they could support. Thank you.

The following is part of the official verdict of Ann's first trial in January 2013 as transcribed by Reuters:

SAN ISIDRO DE EL GENERAL, COSTA RICA (JANUARY 21, 2013) (REUTERS) COURT IN SESSION ANNE MAXINE PATTON IN COURT GENERAL COURT OFFICIALS JUDGE FRANCISCO SÁNCHEZ, SAYING:

"This court unanimously, and applying the principle of 'in dubio pro reo' (when in doubt, for the accused), moves to declare Anne Maxine Patton acquitted of all responsibility with regards to the homicide of John Feliz [sic] Bender that was attributed to her by the Public Ministry. It is ordered that all precautionary measures that had been imposed be removed."

Ann was acquitted. There was no motive. No Evidence. Nothing.

I was present at the first trial. I saw and heard everything.

An appeal was immediately filed by the DA, resulting in the court of appeals ordering a retrial, which took place just now. Ann's testimony never changed, neither did the Defense witnesses. She is innocent. Nothing has changed. However this time the new three-judge panel read out a one-hour verdict accusing her to be a monster who killed her husband, ordering twenty-two years in prison with immediate effect. This is pure insanity and a blatant miscarriage of justice. Ann never ran, she always told the truth. John committed suicide and she tried to prevent it. The police did a sloppy job at best—no fingerprinting of the gun, for instance! And this is just one example. Discussions about the position of John's body abound. But Ann was taken away from the bedroom when help arrived. It is not her fault if the body, or the gun, were moved. By anyone. At anytime. A re-enactment was organized by the police. Ann, the only witness, was absent and not even informed. The house was raided by police a few days after the suicide, and emptied of all its contents; down to the microwave and fridge. Where are all these items now? Not important. Just goes to show the corrupt police work. There are inconsistencies everywhere. Again. No motive. No proof. Circumstantial evidence.

Everything about this is wrong. This is about corruption. Greed. Theft.

John's and Ann's money was, and is, in a trust. They earned their money together, chose to move from the U.S. to Costa Rica. Did everything by the book. The Costa Rican trustee, a lawyer named Juan de Dios Álvarez, stole from them, from day one. John dying was the trustee's ticket to owning everything. The money, the Refuge... He wanted Ann out of the way. And miraculously got just what he wanted. You work it out.

Ann completely collapsed after the verdict and is now in an ICU, gravely ill. I ask my friends, her friends, anybody who is interested, to hook up to her Facebook page, which her brother Ken is now running, giving news.

We, family and close friends, are doing everything in our power to end this nightmare. And we need all the help we can get. Thank you for your kindness, support and prayers. Please help make this story go viral. An innocent woman is dying and we can make this right. We can.

I will never give up.

UPDATE AS OF SEPTEMBER 1, 2014
Kathy Turetzky - Brighton, MI

SEPTEMBER 1, 2014 — Ann Patton-Bender remains in a Costa Rican prison, convicted for murdering her husband by a corrupt Costa Rican court in Pérez Zeledón on May 27, 2014. Ann Patton committed no crime. CBS forensics experts have—not surprisingly—recently concluded that Ann did not murder her husband.

http://www.cbsnews.com/news/american-charged-in-husbands-costa-rica-death-experts-question-case/

Corruption is the rule, not the exception, in Costa Rica. Corruption is completely institutionalized in that country.

Ann Patton's conviction is all about money. If the Costa Rican legal system manages to keep her imprisoned, the Costa Rican state and several individual Costa Rican citizens who Ann once trusted to manage her financial affairs will manage to steal approximately $100 million in assets that rightfully belong to her. Ann's conviction had nothing to do with justice. It was all about greed by a band of cowards who took advantage of Ann in her unfortunate circumstance.

Ann Patton's freedom is now at the mercy of an appeals tribunal in Costa Rica. On June 23rd, her Defense attorney filed an appeal to her conviction, and she now awaits their response. Justice for her depends on that tribunal's competence to see through the corrupt police investigation of her husband's death and the corrupt verdict of the lower court system. Justice for Ann is now entirely dependent on the capacity of another Costa Rican judicial entity to act in a competent and responsible manner. That this will happen is certainly very questionable in a country where corruption is expected of government officials when money is at stake.

All of her money has been stolen by Costa Ricans she once trusted. She needs a strong legal Defense throughout the appeal process to defend herself against this systemic attack on her rights and property. She does not belong in a Costa Rican prison. She is a kind, honest, dignified human being who absolutely does not deserve the disgusting abortion of justice that has taken place to her detriment in Costa Rica. If the Costa Rican judicial system fails to do justice, Ann Patton will not survive her corrupt 22-year sentence.

Aftermath of a Catastrophic Second Trial

"In that Macondo forgotten even by the birds, where the dust and the heat had become so strong that it was difficult to breathe, secluded by solitude and love in a house where it was almost impossible to sleep because of the noise of the red ants. Aureliano, and Amaranta Ursula were the only happy beings, and the most happy on the face of the earth."

Gabriel García Márquez – *One Hundred Years of Solitude*

John Bender died on January 8, 2010, and Ann Bender was unanimously convicted by the Costa Rican court of his murder on May 27, 2014—four years and four months after John passed away. Neither she nor Team Ann could possibly have been prepared for that second trial, and the conviction and sentencing outcome.

How was this possible?

Ann was led away by court police guards, but only barely exited the main courtroom before fainting, collapsing in boyfriend Greg Fischer's arms. She was taken by ambulance to the private hospital in Pérez Zeledón, Clínica El Labrador, where she remained for ten days on round-the-clock suicide watch. She was then transported to El Buen Pastor Women's Prison to serve out her 22-year prison sentence.

Greg Fischer said, "I don't think she's gonna live. I don't think she's gonna survive." In all likelihood, Ann would *not* have survived had it not been for the kindness of her fellow prisoners and the devoted support of Greg, her North Star. A North Star is someone who is constant and dependable in an ever-changing world, and for Ann, that was unquestionably Greg.

During their short-lived love affair, Greg and Ann had become aficionados of all things Tico: the culture, the cuisine, the language, and the arts. Together they had been reading the books of one of Costa Rica's most iconic writers, José León Sánchez. Greg made sure that Ann had the author's most famous book to read for inspiration while in jail: *La Isla de los Hombres Solos* (*The Island of Lonely Men*). This book describes León's own horrendous 30 years in prison on the Island of San Lucas for a crime he swore he never committed. San Lucas has since been converted into a national park, where visitors can see graffiti written by prisoners in their own blood: lots of provocative girlie drawings. It was a heroic tale of overcoming adversity and surviving the nightmare of jail, then later triumphing as a free person on the outside. León's story gave Ann courage.

Costa Rica's patron saint is the Virgin of Los Angeles, a saint fondly known as "La Negrita" by the many Catholic worshipers in the country. The legend tells us that on August 2, 1635, a young native girl was out looking for firewood when she stumbled upon a black stone figure, which seemed to depict the Christ Child being held by his mother. It was a small (less than one meter high) statuette, and the young girl eagerly took it home to show her family. The next morning, the statue was mysteriously right back where it had been found. Then it happened again. Folks considered it a miracle of God, and eventually a cathedral was erected in Cartago to honor and protect the statue, the Basílica de Nuestra Señora de Los Ángeles. August 2nd is celebrated as a national holiday when hundreds of thousands of pilgrims flock to Cartago, often by foot from long distances, to leave tokens of gratitude for the blessings of the Virgin. Coins, charms, trinkets, and jewels are left at the feet of La Negrita.

There is some historical disagreement over the racial background of the small girl who originally found La Negrita. Amateur historians claim that rather than indigenous, she was a *parda*, or free black person of African descent. Either way, she remains famous—yet often nameless. Some historians have claimed that La Negrita was found by Juana Pereira, an unsung bi-racial heroine. La Negrita is one of Costa Rica's most recognized icons, and is usually portrayed as a mother and a child, very reminiscent of the Virgin Mary and Christ Child, standing on a rock with "Virgen de Los Ángeles, Patrona de Costa Rica" (Virgin of Los Angeles, Patron Saint of Costa Rica), carved into the stone supporting them.

In 1950, gunmen broke into the Basilica of Los Angeles, killed one watchman, and stole millions of dollars' worth of jewels from around the La Negrita statuette. Ticos went wild at the sacrilege and the violation of their religion, culture, and the Virgin Mary herself. They found the perfect scapegoat in the future author José León Sánchez, who the newspapers dubbed "The Monster of the Basilica." León is now considered a master of Tico literature. What a divine reversal of fortune!

CRAZY JUNGLE LOVE

León was born in Cucaracho del Rio Cuarto in Puntarenas, a poor small town where his mother was one of two prostitutes servicing the pueblo. His mother had birthed seven children before José León, selling them all because she could not turn enough tricks to support them. León arrived into this world visibly sick, severely jaundiced, described by the hospital as being "yellow as an egg yolk." His mother could not even manage to trade him for a bag of salt, given his sorry look, and ended up just giving him to the salt merchant—who kindly took him to the hospital. Once he was healed, León was delivered to an orphanage where he lived until his escape at age ten. León lived on the streets of Cartago until the age of nineteen, when the group of robbers of the Basilica told the police that it was León who had robbed the Basilica and killed the guard, thereby saving their own hides.

The police forced a confession out of León by sticking lit matches into his ears, and yanking out some of his teeth. They were desperate for an arrest, and León was the perfect defenseless victim. At the age of twenty, León was given a life sentence for his crime, and became the youngest person ever to be thrown into the slave labor prison on the Island of San Lucas, off the Pacific coast of Costa Rica. The treatment and food there made Buen Pastor look like a Hilton, and he was only allowed one hour of sunshine daily.

Eventually León was transferred to the maximum-security prison in San José (now the Children's Museum), where he began to write *La Isla* about his horrendous years on San Lucas. Several other books followed, many of them award-winning, and after thirty years of false imprisonment, León was released and declared innocent by the Costa Rican government. The Catholic Church gave him an official apology. His next book was *God Was Looking the Other Way*, a sentiment keenly shared by the Bender family. José León is still alive, residing and writing in Heredia. He continued to write, and is credited with establishing Costa Rica's first blood bank, among his many other accomplishments.

<<>>

The cash value of the jewels and trinkets that José León was accused of stealing was trifling compared to the cash value of the jewels that the Benders were accused of smuggling. When asked by a reporter what the deal was with all the jewels found at the crime scene, an employee of Ann's responded, "Doña Ana just really likes shiny, sparkly things—like the lamps, and the cut-glass art, and of course, her jewels."

Extreme collecting and hoarding are both associated with major depressive disorders or obsessive-compulsive disorder, so it's much more likely that the jewel collection was a manifestation of both Ann's and John's mental frailty than any illegal pursuit. According to recent British researchers, up to one-third of adults engage in some form of collecting, but only between two and five percent of the adult population would meet the criteria for a diagnosis of hoarding. That was not an easy issue for the defense team to explain to the judges at Ann's trial.

The Benders collected jewels, animals, Tiffany lamps (worth from $80 to $12,000 each), and art-glass artifacts. It should not be surprising that they did not collect Beanie Babies or Barbie dolls. Some suspicious neighbors at Boracayán accused them of flying in wealthy clients to parties at Bender Dome to sell them jewels, but there is no evidence that they ever parted with any jewels, just accumulated more and more. Reportedly, Ann made between twelve and fifteen trips out of Costa Rica in pursuit of more jewels for her collection. She returned to San José without any complications, and had no problems at Immigration and Customs. She declared them as purchases for her own private collection. John had stated all along that the jewels were his liquid assets in case of a financial crisis. John and Ann were neither hoarders nor illegal jewel smugglers. They were extreme collectors. They never even shared their hobby with other collectors—it was all about their shared passion for their private collection. It was all part of their madness.

Pete DeLisi explained, "Both John and Ann had a passion for gemology and took advantage of the 'fire sale' prices that were the result of the 2008 global economic meltdown. Like any art or collectible, the gemstones were for their personal enjoyment, but obviously an investment. They did not buy them to speculate like one would buy a stock or real estate." John had maintained an interest in minerals and gemology since grade school. It was only logical that as an almost-billionaire he would entertain his passion to the fullest, and keep his sweet bride happy at the same time. Ann was his most valuable jewel.

Ann was unfortunately caught in a new push by the Costa Rican government to cut down on the flow of contraband goods into the country. In August, 2014, authorities said that smuggling costs the country up to $100 million annually from lost tax revenue. The Vice Minister of Finance claimed that contraband was a bigger problem than drug trafficking. There was renewed vigor to catch smugglers and put them into prison. Most of the contraband being smuggled was alcohol, cigarettes, and illegal medicine, but Ann was painted with the same broad brush. It became mandatory to face prison time for being found with $50,000 or more of contraband—Ann was accused of possessing over $7 million of smuggled goods. Her case was very serious indeed.

Costa Rica is often called "The Jewel of Central America," but there are no native jewels or gems in this tiny country— only the richness of the environment. Costa Rica means "Rich Coast" in Spanish, supposedly named by the first Spanish conquistadors who got their greedy hopes up when they saw the indigenous wearing gold ornaments. Unfortunately for the Spanish, most of the earrings, collars, and necklaces worn by the indigenous had been traded for food supplies with natives from South America, and there was very little gold for the taking in Costa Rica. Ann Bender seemed to have brought in enough bling for almost everyone. Now *that's* some extreme collecting!

This fortune in jewels owned by only one couple was incomprehensible for Tico authorities. At first, they tried valuing each jewel, but eventually gave up, and decided to weigh them on a meat scale found in the Bender's chef's kitchen. More jewels kept being located hidden away—not effectively—throughout the fourth floor living quarters. The jewels passed through many hands in this process, undoubtedly some with sticky fingers. Ultimately, the jewels (about 3,000 or so), were packed in four giant suitcases and taken for safekeeping to the vault at BCR, Banco Central de Costa Rica. Authorities claim they are still there. The Bender jewel collection consisted of diamonds, emeralds, rubies, sapphires, tourmaline and opals. Some were beautifully set in rings, bracelets, and brooches. Still many more were beautifully cut, but not yet in settings. Ann really did love her shiny, sparkly things.

OIJ certainly did not see it as a jewelry collection. To them, it looked exactly like a sophisticated smuggling ring for high-roller Americans. This was exactly what police always expected from Ugly Americans. At their police pay scale, and after being called to this freak show in the middle of the night, they decided immediately that Ann had committed murder, and the motive was more than likely to gain possession of *all* these incredible jewels. It was this first impression that Ann would have to fight for the next four years.

The OIJ confiscated the jewelry collection under the pretext of not being able to ascertain the source of the jewels or being able to review legal sales records or proof that taxes had been paid on them in Costa Rica. They wasted no time charging Ann with money laundering, racketeering, and smuggling contraband. She was charged in February 2010, one month after John's death, and well before being charged with John's murder. This speed seems to be an epic first for Costa Rican authorities. According to Costa Rica's Intelligence Agency (DIS), about $4.2 billion in cash is laundered annually in the country, yet in 2014, only twenty-one people were formally charged with this crime. The OIJ strongly suspected that the jewels had been acquired on the black market.

The authorities were convinced that Ann's jewels had been unlawfully purchased and imported, many from Africa, including many alleged "blood diamonds." Blood diamonds (or conflict diamonds) are diamonds that were mined in a war zone, the proceeds of which are used by rebel dictators to fund wars against legitimate governments. Costa Rica had signed onto the Kimberley Process in 2003, which prohibits the purchase or import of these tainted jewels. The OIJ felt that Ann was importing unlawful jewels and selling them at millionaires-only parties with fancy auctions at Boracayán. Bender employees claim that no such parties ever occurred, and that the staff would certainly have been aware of fancy folks being flown or 4-wheels driven in on the painfully poor roads leading to Bender Dome. Everyone would have seen them arrive—and gossiped about it. The farmers near Boracayán said it never happened.

Nonetheless, Ann certainly did love her diamonds. Neighbors at Boracayán claimed that her initial attraction to the property was that it overlooked the magnificent, shiny, sparkly, six-hundred-foot waterfall Catarata Diamante, or Diamond Waterfall. This is one of Costa Rica's tallest waterfalls, and after hiking to the top of it, one can spend the night in a cave, in the fresh air, listening to the swish of the falls, and wake the next morning to one of the nicest views in the Southern Zone. For many years the falls and cave were used as the site of a drug rehabilitation program, with young drug addicts working to construct the many steps leading up to the cave and acting as guards at night to prevent squatters from taking over that beautiful spot. A local family has taken charge of the tours to the top of Diamante, and the tours include informal lessons on the flora and fauna that can be seen on the hike to the summit. John Bender would be glad that people can still enjoy this part of his land and his view of the spectacular waterfall.

The police snapped photos of the magnificent jewel collection strewn about the Bender bedroom. Wowzer! Included in the loot was a dazzling red diamond, which Ann claimed they had bought in a lot with other jewels for $2.2 million. There were shiny opals and sparkly emeralds. All told, the collection was worth about $15 million, according to Ann. She uses this figure to refute the prosecution's claims that she killed John for the jewels. Ann elaborates to *Outside Magazine*, "The reason I bring this up is, how do you make this work with this theory that I killed my husband to be able to run away? This is $15 million. I *left* them. Right on the counter." Ann's personal preference for the jewelry she chose to wear was quite simple: she liked silver jewelry with nature motifs and animals.

Friends of Ann's are quite sure that the collection has been ransacked, and the OIJ now declares the current value to be only $7.5 million, about half of what it was at the time of John's death.

<<>>

The accusations of money laundering and racketeering were dropped in 2012, but not the contraband charges. A spokesperson for the Special Prosecutor's Office for Organized Crime indicated that her office was moving forward with charges against Ann for "violating Costa Rica's General Customs Law," allegedly for acquiring and storing jewels that had entered the country by eluding customs control. At the heart of that accusation was the issue of exactly how and when the jewels had entered Costa Rica, and for what purpose. Amazingly, the law Ann was accused of breaking was amended a short two months later. The prosecution no longer had a case.

At this point, the custody of the jewels was turned over to the General Customs Office, with an accompanying appraisal by a court-appointed expert of $7,234,990.77. The General Customs Office was tasked with collecting whatever corresponding taxes had not been collected at the time that the jewels first entered the country. The

Prosecutor's Office claimed that taxes were owed to the tune of $1,538,759.63.

Ann had always maintained that the gems were personal items, like traveling into Costa Rica with a fistful of watches, and were therefore not subject to being taxed. Pete DeLisi (now acting as Ann's spokesman) maintains that customs officials never questioned Ann and John about the gems when they entered, never demanded tax payments, and added that the Benders had always declared everything on their customs forms. Unfortunately, like lots of things in Costa Rica, customs laws regarding entering the country with personal possessions are open to widely differing interpretations. And that's the catch-22 dilemma in which Ann found herself. Then the Central Customs Office began making noise that the gems might not even truly belong to Ann.

In her state of being completely *desplatada* and not agreeing that she in fact owed any taxes, Team Ann nonetheless made a verbal agreement with the Manager of the Customs Office at the time, Enilda Ramírez, to pay $1.5 million in taxes to Costa Rica in return for all her jewels—or what was left of her jewels. Ramírez met with Ann's lawyer, and reviewed all the steps which Oconitrillo and Ann would take to complete this transaction. Ann dared to hope again. Besides, no other individual or corporation had ever come forward to try to claim ownership of the gem collection.

She had begun to hope too soon. Ann was called back to her second trial in May of 2014, and this time, as we know, the verdict was catastrophic.

Americans who had not been very sympathetic after John's death seemed to rally around the injustice of Ann's situation, and their comments about Costa Rica's handling of Ann's case were brutal. Said George of Uvita in an email to his neighbors,

> "Can you believe these motherfuckers? This poor lady comes to town, helps the local economy by building a mansion and bringing in water to the whole area, is a little off her rocker—who isn't—collects fine things for her personal enjoyment, creates a lovely national park, and what does Costa Rica do? They accuse her of killing her own husband, then take all her fine things away, then they fucking throw her in the slammer. On what planet is THAT Pura Vida? I'm moving to Panamá."

When Randall Baldí, one of the principal taxi drivers who helped transport Team Ann around town was asked his opinion on the confiscation of Ann's gems, he had but one slang response, *chorizo*, literally meaning sausage, but in slang meaning illegal business, a scam, or corruption: bullshit. Expats in San Isidro agreed.

Love Flames, then Dies

"There is always something left to love."

Gabriel García Márquez – *One Hundred Years of Solitude*

With Ann now in prison, Greg Fischer was completely alone. The nearly two-year affair with Ann had filled him with joy and a deep, enduring love. He missed her from the time his eyes opened at sunrise, to his last thought before sleep. Ann was the love of his life—forever. Greg knew deep within his heart that he would not survive the 22-year sentence without her. She was his Ana, or as he sometimes called her, his Iliana.

During their emerging love for each other, and growing love for Costa Rica, Greg and Ann had learned about one of the most popular myths in Costa Rica: How the rualdo bird lost his song. This myth tells of a beautiful young indigenous girl named Iliana, who lived in the lush tropical rainforest near her tribal home, at the foot of Poás Volcano. One day, as Iliana was out exploring the forest, she came upon a rualdo bird (golden-browed chlorophonia), a brightly colored bird found in both Panama and Costa Rica. Seeing that the girl was completely alone and lonely, the rualdo bird adopted Iliana and began to follow her everywhere. They became best friends. Iliana was always accompanied by the sweet song of her rualdo bird companion.

One day, Iliana's father—a powerful shaman in Poás—became very concerned with the rumblings and groans emerging from the volcano. He knew from stories passed down by his forefathers that this volcano could erupt, sending lava, ash and molten rock into the air and down over his people, destroying his village and tribe. He decided to climb to the summit of Poás to negotiate with the powerful spirit there. The Poás spirit said it would only be appeased if the father sacrificed his only child to the volcano. Iliana would have to die to save the tribe.

Iliana was bound and gagged, and dragged kicking and screaming to the mouth of the volcano, now roaring with anticipation of the human sacrifice. Suddenly, the rualdo bird took flight, diving deeply into the scalding cauldron of the volcano, to plead firsthand for Iliana's life to be spared. He offered to trade the only thing he owned—his lovely song—for Iliana's life. The rualdo bird filled the fiery cavity with his music, singing of friendship, faithfulness, and the beauty of his native land. His song was so beautiful that the volcano wept a million tears, thereby flooding the crater now known as the Botos Lagoon of Poás. Iliana's village was saved.

Volcán Poás is considered one of the most breathtaking sites in all of Costa Rica, and had erupted 39 times since 1828. It is still an active volcano and is located about an hour and a half from Greg and Ann's apartment in Escazú. Rualdo birds are still plentiful, but their call is only a sad, soft, low whistle.

The myth of the rualdo bird and Iliana touched Greg's and Ann's hearts, as their love for each other flourished.

<<>>

Greg's song was nowhere close to being silenced. He launched himself into an extensive search for ways to help Ann out of her predicament. He contacted the US Embassy; they were sympathetic and willing to check on Ann in prison, but unable to intervene in a foreign country's legal process. They did impress upon the Tico authorities the importance of maintaining Ann's fragile health. The prison doctor was put on notice to help Ann in any way he could, which he did. The Embassy sent pairs of female Embassy officials to look in on Ann from time to time in prison, but their visits, Greg felt, were useless, and perhaps depressing rather than energizing to Ann. Ann had truly been sent "up the river," as the American expression goes, sent far away to jail.

Along with Ann's brother Ken, Greg began contacting US senators and congressmen to see if they could help. They could not. Costa Rican presidents and senators were approached; no help there. American companies who specialized in asset recovery, some operating in Costa Rica, were contacted to see if they could help retrieve Ann's fortune. Still no luck. It seemed to many as though Ann was fighting a losing battle, and a hugely complicated and dangerous one at that. The danger aspect never seemed to deter Greg, who continued to fight on valiantly against the odds. He actually felt safer personally with Ann in jail. Most suspected that whomever was framing Ann—if that is what was happening—was hopeful that she would die in jail and the problem would be solved. They did not realize what a consummate survivor Ann had always been, and continued to be. No one could have predicted that it would be Greg Fischer who would die mysteriously while Ann was in prison. That was a huge surprise to most everyone.

Greg devoted himself to all the details and tasks involved with making sure Ann could manage while incarcerated. He brought her clean clothes, food, emails from friends, encouraging news and funny articles from newspapers, the latest tallies on her *GoFundMe* page and her *Petition to Free an Innocent Woman*, missives from her family and legal team—anything he could think of to cheer her up and lift her spirits. He was her caterer, wardrobe manager, secretary, psychiatrist, and above all, knew exactly who he should bribe and reward to keep her safe at El Buen Pastor Prison. The reporter from *Inside Costa Rica* declared that Greg was the ONLY thing keeping Ann together and alive in Buen Pastor, and wondered what others without such a support system would do to cope while in prison. It was frightening to contemplate.

Greg's next brainstorm was to begin researching Americans with deep pockets who could possibly help, especially those who might have at one time found themselves in similar legal situations in Costa Rica. He found the idea of approaching these people humiliating, but was willing to do it for his beloved Ana. The financial situation of Team Ann was truly alarming, and a fast influx of cash could be of great help to all those involved in *la lucha*, or the struggle. One name kept popping up in his research—Calvin Ayre, a Canadian.

Calvin Ayre (pronounced Air), had set up his online gambling operation in Costa Rica in 1996, two years before the Benders began purchasing the huge chunks of property which were to become Boracayán. He was a fabulously wealthy entrepreneur and playboy billionaire who founded an online gambling empire headquartered in San José called *Bodog.com*. By 2006, Ayre turned up on the cover of the "Billionaire's Edition" of *Forbes Magazine*, featured as a business genius who had purchased a $3.5 million estate in San José, possibly to hide from US tax agents, and reputedly had already bedded some 8,000 women. The *Forbes* cover read, "Catch Me If You Can."

Ayre described having read in 1992 about a Caribbean-based company offering betting services over the phone. Ayre said he heard, a "…a loud bang in my head, and the whole universe came together." His epiphany was that gambling was absolutely tailor-made for the internet, something which no one else seemed to be exploiting. *Bodog.com* was born, with Ayre becoming the face and lifestyle model for his company, in an era where online gambling was largely secret and faceless. He threw wild parties with wild women, and by 2006 was worth probably $1.2 billion, all of it beyond the reach of the IRS or any other tax-collecting entity. He drove around San José in a Humvee with an armed driver who had been trained by the Canadian Army and had served in war zones throughout the world. In 2005, Ayre began the *Calvin Ayre Fund*, a not-for-profit organization in Costa Rica focused on animal welfare and the environment. The fund and grown considerably by 2010 and had helped various causes throughout Costa Rica. He was the perfect person to help!

Only he wasn't. By February 2012, Ayre and three other Canadians were indicted in the US for unlawful internet gambling. Ayre vamoosed to Antigua. His San José property was taken over by squatters, and the price of his property was dropped from $6 million to $3.5 million, with experts saying he would be lucky to get $2 million—after a long, drawn-out fight with the folks living on his property. Squatters in Costa Rica have incredible rights.

Also of interest to Greg was the pair of Atlanta, Georgia land barons who had bought 1,200 acres of land in Costa Rica's Guanacaste province. The property consisted of rolling hills, a lovely crescent beach, and the requisite number of monkeys needed to amuse American tourists. One partner was a 53-year-old Atlanta internet millionaire named Charles Brewer,; the other was a fellow Atlanta hedge fund billionaire, the 61-year-old Tom Claugus. The project was to create an eco-town called Las Catalinas, consisting of a high-end hotel and million-dollar second homes for Americans and Europeans.

By the time Greg had his ducks in a row in 2014 to make a move on these potential benefactors, the project had stalled out with no hotel, only ten houses and a very modest restaurant and shops. It was a rough time to launch a resort project while the world economy struggled out of crisis, and Brewer and Claugus were having a hard time enticing investors into plunking down between $500,000 and $2 million on a house accessible only by a dirt road. Additionally, the courts had put a work-stoppage injunction against Las Catalinas for disturbing the environment and possibly obtaining water permits illegally.

Brewer and Claugus were not easily deterred. Brewer had founded the Internet company MindSpring, which merged with Earthlink, Inc., earning Brewer a cool $50 million. Claugus, who had planned to be a millionaire by age fifty-two, achieved his goal by age thirty-eight. These were not men who would easily cry uncle. As of the summer of 2016, the Casa Chameleon Hotel Mal País at Las Catalinas had still not yet been built, but there were more villas now under construction or completed. The partners were enjoying their investment as a getaway for their friends and families. They were still not at a level of accomplishment in 2014 to focus on any philanthropic ideas for people they had never even met. Greg refused to be discouraged; this was a fight to the death for his lovely lady Ann.

Casa Chameleon Hotel Mal País features a magnificent 360-degree, zero-edge swimming pool perched on top of a cliff, with a poolside bar overlooking the Catalinas Islands. Their brochure states, "Casa Chameleon Hotel is all about an intimate, unique, and eclectic atmosphere, where cookie-cutter is never the go-to." Sounds about right for high-roller tourists to Costa Rica.

Ann's own family and friends had contributed all that they could financially to her defense. Sadly, Ann's dear grandfather passed away while she was in the midst of her turmoil. In July, 2012, Walter Hibbard Esworthy, Ann's grandfather on her mother's side, died at the age of almost ninety-four. Ann had been named after her grandmother Ann Esworthy—Ann is Hannah in Hebrew and means grace. Walter died at home while holding his wife Ann's hand. Walter had a distinguished career as a submarine naval officer and had retired to the family estate, Alemquer, in Sarasota, Florida, where he and Ann spent forty-two years tending the lovely botanical gardens and contributing to the nearby Selby Botanical Gardens. Selby Gardens played a big part in helping with the botanical discoveries and lab work done at Boracayán. Ann Bender even named a newly discovered gesneriad (similar to an African violet) for her grandmother—just one of several botanical contributions Boracayán made in the years Ann resided there.

A team of botanical scientists from the Marie Selby Botanical Gardens of Sarasota Bay, Sarasota, Florida, had visited the Benders at Boracayán in 2003. Marie Selby Gardens are the only botanical gardens in the world dedicated to the display and study of epiphytes, especially orchids and bromeliads. An epiphyte is a plant that grows harmlessly upon another plant and derives moisture and nutrients from the air, rain, and sometimes the debris accumulated around it. These plants usually flourish up high to reach the sunlight, using the tree for support, yet making all their own energy through photosynthesis. They are reproduced via spores transported by birds or the wind.

Selby Gardens is located on the grounds of the former Sarasota home of Marie and William Selby, and features 20,000 unique plants including 5,500 varieties of orchids and 3,500 species of bromeliads. William Selby made his fortune as co-founder of Texaco, and he endowed Selby Gardens and donated his mansion for the Gardens' not-for-profit use. Marie Selby is famous for being the first woman to cross the US in an automobile. Ann Esworthy, Ann Bender's grandmother, was a dedicated contributor and supporter of Selby Gardens. She and Ann's parents helped to endow a small laboratory at Boracayán, for the use of both John and Ann for their own scientific study, as well as for the use of visiting scientists with an interest in the rainforest and its canopy ecosystem. Both the nature reserve and its tiny lab showed great promise for new scientific discoveries in the Southern Zone. Lawyer Álvarez allegedly cleared out the lab to take the contents home with him at the same time he removed the art from the Bender sculpture garden.

So promising was the scientific potential of Boracayán that in the year 2003, Selby Gardens sent an international three-person research team to help establish the Walter H. Esworthy Botanical Laboratory, named after Ann Bender's grandfather. The team was comprised of Bruce Holst, Laurie Birch, and Angel Lara, as well as the world-renowned orchidologist Dr. Robert Dressler. Although only on the reserve for one week, the Selby team managed to discover four new species of plants. The rarest orchid found they chose to name in honor of Ann Bender's grandmother and the Boracayán Reserve. They called it *Gongora boracayánensis*. It is a delicate white orchid with red splatter—like blood spatter—scattered over the delicate flower top.

They described their orchid discovery in the Selby Gardens scientific magazine *"Selbyana"* in an article titled "An Old Species Finally Named and Described," as follows:

> "During a preliminary plant inventory in May 2003, of the Boracayán wildlife Refuge in south western Costa Rica, owned and managed by Ann Patton and John Bender, a Lycaste plant was collected by staff of the Marie Selby Botanical Gardens, in collaboration with Lankester Botanical Garden. The Lycaste was brought back to Selby Gardens with numerous other collections and placed under the care of horticulturist Angel Lara. The plant was re-potted in 2004, when a small and different looking orchid seedling was discovered among the pseudo bulbs of the Lycaste. The seedling resembled a minute Gongora and was therefore placed in a hanging basket to allow any future and pendent inflorescences to develop freely. The first flowering of the Gongora took place in 2006 and some flowers were photographed and preserved in alcohol for identification at the Orchid

Identification Center (OIC). Since the curator of the OIC was out of the country at the time of flowering, the jar with the Gongora flowers was temporarily placed on a shelf where it remained unidentified for a while. Eventually, an attempt to identify the plant resulted in the conclusion that it represented what Jenny (1993) describes as a frequently cultivated but misidentified species, known in horticulture as *Gongora quinquenervis Ruiz & Pav.* A photo of the misidentified species can be seen on the cover of his monograph of the genus. Since Jenny has established that the real *Gongora quinquenervis* represents a different species, the plant from Boracayán hence needs a new name."

The new chosen name became *Gongora boracayánensis.*

<<>>

Next, Greg put on his thinking cap and began to look for possible sources of financial aid from within Costa Rica, by seeking help from Ticos themselves. There were 85 Tico millionaires living in Costa Rica in 2012, with an accumulated wealth of $12 billion, according to Wealth-X, who tracks this sort of thing. That number was fewer than any other Latin country except Cuba—Costa Rica is a more equitable country than most in terms of wealth. Although the Benders had not been personal friends with any of these millionaires, Ann's case had gotten lots of press before, during, and after her conviction. The case gave all wealthy folks living in Costa Rica a little shudder. Most of these Ticos were American-educated and would at least understand the situation and the dire need for financial assistance. It was a long shot, but Greg was willing to take a chance and pursue some of these people to ask for help. Ann's lawyers needed to be paid, and Boracayán was floundering with no paid staff to keep it going. Greg felt this was his only choice.

Greg had now added fundraiser to the collection of hats that he wore. He chose three families to approach out of the 85 millionaires in the country.

First was the Arias family, considered "old money," having made their colones the old-school way through coffee, sugar plantations, and real estate. Oscar Arias was a former president and a Nobel Laureate Peace Prize winner, amazingly well-known and popular in the country, and apparently the owner of a Morgan Stanley US account alleged to be worth $570,000, divided among his various business groups. This was a fairly typical practice among wealthy Ticos—make your money, then stash it away in the US. Seems everyone wanted their nest egg out of reach of possibly unscrupulous Tico government officials. The Arias family now owns several shopping malls and gated gringo-attracting housing complexes.

Second was the Figueres family, begun by the iconic José Figueres, a key figure in the Costa Rican Civil War, and responsible for abolishing the military in 1948. Figueres spawned a whole dynasty of politicians and successful business leaders, each son and daughter more successful than the last. Figueres had begun with a humble coffee farm called La Lucha and had gone on to become president twice, to forge ties with the C.I.A., and even to arrange for fugitive businessman Robert Vesco to be granted asylum. Everything the Figueres family touched turned to gold. Their business ventures are now in real estate, agriculture, and financial investments. Numerous Ticos did very well selling real estate to American investors over the years. This family certainly had the funds and contacts to help.

A third possibility was the Tico hero Dr. Franklin Chang-Díaz, the third Latin American ever to go into space with NASA, now retired to Costa Rica with his own company called Ad Astra Rocket. The doctor had developed the VASIMAR engine for manned space missions to Mars—and stood to make a fortune from this venture.

Additionally, Dr. Chang-Díaz had worked as a young man in an experimental community helping mentally ill patients with chronic conditions—including those with bipolar disorder. He could be the perfect power person to help Ann out of her predicament.

Sadly, none of these possible benefactors were ever fully developed, as Greg Fischer's death ended the search. The one person keeping Ann alive was gone, and Ann was on her own—again—and in jail serving out her 22-year sentence.

The tradition in Costa Rica when someone dies is to have a celebration called *la Novenaria*, a nine-day event beginning usually on the day following the death. Every night for nine days, the community comes together to say a rosary and pray for the deceased who is believed to be resting in purgatory. Candles are lit, prayers are offered, and it is believed that this ritual enables a loved one's spirit to be elevated toward heaven. The nine days represent the nine months that an unborn child is in the mother's womb. It is believed that after those nine days the soul of the deceased is then "born" into heaven.

Coincidentally, Ann Bender was in jail for exactly nine months, which certainly must have felt like being in purgatory. She was unable to fully grieve for the passing of her lover and friend; however, her fellow prisoners in her cell barracks managed to persuade the guards to let them smuggle in some illegal votive candles to be able to honor Greg Fischer on the ninth day of the Novenaria. Ann's cell mates wept with Ann, the rosary was said, and Ann truly hoped that Greg's soul would now find peace in a better place. Ann had become convinced that her husband's soul had found no peace yet, and she received proof of that at her third trial when a medium was able to contact John via a pendulum and reveal the true condition of his torment.

A memorial service was held for Greg on December 6, in West Islip, New York. No one from Ann's family was able to attend. Ann mourned among her fellow prisoners at Buen Pastor. This was probably the toughest time for her in prison; it was total sorrow and sense of gloom. She was inconsolable.

A friend of Greg's wrote in his condolence book at the memorial service,

> "Condolences to Greg's family and to Ann and her family. Greg's loving smile and larger-than-life presence are missed by his friends here in Costa Rica. He was such an inspiration to all who knew him. His love of life and dedication to Ann were true examples of how he showed others through his actions. I know if he were here he would

tell me to have faith and that everything is going to work out for the best."

Greg Fischer's brother Brian simply wrote,

"Another journey begins…"

Crazy Jungle Love

"The only regret I will have in dying is if it is not for love."

Gabriel García Márquez – *Love in the Time of Cholera*

Ann Bender had been lucky enough in her life to have experienced two epic love affairs. But there was still one more passion filling her heart and bringing her much joy: the Boracayán Wildlife Refuge. She had heard from the tiny remaining refuge staff that all the animals she had so enjoyed at Boracayán had passed away, including her beloved Millie, the German shepherd. They were old—Ann felt old at forty-seven—and she had almost died several times herself in recent years. Ann had lots of time to reflect while at Buen Pastor, and she found herself reliving her favorite walks through the reserve, her favorite spot to stop and gaze at Diamante Waterfall, her favorite moments with John on their balcony at sunset, and her lush life in that magnificent nature reserve with all its hopes and adventures. The dream of returning to Boracayán gave her strength and courage to fight on for her survival—and for the future of the reserve.

Foreigners often say they visit Costa Rica for the surfing, beaches, kayaking, zip-lining, mountain hiking, fishing, wildlife, ecological touring, and to experience the relaxing *pura vida* lifestyle. John and Ann Bender came with a much more altruistic and philanthropic agenda. The Benders came to build a private nature preserve. Many say it was a miracle that they achieved that goal given the red tape, government obstruction, and conflict with their pugilistic neighbors. Nonetheless, in 2002, the rustic carved wooden signs marking the boundaries of the wildlife refuge were hammered into place, and a new private reserve was born. It currently sits dying a slow, sad death, abandoned by everyone.

Costa Rica has done an amazing job of preserving its national resources, even though those efforts were often at odds with slash-and-burn farmers, poachers, squatters, resort developers, ambitious tour operators, gold miners, and rich foreigners who thought money alone should entitle them to endangered portions of paradise. Costa Rica accounts for only three-tenths of one percent of the earth's surface area, yet contains roughly six percent of the world's biodiversity. It counts among its national treasures active volcanoes, beaches, forests, rainforests, hot springs, caves, river canyons, waterfalls, a multitude of animals—rare and magnificent—and jaw-droppingly beautiful foliage and plant life. The Benders arrived fully committed to preserving and protecting their slice of paradise, and John was convinced that the secret to curing his beloved Ann's Lyme disease lay hidden in the wilds of Boracayán.

Between 2011 and 2013, an amazing 5,000 new species of plants and animals were discovered in Costa Rica as part of the country's National Biodiversity Strategy (ENB in Spanish). This program follows the very reputable United Nations Strategic Environment Program Plan for Biodiversity. Among the wonderful new discoveries were orchids, mushrooms, mollusks, fish, reptiles, and birds—

and of course, a new venomous snake, the Talamanca palm pit viper. No environmental party in the Southern Zone would be complete without a good new poisonous snake! The good news for southerners is that the hospitals and clinics tend to be well-stocked with anti-venom.

Some of the more whimsical discoveries were a new fairy fly which measures 250 microns in length, about 2.5 times the width of a human hair, which they named *Tinkerbella nana*. Also discovered in 2015, was the glass frog, which lacks pigmentation so that it looks transparently glass-like. Most interesting for the bird-loving Benders was the *Touit costarricensis* (red-fronted parrotlet), a small bird which likes to nest in termite mounds found in trees and makes an enormous racket when it takes flight. The touit (cotorrita costarricense in Spanish) is named for the call it makes— tou-iiiitt, tou-iiiitt—and it also makes odd chattering sounds when not flying.

Costa Rica has protected about 28 percent of its lands in national parks, reserves, and wildlife refuges (like Boracayán). Two parks have even been declared World Heritage sites by UNESCO. The Costa Rican environmental protection program breaks down as follows:

~27 national parks

~58 wildlife refuges

~32 protected zones

~15 wetland/mangrove areas

~11 forest reserves

~8 biological reserves

~12 other conservation areas

All this is in a country the size of West Virginia!

This vast accomplishment has been achieved just since 1970, the year that the National Park Service was established with the mission of "conserving natural or scenic areas of national interest, perpetuating natural resources, and fostering environmental education and scientific study." Tiny Costa Rica has built a world-renowned national park service in the past few decades and has become a model for other developing countries striving for sustainable development. And not a minute too soon, according to environmentalists. During the last fifty years, Costa Rica tragically lost about fifty percent of its forest cover—not chopped down for timber to build houses for its citizens—but burned off to create grazing grounds for low-grade export beef: think McDonald's. Now Costa Rica actually has a positive forestation rate and recently passed 50% forest cover for the first time in fifty years.

Sadly, the government funding and manpower needed to monitor these protected sites is not yet in place, and there have been scandalous reports in the local press involving park rangers assisting with the planting and harvesting of marijuana on Park Service grounds. Rangers were allegedly paid to water, fertilize, and harvest the plants for the *mecheros*, or marijuana dealers. This money certainly helped to augment the meager pay of park rangers, some of whom were bribed to look the other way when they found marijuana growing on park lands. It is illegal to grow marijuana for sale in Costa Rica, but that transgression does not carry the same stigma as it does in some other countries. It makes it easy to understand, however, why the Benders and their staff found it necessary to be armed at all times on their reserve. There were always drug smugglers on the lookout for new and better places to cultivate their crops, and new underground railroad routes to transport their bounty without detection by police.

Although John and Ann had not taken much notice of fellow expat sources of information before their arrival, they had made themselves keenly aware of environmental challenges in Costa Rica, and of the history and importance of national parks in preserving national resources. They were especially aware of the hero known as the founder of the Tico park service movement: Nils Olaf Wessberg. They had read *The Quetzal and the Macaw: The Story of Costa Rica's National Parks* by conservationist and environmentalist David Rains Wallace. From a distance, it appeared as though the Benders were following in the footsteps of Wessberg and his wife Karen Morgenson. They would soon find out that these were exceedingly dangerous footsteps to follow.

<<>>

Nils Olaf Wessberg, known as Olle to his family and friends, is credited with creating the Costa Rican National Park Service, beginning in 1963 with the oldest park, Reserva Natural Absoluta Cabo Blanco, a 1,250-hectare (3,090-acre) reserve. He would later found and develop the dangerous and mystery-filled Corcovado National Park, a 42,000-hectare (103,780-acre) park with thirteen distinct habitats, and most of the remaining endangered jaguars and pumas prowling the country's forests. Folks disappear in Corcovado National Park—quite frequently. The well-known National Geographic explorer Roman Dial's twenty-seven-year-old son Cody Dial, himself an expert explorer, disappeared there in 2014, and some of his belongings, along with some of his bones were eventually found two years later. They were discovered by Ngöbe Indians, a tribe very familiar with the park and how to navigate it safely. His death, along with numerous others that occurred in Corcovado, remains a mystery. His father has stated that he believes Cody was killed by a falling tree.

Olle was born in 1919 in Germany, but was raised in Sweden and always considered himself a Swede. He lost his mother to brain cancer in 1947, and for his whole life was convinced that her death was the fault of poor diet and substandard foods. He suspected a link between the environment and cancer, a theory reconfirmed when his sister also died of brain cancer. Olle became an avowed vegan. Both his family and neighbors considered him odd as a result of his dietary habits and beliefs.

Olle worked at his father's side, learning about nature and animals, and forming his own slightly offbeat ideas about Mother Nature and our relationship to her. One night, at a raw-food get-together, Olle was introduced to Karen Morgenson. Like with the Benders, it was love at first sight. Karen said, "I saw him standing in the sunbeams, his white hair shining in the light, and I knew immediately that this was the man I wanted to share my life with." They discovered that they shared an interest in biology, environmental and health education, and exploration of foreign countries. They were married shortly thereafter, and in 1954, embarked on their odyssey to Costa Rica on a banana boat—never to return to Sweden again.

Olle's father Hugo described his son's life in Costa Rica, "Olle lived like a monkey in the trees—he will probably never come back." Actually, the couple found their paradise in a palm-leaf hut at the southern tip of Nicoya Peninsula, in northern Costa Rica. Their nearest neighbors were one-and-a-half miles away from them. They immediately planted thirty-two fruit trees, but had to forage in the forest like animals while waiting years for the trees to produce fruit. The couple would carefully observe what the monkeys ate, and eat it also, assuming it would not harm them. Hugo shipped them vitamins and supplements to augment what they found in the forest. The first two years for the couple in Costa Rica were filled with hunger and suffering. They were sustained, however, by their passionate tropical love for each other, that same co-dependent love as the Benders: that crazy jungle love, that *amour fou.*

Karen made a drink from several of the leaves she had seen the monkeys chewing, and called it monkey juice. She and Olle drank it every day, and it seemed to keep them healthy. Like the Benders, Olle and Karen never had children, but tended to a posse of animals that they rescued. After twelve years in the rainforest, they decided to celebrate and preserve it by making it into a national park. Olle traveled to San José twenty-three times, over dangerous and often impassable roads, to lobby for his park, and finally, in 1963, Central America's first national park was founded: Absolute Nature Reserve Cabo Blanco (white cape). Both the main trail through the park (Sendero Sueco), and the park's beach (Playa Sueco), were named after Olle, the *sueco* (Swede).

In July of 1975, Olle went to the Osa Peninsula to write an important report, promising to return in time for Karen's birthday on August 4. Karen had frightening nightmares while he was away. When he did not return for her birthday, Karen knew immediately that something terrible had happened. She hired a broken-down, beat-up aircraft and pilot and went looking for Olle in his latest project location: Corcovado Park.

Karen found the couple with whom Olle had spent the night before entering the park with his hired guide at his side. It is illegal, for reasons of safety, to set foot in Corcovado Park without a licensed guide. Despite days of flying back and forth over the park, there was no sign of her love, Olle. Then Karen hired some local farmers to go look for him, and they fairly quickly found Olle's compass, shoulder bag, and his machete stuck in a tree. The forest animals had devoured all of Olle but some of his bones. Karen lovingly gathered up the remaining bones to bring home to bury in her garden, where they would be near her always.

Much later, it was discovered that the guide Olle hired had murdered him at the request of some residents of Corcovado who were vehemently against the formation of a national park on that land. They wanted to continue digging and panning for gold, and planting banana trees for fruit they could sell. The guide was sentenced to prison, and was murdered by a fellow inmate while there.

The president of Costa Rica eventually held a televised speech in which he said, "The Swede has given his life to protect our rainforests. Now it is Costa Rica's duty to realize his dream of a national park in Corcovado." The Swede would have been heartbroken in the 1980s when a twenty-five-pound gold nugget was found in Corcovado Park, causing such a tremendous gold rush that government officials decided to close the park for several years to evict all the prospectors who had taken it over illegally.

Hats off to Olaf and Karen, the visionaries who created Corcovado National Park. It is home to over half of the country's endangered species of both trees and plants, including the largest tree in Central America, the giant silk cotton tree. Corcovado is home to one-hundred species of mammals, three-hundred-sixty-seven species of birds, fish, reptiles, and amazing insects too numerous to count. Unfortunately, the park continues as a hideaway for illegal loggers, hunters, and gold prospectors. The Swede ultimately triumphed over all of them, and someday Costa Rica may have the budget to adequately protect his creation.

Karen Morgenson died in 1994 at the age of sixty-eight, thirty-nine years after she and Olle had arrived in Costa Rica on that banana boat. She died of Olle's biggest enemy:

cancer. She and Olle are buried together near their first reserve.

<<>>

Still another example of crazy jungle love in Costa Rica—with dire consequences—ended six months after John Bender's death, in the person of the Canadian pioneer settler and hellcat, Kimberley Ann Blackwell. Kimberley discovered Costa Rica in the '90s, driving down from her native Canada in an old beat-up truck, then deciding to move to the Osa Peninsula permanently. When the Greenpeace ship *Rainbow Warrior* docked near her in Osa, Kimberley met Christopher Hoare, a handsome Australian ten years her junior, who was working aboard the *Rainbow Warrior*, and they both apparently saw stars and rainbows. Said Hoare, "You could say it was love at first sight. We had similar ideas about how we wanted to live our lives—clean air, clean water, and clean food, away from the crazy world."

Soon after their meeting, Hoare sold his condo in Sydney to enable them to buy a $150,000 plot of Osa land with a panoramic view of the ocean. The couple built themselves a shelter on their new property: no walls, but a sturdy waterproof canopy overhead, which, like Bender Dome, was open to all manner of animal visitors at all times of the day and night. Kimberley, like Ann Bender, rescued a baby sloth and bottle nursed it for several months, allowing it to sleep in bed with her and Christopher. Friends dubbed her "sloth mother."

Christopher and Kimberley set up a homestead near Puerto Jiménez, almost at the entrance of Corcovado National Park. Their land had a road, a freshwater well, lovely mature mango and wild banana trees, and amazing wild cacao growing throughout the property. This was paradise! They had lived there several months before they realized a troubling detail: their farm was a notorious cut-through for illegal gold miners, *oreros*, entering Corcovado to pan gold to sell in Puerto Jiménez. Osa was famous for still having a few un-mined gold reserves, mostly found in and around the river bed of the Rio Tigre. Gold mining had supported residents of Osa for over fifty years, and despite Costa Rica declaring it illegal, was still an occupation for many third- and fourth-generation oreros in the park. These gold miners were tough customers—uneducated, unruly, heavy drinkers, and not interested in any good-neighbor programs. Nowadays, several of the oreros have been cleaned up and retrained as tour guides for the *other* gold in Costa Rica: ecological tourism.

After discovering delicious wild cacao trees on their property, Kimberley launched Samaritan Xocolata, a chocolate company incorporating cacao from her farm, authentic Mayan recipes using chili and other exotic flavors, and Osa labor to support the local economy. Kimberley always stated to her friends and neighbors that she fervently hoped that her chocolate company, with its well-paid employees, would put an end to folks near Corcovado Park poaching wild animal meat from the park, further reducing the numbers of animals—particularly endangered animals like jaguars and pumas.

Kimberley also enjoyed preaching her own brand of feminism to the local female population. This included informal lectures on birth control and other topics not welcomed in such a Catholic country. "Osa" in Spanish means female bear, and Kimberley was that in every possible way. For several years, Christopher was her biggest admirer and supporter. Then the love affair began to falter under the pressure of increasingly hostile neighbors, hunters, and oreros.

Kimberley and Christopher often found it difficult to understand that they were trying to change a generations-old custom of poachers hunting in Corcovado Park, who used Kimberley's property as a cut-through to access the premium hunting grounds. These were exactly the same cultural challenges faced by the Benders at Boracayán.

These customs and traditions do not change overnight, and they certainly don't change because gringos think they should. The animosity and mistrust between the locals and the foreigners began to escalate. Meanwhile, scientists from the Universidad Nacional de Costa Rica warned that the poaching behavior, if not stopped, would mean curtains for many animals in Corcovado Park, including jaguars and tepezcuintles (spotted paca). Kimberley became more and more agitated by poacher activity on her property. She would often go out alone at night with just her dogs as backup to confront the poachers and demand that they leave immediately. She was a tiny lady, about 5☐ 3☐, with a thick mane of curly black flowing hair. The poachers called her *la bruja,* the witch. Latin men don't seem to like being told by women what they can and cannot do, especially foreign women, and Christopher and Kimberley were beginning to feel the heat from the aggressive and angry poachers.

Soon the conflicts with oreros began to also escalate. The Osa Peninsula has been a large and prolific gold-bearing region since the 1930s with some nuggets and chunks so large that they are on display now at the National Gold Museum in San José. Gold hunting in Corcovado Park has always been a hugely dangerous and risky proposition, and it's getting more competitive and less lucrative as many more areas are almost tapped-out. In 2014, a movie was made by a Tico film maker named Alvaro Torres Crespo, about the grueling life of oreros, titled *El Lugar Indeseado* (*The Undesired Place*). It won in the Best Short Documentary category at the Ícaro Central American Film Festival. The movie is a gripping, dark portrayal of a dying breed of Tico gold hunters. These were the characters who traipsed through Christopher and Kimberley's land, mostly under the cover of dark and dangerous nights.

After a decade together, Christopher upped and left to return to Australia. He was fed up and afraid, and seemingly over his crazy jungle love for Kimberley. Kimberley stayed on all alone. Then a hunter neighbor of Kimberley shot and killed her dogs. She retaliated by running him over in her car and breaking his leg. Her family sent money from Canada to pay for his medical treatment and lost wages. Next, she shot a man in the back with a BB gun, thinking he was a poacher. Things were not pura vida for Ms. Kimberley Blackwell.

She wrote in her diary, "Not being like everyone else can make life difficult." She also hand-lettered inspirational notes to herself. For instance, "You are lovable and loving, always." These were found by her friends in her house after her death.

After twenty years of living in Osa, the fifty-three-year-old Kimberley was found by a park ranger on February 2, 2011, beaten almost beyond recognition, sprawled in her own blood and shot execution style in the back of her head, near the entrance to her property. Her friends lobbied and pressed authorities to find the killer(s), and eventually some poor soul did do prison time for her murder, though it was widely rumored that he was paid to do prison time by the people who were really the guilty parties. Her family members never agreed with the conviction, and have commented that their daughter had simply joined the many other unsolved murders of Corcovado National Park.

The forensics of Kimberley's murder were equally messy as those of John Bender. Her body was taken to the closest hospital where she was put on ice to await the coroner's investigation. The coroner had a birthday, then a vacation, then someone lost the key to the ice vault. By the time the coroner was nagged into doing his job, the corpse was degraded to such a state where an accurate autopsy was virtually impossible.

The day after Kimberley's death, the previous owner of her house and land moved his entire extended family back into her home. This is completely legal under Costa Rica's squatters' rights. All of her possessions were appropriated, sold, or given to relatives. Later that year American Lisa Artz, resident manager of Casa Tres Palmas, an eco-lodge near Corcovado, was found tied up with a bag over her head, presumably dying of asphyxiation. Some of Kimberley Blackwell's electric appliances were found in the homes of the accused killers of Lisa Artz. The truly responsible parties have never done any time in preventive detention for either Blackwell or Artz's murders.

A blogger named Mark Meadows, who lives in Osa and blogs under *Eco-Tourists and Gold Miners*, tried to understand these senseless killings:

> "Kimberley (and Lisa Artz, and many others who come to Costa Rica) arrived in Costa Rica and wanted to, in some small way, make a difference. They wanted to improve the world, make it a little better. But their neighbors weren't into it and this caused a social snag. Culture's a great social machine of cogs that fit together, people working together, spinning in a complicated symphony. But if the social gears get stuck, then a little blood seems to help lubricate things.

> "Eventually Canadian detectives came down [to Osa], sniffed around, rattled the cages over at the Juzgado Penal de Golfito [enforcers of the laws of Osa], and a couple of people were accused, busted, imprisoned, then quickly released. The felonies were treated as misdemeanors. But the

misdemeanor, or whatever demeanor which isn't working, is *El Gringo's*. Not according to the law, but according to the culture, history, and majority rule. It is a question of cultural compatibility.

"In the end, the rule of culture is *always* stronger than the rule of law."

Yet another blogger at the time of Kimberley's death proclaimed, "Costa Rica now leads the region in deaths of foreigners."

<<>>

The truth of the matter regarding Americans who die of unnatural causes while abroad is much less dramatic. The US Government doesn't keep comprehensive records of civilian deaths of Americans who die while abroad. It is, however, required to collect and publish information on Americans overseas who die of unnatural causes. The figures are updated every six months. They have recorded over 8,000 deaths while abroad for the years 2005-2015, or only about 827 deaths per year. These figures seem stunningly low when you consider that some 68 million Americans travel out of country each year.

In Costa Rica, the primary causes of unnatural death among Americans are drowning and traffic accidents. Very often these are exacerbated by the consumption of alcohol. There is no law in Costa Rica requiring lifeguards on beaches, and most swimming in either rivers or the ocean is at your own risk. Costa Rica has had 101 American drownings since 2002, out of 937,000 foreign visitors per year. The US Embassy sends out bulletins each year warning Americans residing in-country, or just visiting on vacation, to be mindful of riptides and strong currents.

Americans are known to go a little loco while in Costa Rica, in a condition known as "leave your brain on the plane." There is no treatment or cure for what happens to you when you tumble head over heels in love in Costa Rica—all bets are off. It's an undertow in which even swimming parallel to the shore won't allow you to survive. It's truly *Love in The Time of Cholera*, and Ann Bender spent her quiet moments in jail mulling over everything that had happened to her while she lived in Costa Rica—and trying to mend her twice-broken heart.

Ann Emerges a Fighter

"Love becomes greater and nobler in calamity."

Gabriel García Márquez – *Love in the Time of Cholera*

As soon as Ann was released from prison at the *algo de pesadilla* (something from a nightmare) Buen Pastor, her legal and emotional support team barely gave her enough time to regain her health before beginning to prep her for the toughest battle of her adult life: her third trial for murder. This was the closest to a life-and-death struggle for Ann as she had ever experienced. It was going to be really brutal. She couldn't afford to lose! At her first trial, Ann had been acquitted of all charges, but at her second they threw the book at her: Murder One—premeditated murder—which resulted in her nine-month stay in preventive detention. Ann felt that if she was forced to repeat that prison experience, she would rather die. It was that simple for her. Win or die.

In the three years that had passed since her first trial and acquittal, Ann had wised up and toughened up quite a bit. She had to—there was no more John or Greg to protect her. She often found herself feeling like the bull she had seen at a Costa Rican bullfight, a tight rope cinching its midsection, starved for twenty-four hours before the battle, and mad as hell. That's just how she felt. She was mad as hell. She was no longer assuming the role of victim, she was coming out swinging. As she told *Outside Magazine*, "I'm angry. And when I'm angry, I do a lot better than when I'm sad. Sad means passive. And that's exactly how the powers-that-be want me."

CRAZY JUNGLE LOVE

<<>>

In Costa Rica bullfights are called *corridas de toros*, and are a combination of a rodeo, bullfight, and the running of the bulls in Pamplona. The rules are that no one can hurt the bull, but the bull can impale, toss, trample, or kill anyone. It's a tradition that dates back to at least 1868 and is hugely popular at various times of the year in Costa Rica, especially around Christmas. The bull is called the *violador*, and the mixture of professional and amateur bullfighters are called *improvisados*. The only rule is that no one hurts or kills the bull (no need to waste good meat), but the poor bull is tormented and teased by fifty or more aggressive participants.

Young men (and more recently women), just everyday people, screw up their courage, often wearing costumes of Batman or Superman or Spiderwoman, and jump into the ring without protective gear or weapons to tease and torment the bull in the most daring and audience-pleasing ways possible. They slap the bull's face, or spank the bull's bottom, or tug the bull's tail, anything to really annoy and torment the poor animal. It's called "Toros a la Tica," and it is very popular all around the country. Lots of money is bet on the improvisados, and lots of drinks are sold to audience and participants alike. Medical teams and ambulances are always standing by. Participants have to sign hold-harmless agreements with the organizers, and prove they are current with their health insurance payments. People for the Ethical Treatment of Animals (PETA) are always protesting, and there have been many unsuccessful attempts to ban these events. The corridas can always be seen on television if you can't be there to watch the events live. The foremost corrida is the largest annual bullfight, in Zapote, San José, held just after Christmas, which draws people from all over the country, as well as from the neighboring countries of Nicaragua and Panama. It's a once-in-a-lifetime experience—tourists love it.

The final thing the bull hears before it is released into the ring is *PUERTA!* (DOOR!), which is the signal that the battle is about to begin, and Ann heard that loudly and clearly before she began her third fight-to-the-finish battle with the prosecution and the justice system of this tiny nation which saves bulls, but might not be willing to save a (probably) innocent American lady. She would be prodded and poked and tormented, but never killed. There is no death penalty in Costa Rica.

<<>>

The Costa Rican Judiciary, "El Poder Judicial," was created in 1821, the same year Costa Rica declared independence from Spain, and has been functioning ever since. Costa Rica follows the United Nations guidelines and recommendations regarding murders, referring to them as "intentional homicides." Ann was charged with an unlawful killing that was both willful and pre-meditated, meaning that it was committed after planning or "lying in wait" for the victim. In 2010, the year of John's death, there were 525 deaths by homicide in Costa Rica. In subsequent years this rate dropped slightly, and then rose again, probably because of better tracking of homicides by the police and their push to enforce a *"mano dura"* (iron fist) policy toward intentional homicides.

In Costa Rica, like in the US, the person accused of a crime has certain basic rights, for example:

~ the right to an attorney

~ the right to know what charges are being filed

~ the right to obtain bail if it is authorized

~ the right to address the court during the trial

~ the right to a speedy trial

This last right is constantly scoffed at by foreigners because the backlog of legal cases is so immense that most people wait years before going to trial.

The accused individual does not have the right to a trial by a jury of his peers under the Tico legal system. As mentioned earlier, the judgment in an intentional homicide trial is made by a panel of three judges. A lesser crime would be adjudicated by only one judge. Eighty-five percent of those awaiting trial in Costa Rica are released on their own recognizance. Only those who have been judged dangerous, likely to flee, or uncooperative in pre-trial procedures are detained in a holding facility. Time served in holding facilities is deducted from the sentence if the accused is found guilty. Ann's time hospitalized in the psychiatric ward at CIMA Hospital was deducted from her total sentence, as well as her time spent incarcerated at Buen Pastor. The concept of plea-bargaining is seldom seen, and unlike the very common practice in the US judicial system, there is never a lighter sentence given for ratting out a fellow criminal. That being said, the judges have a lot of leeway in their sentencing practices.

Evidence in a Costa Rican courtroom is presented to the judges by live witnesses who have been vetted and pre-approved by both the prosecution and the defense teams in advance of the trial. Another significant difference from US law is that there is little restriction on hearsay evidence.

Cross-examination cannot include leading questions. Finally, experts may be appointed by the Court to consult on technical matters, as was the case in Ann's trial.

The Costa Rican Judiciary has fallen under criticism in recent years for allowing criminals to enjoy more and more impunity for their crimes. There is even an annual study by a former Minister of Public Security called *"el impunómetro"* (impunity meter), which is published annually. El impunómetro uses figures from the Ministry of Public Security (MSP) to determine what percentage of crimes remain unpunished at the end of each year. For example, by 2016 only 109 of the 477 cases of intentional homicide in 2014 have resulted in convictions. Fifty-eight percent of cases remain unresolved one year later.

Despite these underwhelming statistics, the Judiciary had succeeded in finding their fall guy for the murder of John Bender, in the person of his adoring wife Ann Bender—and they were not letting her go. Plus, it was rumored that there were other forces and interests at play in this trial. Juan de Dios Álvarez, the trustee of the Bender estate and wealth, was the unseen elephant in the courtroom. The Judiciary was acutely aware that the eyes of the world were upon them. They, like Ann, could not afford to lose. It would be a *Battle of the Titans.*

To quote José Pizarro, the former head of security for the Benders, "This case is—how you say? —Bullshit. Bullshit from motherfuckers, sí?" Pretty much summarized how most Americans felt about it.

It was puzzling to many at the time of the trial, and in the following years, that Ann's lawyer did not suggest either self-defense, or mental incapacitation. Either finding would have resulted in Ann not being legally liable. Even second-degree murder seemed more appropriate to foreigners who were following the case: a crime that happens in the heat of the moment, which does not involve premeditation. The whole concept of Ann "lying in wait" seemed far-fetched and ridiculous. Ann herself, when asked how she thought the judges would rule said, "Last night I was lying in bed, and I was thinking: *What would I have done if I'd been in the prosecutor's position?* I would have said, *'She's crazy, something set her off, and BOOM! She killed him in a fit of craziness.'* But no, he goes for the whole enchilada, which is really crazy." The whole enchilada was, of course, Murder One.

At expat parties the topic of a possible assassination was discussed. Contract killers had made the news quite a few times in the months preceding John's death, and many felt that was a possible scenario in the case of John's death—and also that of Greg Fischer.

According to *Inside Costa Rica*,

> "Costa Rican assassins and contract killers are traveling to Mexico to receive specialized training from that country's cartels, including the infamous Sinaloa cartel. Costa Rican hit men are traveling to Mexico to learn skills such as tactical pistol skills, intelligence gathering, escape tactics, and how to use high-caliber automatic weapons."

That certainly seemed as likely—even more likely—than the petite, de-conditioned Ann picking up John's Ruger, and blasting him in the back of the head.

The trial ahead would certainly be one of the most interesting in Costa Rica's history.

<<>>

At this point in Ann's legal history in Costa Rica, her trials were numerous and detailed enough to merit their own curriculum vitae (CV), given all the twists and turns, characters, and shadowy behind-the-scenes shenanigans. In 2013, at Ann's first trial, she was acquitted, but at the insistence of the prosecutors an appellate court ordered a retrial. The retrial was held in May of 2014. At that second trial, Ann was found guilty of murder, and she was sentenced to twenty-two years in preventive detention, reduced from the original 25-year sentence. Ann served nine months in the slammer, before an appellate court in Cartago threw out the guilty verdict for wrongly assessed evidence. They then ordered Ann to stand trial a third time. Triple jeopardy, how amazingly unfair by American legal standards.

The third trial began on August 10, 2015, again at the Pérez Zeledón courthouse, which had been repainted, two new parking spots added out front, and a snazzy new imitation cappuccino coffee maker installed in the lobby coffee kiosk. Otherwise, the scenario was depressingly similar to the previous two trials. Ann commented to the reporter Zach Dyer, "It is my opportunity to finally, hopefully, get true justice. I have faith that justice will finally be served."

Also new was the assignment of a fresh team of three judges who would preside over Ann's trial: head judge Esteban López Cambronero, Ericka Cordero Marroquín and Manuel Morales Vásquez. They were exceedingly polite to Ann during the entire trial, never antagonistic, and López as chief judge conducted the trial smoothly and efficiently, making sure that all three judges had their questions answered thoroughly and that Ann understood the proceedings despite Spanish being her third language, after her native Portuguese and English. There was a translator standing by for Ann (paid for by the defense), if she needed it, as well as for the forensic experts from the Netherlands. For some unfathomable reason, however, Judge López made no effort to squelch the anti-American, anti-wealthy, and anti-genius tirades the prosecutor launched against the Benders repeatedly, while onlookers squirmed in their seats. The prosecutor was the infamous Edgar Ramírez, known to be a colossal SOB.

Ann's lawyer, Fabio Oconitrillo, impossibly more dapper and better dressed than at the previous two trials, opened with a statement addressing the incalculable damage Ann had suffered during her time at Buen Pastor, and during the two previous trials in Pérez Zeledón. "We will demonstrate for the third time that Ann committed no crime. We have no way to calculate the wounds to her personality which she suffered during her nine months in preventive detention." He did not let on during his opening statements that Team Ann now had a new weapon at their disposal: the world-class and renowned Dutch medical forensic reconstruction experts, Richard and Selma Eikelenboom.

The Eikelenbooms had their own style of crazy jungle love going on, first in the Netherlands, then in Colorado at a lab they co-founded called Independent Forensic Sciences. They are a very intense couple, and have been described as

"The most diligent, painstaking skin cell research team you could hope to find," by a defense lawyer who has worked with them and watched them in action. They consulted on both the Casey Anthony and JonBenét Ramsey cases. It was the Casey Anthony case that first brought them to the attention of the American public. Casey Anthony was the mother who was accused of murdering her two-year-old daughter, Caylee. JonBenét Ramsey was the six-year-old beauty queen who was found murdered by asphyxiation in her home in Colorado. In both cases, as with the Bender case, family members were accused of the crime. The Eikelenbooms called that assumption "tunnel vision." They were contacted in all three cases because of their highly sophisticated forensic technology, not yet available in most US labs.

At the time of John Bender's death, the Eikelenbooms had already relocated themselves from the Netherlands to their new home and lab in Colorado. They referred to it as the "Crime Farm." Their US accommodations were a vast improvement over where they had been working in the Netherlands; they had been operating out of their own home, using every room except their bedroom and bathroom. They rarely had people over to visit for fear of contamination of evidence. There wasn't even a proper place to eat or drink. That's the way they liked it: staging crime scenes all day and working on DNA recovery and lab analysis, until it was time to curl up together in the evening to watch their favorite American television shows, *CSI* and *Law & Order*. They matched the Benders in intensity, intelligence, and eccentricity. And love.

The Eikelenbooms tucked very contentedly into their new Colorado home and lab, along with their one cat and two German shepherds. Richard described why they preferred living in the US: "America is much bigger [than Holland]; you have more cases, and more interesting cases. People can go from state to state to kill and dump. In Holland, we have 16 million people living in a 50-by-100 mile area—it's harder to dump a body."

The Eikelenbooms built their reputations by specializing in several areas of forensic evidence, blood-stain analysis, and DNA testing. They became known as "The death-obsessed couple revolutionizing DNA." All of their skills were put to use in their careful examination of the evidence from the Bender case.

Obviously, their efforts were even more challenging given the poor evidence recovery performed by Costa Rican authorities. The Eikelenbooms excelled above all else in contact DNA testing. Here is how an American expert in the field describes that science:

> "Contact DNA testing involves attempting to obtain blood, sperm, saliva, sweat, or epithelial cells (i.e. skin cells) that belong to

a perpetrator and were transferred to a victim or an item of, or connected with, the murder of the victim during the commission of the crime. In other words, when you touch something or someone, you almost invariably transfer some amount of yourself (cells) to that surface. In the case of skin cells, the issue is that they usually are very problematic in producing a full DNA profile unless you get a significant amount. But if you can get enough of them and you can perform an adequate number of cycles of amplification, you have a chance of producing a usable profile for DNA identification."

The Eikelenbooms' work in the landmark case of Timothy Masters resulted in the first touch DNA exoneration in the United States. Masters was convicted of killing Peggy Hettrick in 1987. With the detailed forensic work of the Eikelenbooms, Masters was exonerated and released from prison in 2008.

Ann had a real pair of heavy-hitters backing her up this time, courtesy of the show *48 Hours*; and the Costa Rican forensic scientists were about to be thrown into the deep end of the pool, with no flotation devices.

CRAZY JUNGLE LOVE

<<>>

The other of the defense's powerful weapons was apparent to all: a second team of lawyers from the British law firm Seven Bedford Row, led by Barrister Stephen Baker, assisted by the completely bilingual Barrister Gary Pons and the equally bilingual American lawyer Sonia O'Donnell.

They sat together in the front row, entering every word into their computers, whispering among themselves, and consulting with Oconitrillo during breaks. This time the defense also took full advantage of the talents of Marissel Descalzo, a rising star attorney who thoroughly prepared Ann and other expert witnesses for trial.

The prosecutor, Edgar Ramírez, was in for a tough uphill battle to try to prove Ann's guilt. This time she had brought the cavalry. It seemed to many that Ramírez had not brought his A game, just a lot of posturing, insults, and bravado. Ramírez was confronting the best legal and forensic teams available, and it would not have happened without the intervention of an American TV crime show: *48 Hours*. Susan Spencer, a *48 Hours* correspondent, had done a television special on the Bender case in September,

2014, and remained intrigued and amazed by the whole saga. She told Jonah Ogles of *Outside Magazine*,

> "I have never had a story like this, ever. I've been doing this a long time, and when you think about the money, the house, the jewels, this idea of starting a sanctuary for wildlife, the mental health issues, every time you turn around there's another aspect to it that could be an hour show in itself. The confluence of these things coming together and resulting in one person being dead is astounding. But then you look at the sequence of events, and maybe it's not that surprising at all."

Susan Spencer was assigned to the case, along with *48 Hours* producer Josh Yager. Together they toured and filmed Boracayán, documenting the ravished interior of the mansion; the OIJ had left only some of Ann Bender's clothes dangling mournfully off their hangars. Spencer described the visit to Bender Dome,

> "The phrase 'over the top' doesn't begin to do the house justice. It's some bizarre combination of Disneyland and art museum and something you'd really only see in a James Bond movie."

Spencer became convinced that the whole case against Ann hinged on forensic evidence, and she knew the best folks in the business on that topic: the Eikelenbooms.

Richard and Selma Eikelenboom are a striking, good-looking couple, which played well on TV. They are both tall and slender and elegant, and provided a nice visual contrast to the prosecutor with his sweat-stained, rumpled shirt straining across his rather large gut. Selma had a tidy pageboy haircut, and Richard is going bald. They both wore suits to court and provided a gravitas which helped legitimize the defense's case. It was looking again like a class warfare-tinged scenario in that Pérez courtroom.

As mentioned previously, the Eikelenbooms are both experts in what is called touch DNA. It is called touch DNA because it only requires minuscule particles of DNA—only seven or eight cells—for analysis. That is also its drawback, as a minute quantity of DNA could be left by anyone just brushing past an object, or might have already been on the object. The couple also has expertise in ballistics and blood science. *48 Hours* had provided the defense their own CSI!

48 Hours hired the couple and furnished them with Costa Rica court documents and police photos to review in detail at their Colorado lab. That work lasted one month. Then they were brought to Bender Dome to conduct tests on location and do a forensic reconstruction of the shooting, in the actual room where it happened, with all the influences of temperature, wind, humidity, and sun as authentically correct as possible. The Eikelenbooms are fanatical about even the minutest details.

The Eikelenbooms immediately pointed out four whopping errors in the investigation of the crime scene by Costa Rican detectives:

~Failure to photograph the crime scene accurately.

~Failure to test the bloodstains on the sheets and headboard.

~Failure to fingerprint the gun.

~Failure to fingerprint John Bender.

Meanwhile, the new legal team could not have been more prestigious and competent. The team was led by Fabio Oconitrillo, but now included the two British barristers who were experts in criminal cases and Sonia Escobio O'Donnell, an American who had worked on the Manuel Noriega trial and was well-schooled in Latin American courtroom drama and possible legal corruption. The reporter from *Inside Costa Rica* commented, "Wow, lots of depth on the bench this time, unlike last time. Ann's got a much better chance this trial."

The prosecution, however, accused the defense of bringing in foreign team members to try to cast the Costa Rican justice system in an unfavorable light.

Those were the teams assembled to argue the fate of frail Ann Patton Bender in August 2015. Ann herself was accompanied by her mother and father, her brother Ken, Osvaldo Aguilar (the remaining custodian of Boracayán whose loyalty never diminished for doña Ana), Pete DeLisi , Paul Meyer (next door neighbor at Boracayán), and a bevy of neighbors from Boracayán who came to support and help if they could. There was also a lot of local press and many curious onlookers looking to be entertained.

Ann entered the courtroom wearing all black, with a single long strand of pearls, conservative high-heeled sandals, and a long cardigan in anticipation of the always-cold courtroom. She did not look around or greet anyone. She just leaned on her cane and the arm of one of her legal team as she navigated down the treacherous courtroom steps to join Oconitrillo, his assistant, and the translator at the foot of the steps. Now, when she moved, she always looked as though it required much effort and concentration. She would open and close her hands and stretch her feet frequently during the proceedings. Her Lyme disease seemed to have gotten worse since the last trial, and she looked to be in pain most of the time.

What Ann heard that first day in court was "PUERTA!" and she was ready to take her stand this time—and triumph.

The Third Trial

"Courage did not come from the need to survive, or from a brute indifference inherited from someone else, but from a driving need for love which no obstacle in this world or the next will break."

Gabriel García Márquez -- *Love in the Time of Cholera*

Ann Bender's third murder trial began on Monday, August 10, 2015, and lasted until Monday, September 7, 2015—almost a full month—when her verdict was read to a packed courtroom. They had waited several hours for the judges to appear to read the official verdict. This scheduling is called *la hora Tica*, which means things always begin and end late. It would be referred to as "island time," if only Costa Rica were an island—many foreigners actually believe it is—or maybe they confuse it with Puerto Rico.

Ann was among the first to testify. The defense wanted to set the tone for their case with the fragile-looking and humble Bender. They also wanted to use her at the beginning of the day before her limited energy and stamina began to dwindle. In Costa Rica, women do not take their husband's names in marriage, so she was sworn in as Ann Maxine Patton, her maiden name.

Ann spoke in short, soft sentences, punctuated by small head-nods which seemed to have gotten more pronounced since her previous trials. She no longer had a medicine port in her chest. The only two times she required the translator's help were for the terms "Wall Street" and "hedge fund manager," two terms she used in her description of John and his occupation. Both terms are mostly unknown in Costa Rica. John's career and successes were very difficult to understand for Pezeteros (folks from Pérez Zeledón), which is a largely agricultural town. Ann might as well have been describing life on Mars. The audio visual tech kept stepping in to adjust the microphone. No one wanted to miss a single word of her testimony, and her voice was painfully soft. Her testimony, however, was unwavering, seamless and varied very little from previous trials. Ann was speaking her truth.

Ann began by describing the kind of man and husband John Bender had been. She spoke of his devotion to her, despite her various ailments, and his commitment to trying to cure her of her Lyme disease and find a cure for her bipolar disorder. He had hoped to find the cure for both illnesses right in the jungle of the Boracayán sanctuary. She described how frustrated and depressed John became when he was unsuccessful in finding help for her. She described how hard John had fought to protect her and the reserve from poachers and other threats. She told of how he had renounced his American citizenship, wanting to fully embrace his new country of Costa Rica. They were once both so full of boundless hope. They had never faltered in their love for each other.

Ann described John's fantastic successes on Wall Street. She spoke of his mathematical genius and other-worldly ability to choose and manage winning stock portfolios. She mentioned John's work for George Soros, the billionaire Hungarian-born financier known as "The man who broke the Bank of England," because of his short sale of $10 billion during the 1992 Black Wednesday UK currency crisis. That made Soros $1 billion in one fell swoop. Soros was a client of John's at Amber Arbitrage, and when one of the investments John had chosen for him failed, it almost drove John to suicide. John could not tolerate failure in his life, and was always powerfully drawn to suicide as a way out.

In an American courtroom, the defense would probably have used what is called a "psychological autopsy," which involves interviews with family and friends, as well as presenting emails and messages from the deceased indicating just how severe the person's depression was. That task fell almost completely to Ann. She had to explain how demoralized John had become because he felt he had let Ann down as both a provider and husband; that was *so* painful to remember. She hinted that she eventually came to fear for both of their lives. Ann described to the court John's various attempts at suicide during their marriage. Her lawyer was able to submit several emails John had sent to Ann and his family which indicated the depth of his despair at the time of his death. She declared her love for John repeatedly. Several times Ann was fighting back tears and could often be seen trembling slightly in her hands and with her head. She was white-knuckling through the recounting of their lives together and their love for each other. There seemed to be no doubt in Ann's mind that John was destined to kill himself; the question was when and how.

Oconitrillo submitted an email John had sent to Ann while she was away on a gem-buying trip in the US. He said, "I wish I were dead. I deserve to die, I feel so utterly ill that there aren't even words. I haven't been this bad in years." John was clearly circling the drain.

Next, Ann recounted exactly what she remembered of the tragic night of January 8, 2010—the night on which John Bender died. She had told this story over and over again, and the essence and details of it never seemed to vary.

John and Ann finished up their evening ritual of watching the sunset, followed by hours of playing *Fallout 3*. Ann was sleepy and began her agonizing climb up to the fourth floor bedroom. John scooped her up and carried her gently to bed. All of the 550 Tiffany lamps that encircled their bed were extinguished, and Ann began to doze off before John joined her in bed.

Ann was awakened because John, lying next to her, was mumbling something. Ann was still groggy, but thought she heard John say, "You don't know how it feels to wake up with your spouse half dead next to you." That was certainly a statement that could have been uttered by either partner, given each of their debilitating conditions. But that was the first time Ann had ever heard anything like that from John, and she immediately snapped open her eyes to confront the horror of John pointing one of the Rugers at his own face.

She thought to herself, "This is it. He's going to do what he always threatened to."

At this point, the entire courtroom was quiet enough to hear a pin drop, and all three judges were sitting at the fronts of their chairs, gazing down intently at the accused.

Ann continued to describe how she had somehow managed to run around to John's side of the bed. She could not believe her worst nightmare had just happened. She clicked on the bedside lamp and was confronted with a pool of blood already dripping off the bed, and pooling onto the tile floor. She picked up the two-way radio and frantically called the night security staff for help. It was then that she heard John's last breath, a rattle in his throat, then silence.

"Post Five. Help! Help! Help!" reportedly heard the guard on duty, Moisés Calderón. Ann recounted to *Outside Magazine*, "I think I was in shock, because I was running around—which given the state I was in, I shouldn't have been able to do. But I remember I did, like, four laps around the bed as I was waiting for someone to help me."

Moisés recalls having heard what he thought was a gunshot from the fourth floor at about 12:15 a.m. on the night of John's death. As he was trained to do, he immediately radioed his supervisor Osvaldo Aguilar, who was not on duty that night, but sleeping in a house close by. The guards alternated shifts, but were almost always somewhere within the refuge. Osvaldo came running, but it was still several minutes before he and Moisés managed to unlock the elevator to the fourth floor and enter the Benders' private living quarters. Neither of them had ever been up there before. The elevator opened to reveal Ann Bender, covered in blood spatter, and kneeling at John's side weeping, and stroking her dead husband's hand. Near her on the floor, was one of John's two semi-automatic pistols, a Ruger P95.

Osvaldo checked John for a pulse, and finding none, radioed his supervisor at Imperial Park Security to report what had happened. Neither guard was really trained for this kind of situation, but Osvaldo was absolutely sure that the right thing to do was take distraught Ann away from her dead husband's side, and take her to where she could call her family for help. He also needed to call the OIJ and the coroner to come get John's body. In cases of death in the tropics, time is extremely crucial.

Ann took a tranquilizer, wiped the blood off of her hands with paper towels which she tossed in a chair near the computer, and proceeded to email her parents and call her older brother Ken in Michigan. Ken picked up almost instantly, and Ann remembered saying to him, "He finally did it."

<<>>

She'd survived. Ann had once again relived that awful night and described it, and what led up to it, in the very best way she could. After a break (Ann was desperate for a cigarette), the trial resumed with prosecutor Edgar Ramírez doing cross-examination. He reinforced the fact that the Benders were mind-bogglingly rich and eccentric beyond anything seen in Costa Rica before or since. He hinted that not all John's wealth might have been legally earned. He tried to insinuate that the Benders had gone to bed mad at each other that night, and that they had been fighting before they retired for the evening. There was no proof of that. Employees of Boracayán would later testify that they had never even seen the couple argue in the decade they had lived on the Reserve. It was always "puro amor," and John and Ann treated each other gently, and with great tenderness. The Prosecutor's allegation of a fight between the couple having led to John's death did not hold water.

Ramírez drilled down on the jewels found at the death scene. He asked questions regarding the origin of the jewels, but that was ruled a separate case, so the prosecutor had to move on. He had now hinted that the motive for Ann killing her husband was either a fight (unlikely), or that she wanted all the jewels for herself (less likely—they were hers anyway). So the prosecutor was unable to present a reasonable motive for Ann to have killed her husband. He had managed, however, to make his feelings about Americans, especially rich Americans, abundantly clear. The first day of the trial had gone quite well for Team Ann, but it would get much more grisly and difficult in the days ahead. And the prosecutor's disdain for the international press, and rich people, and foreigners, would continue to manifest itself in each exchange between Ramírez and the Benders, or their Dutch forensic experts.

The battle between the prosecution and defense had been clearly delineated. The prosecutor accused Ann of having killed John in cold blood, quite possibly after having premeditated his murder for quite some time. The big hole in the prosecution's case was a lack of a viable motive. The defense claimed that John had committed suicide, as he had always threatened to do, after becoming despondent and failing in his role as husband and provider. The challenge for the defense was the overwhelming forensic evidence which seemed to indicate that Ann murdered her husband, rather than having witnessed his suicide. This would be an epic battle between the two sides, incorporating some of the most dramatic courtroom performances ever to have been seen in a Tico court of law. What the prosecutor lacked in forensic evidence he more than made up for in bluster and bravado.

There were twenty-five witnesses slated to testify at this trial. John's father, the distinguished law professor Paul Bender, was unable to attend but sent a letter of support for Ann. Ann's mother was slated to testify, but was replaced by her brother Ken, at her mother's request. There was Pete DeLisi. Also scheduled to testify was Ann's closest neighbor at Boracayán, Paul Meyer. Ann's psychiatrist, Dr. Arturo Lizano-Vincent, came from San José to testify on Ann's behalf. Many employees of Boracayán and the security team who guarded Ann were called, but the defense could not be sure what these folks would say when push came to shove. It had, after all, been five years since John's death—lots of water under the bridge.

That left roughly twenty people to hear in a trial that could go either way, and often did. The trial that was initially expected to last one week was clearly going to go longer. Some press members were provided with the list of witnesses, but it became apparent fairly quickly that the order of witnesses, and even the attendance of witnesses, was a bit haphazard. For those reporters from the US, the random order of those testifying made the trial seem bush-league.

The truth of the matter was that for some of these folks, this was the third time they had been asked to leave work, come all the way into San Isidro, and make the same statement about the same case—it was getting old. A shadow hanging over the trial who was neither identified nor called to testify was Juan de Dios Álvarez, the lawyer Ann claimed had stolen all John's money, and had accused of appropriating the nature reserve. Most of the key players on both sides knew this lawyer, and everyone was aware that he probably had the funds to attempt to pay off any witness—and perhaps even their testimony.

Never was this proved in court, nor was Álvarez formally accused, but rumors circulated wildly about witness tampering. Many claimed that this happens not infrequently in Costa Rican courts, and people said that next to Ann, Alvarez had the most to lose in this case. Álvarez had long since fled to Nicaragua.

After Ann's lengthy testimony, the court called several employees of the reserve to describe normal life at Boracayán, and shed light on the relationship between John and Ann. The two security employees of Imperial Security testified about the night of John's death, how the crime scene had been preserved, what Ann's behavior had been like before and after John's death. The majordomo testified as to his duties in the Bender household, daily life with the Benders, and how he had noticed John's decline into the severe depression which might have caused his death. These testimonies were almost identical to those at Ann's first two trials. Again, no one could testify to any friction between the couple.

The security employees were questioned at length about the guns the Benders owned. It was established that the two Ruger automatic pistols were purchased legally, and that

John always wore one of them on his hip when he was outside the Dome directing workers or surveying the land. The Rugers were licensed and registered, and both John and Ann had taken courses in handling guns, although Ann was seldom seen touching one and did not carry hers with her when outside the Dome. Target practice for John was a regular routine, along with the security staff, and he was apparently a fairly competent marksman. The two AK-47's, on the other hand, were not purchased legally nor registered; in fact, those guns are strictly illegal to own in Costa Rica.

The security guards were also able to testify where within the Dome the guns were kept, and the answer was that the guns had their own locked cabinet on the first floor, each with their own custom-shaped rest. It was highly unusual, apparently, for the Benders to remove the guns from that closet, unless taking them outside. The idea of John bringing his gun to bed on the night of his death was a total mystery to the security guards, they said.

It was mentioned that John and Ann each had their own ATV (all-terrain vehicle), on which they would tour the property or run down to the outlying employee houses on the grounds. Those vehicles were confiscated by the OIJ soon after John's death, supposedly in connection to the alleged jewel smuggling case. A wise guy American who attended the trial commented that in his imagination, he could see an OIJ employee riding one of those ATVs around his newly purchased farm, a farm that had several nice Tiffany lamps lighting up the tropical evenings, casting light on the lovely jeweled necklace encircling his wife's neck. There was no proof that that ever happened, but some member of the OIJ had undoubtedly benefited from having spent time at the crime scene at Bender Dome. The atmosphere generally among the trial onlookers was anything but jovial—this was Ann Bender's life on the line.

Then the first bombshell dropped in Ann's third trial: an employee completely reversed his testimony and contradicted testimonies given by other Bender employees, as well as his own from the previous trial. At the first trial this employee testified that Ann's condition at the time of John's death was deplorable. He described her as emaciated, unhealthy, and frail. He said she barely moved from room to room within the Dome, and less and less ventured out to walk the property. He described her as leaning heavily on the harness of Millie the German shepherd. He commented that she was no longer taking care of herself physically and not maintaining good hygiene and healthy eating habits. He mentioned the collection of boils and sores visible on Ann's arms and legs, remnants of where John was injecting her with dirty river water, apparently with her permission.

This time, while under oath, the employee described at length how vibrant and energetic Ann had been at the time of John's death. He declared her to be visibly healthy and fit, and seemingly able to move around without any trouble whatsoever. He mentioned a disagreement between the couple on the day of John's death. What? Onlookers whispered during the break that someone had gotten to this fellow in the five years since his last testimony, and most folks felt they knew exactly who had the colones and the *cojones* to produce such a total reversal of testimony. Many onlookers felt that person was probably the unseen shadow hanging over the trial.

This testimony was trivial compared to what was to follow the very next day. The star witness for the prosecution did a complete U-turn regarding one of the most important pieces of forensic evidence: whether John, as a left-hander, could have shot himself in the back of the right side of his head. This reversal of expert testimony by a prosecution witness provided what is known in the US as a "Perry Mason moment," and the expert was none other than Dr. Gretchen Flores—Forensic Medical Examiner, and employee of the Costa Rican government.

Forensics to the Rescue

"Only God knows how much I love you."

Gabriel García Márquez – *Love in the Time of Cholera*

Getting to the testimony of the renowned medical examiner, Dr. Gretchen Flores Sandí, would prove a little tricky. The first week of Ann's murder trial, Dr. Gretchen (as she was called throughout the trial), did not show up at all. She was eighth on the list of witnesses, but failed to appear, no explanation given. It was widely known that Dr. Gretchen was the key witness for the prosecution, had testified at both previous trials, and had examined Ann after she arrived at the police station after John's death. Most felt that the prosecution's case hinged on her testimony. Costa Rica is proud of and impressed with Dr. Gretchen's résumé. Rumors at the courthouse coffee kiosk were that she would be testifying via video conference. Where was she?

Finally in the second week of trial, Dr. Gretchen arrived, amid lots of fanfare, at the prosecution's table. The *fiscal*, or district attorney, introduced her, and explained that she was an incredibly talented forensic pathologist, with a 23-year career with the Costa Rican government, and over 3,000 autopsies performed during her tenure. She looked like an undertaker: dressed all in black, chunky body, messy graying hair, and poor posture. She also seemed to have quite a defensive attitude about her, and did not seem at all pleased to be back testifying in the Bender case—especially up against the world-famous Dutch forensic pathology team who were helping the defense. The word had obviously gotten back to her that the expert Eikelenbooms would be testifying.

People in the courtroom sat up to listen, and there was a new energy in the air. This would be the next best thing to Saturday night *lucha libre*, they thought. Lucha libre is a Mexican style of wrestling where fighters enter the ring in flamboyant capes and costumes, and entertain the crowd with acrobatic moves and pratfalls; it is superbly popular on Tico television.

Dr. Gretchen testified at length about the gun and the bullet from the kill shot. Apparently the gun used in killing John was never tested in any re-creation of the crime scene. Dr. Gretchen explained that after John's death, Ann had been hospitalized for six months which made any crime scene re-creations difficult. It was not explained whether that was because investigators did not have access to the gun, or to the death scene, or to further questioning of Ann. Dr. Gretchen was very eloquent in her description of how she thought Ann had killed her husband. She discussed the bullet trajectory, probable distance from John's head when the gun was fired, the blood-spatter pattern, the position of John's body at the time the gun was fired, and declared that she was convinced beyond a shadow of a doubt that John was the victim of murder. Her conclusion: he was murdered in his own bed, by his own wife, while he lay sleeping on the night of January 8, 2010. She said he never saw it coming. Dr. Gretchen herself was present at the crime scene, and had processed much of the evidence, beginning on the night of John's death.

She reminded the courtroom that John was found with his earplugs still in place, and remarked that it was odd for a person who was about to kill themselves to put in earplugs—wouldn't you want to be listening for anything that would disrupt your plans? She described the position of John's body, which looked very much as though he had been asleep when the shot was fired. John was lying naked on his left side, eyes closed, left arm hanging off the side of the bed, right arm relaxed behind him. In fact, his whole body looked like a person who had just relaxed into sleep in a semi-curled, natural position. Her testimony was illustrated by the same floor-to-ceiling photo of the dead Bender, projected onto a screen which was left up for days on end. People remarked that they had almost grown accustomed to walking into the courtroom to listen for hours on end to testimony in the shadow of Ann Bender's naked husband's photo. The horror of it rolled over people in waves.

The problem with Dr. Gretchen's testimony was that she had made significant changes to it from the first to the second trial, and further slight modifications at this third trial. At first, while on the stand, Dr. G had indicated that there was a very slight, but not impossible, chance that John had shot himself, committing suicide as Ann had indicated. By the next trial—in which Ann had been found unanimously guilty—Dr. G had changed her expert opinion to a very strong view that it would have been impossible for

John to have shot himself. This was the second witness to flip-flop, and testify differently from the first trial. First there was the Bender employee who swore to Ann's perfect health and tiff with John on the night of his death—differing radically from his testimony at the first trial—and now Dr. G reversed herself. Repeated questioning from Ann's lawyer about this flip-flop seemed to generate little interest from the judges. This laid the groundwork for the "Perry Mason" moment in Ann Bender's third trial. This proved absolutely crucial to the defense's case.

In US court proceedings, a Perry Mason moment is said to have occurred whenever information is unexpectedly, and often dramatically, introduced into the record that changes the perception of the proceedings greatly—often influencing the outcome. Obviously named after the mid-twentieth century television series' defense attorney Perry Mason, these moments are very rare in modern US courtrooms where both sides are largely aware of what the other plans to introduce as evidence. An example of a well-known Perry Mason moment is at the trial of O.J. Simpson when Simpson was asked to try on the gloves he supposedly wore when murdering his wife Nicole Brown. He struggled to accomplish this, but the gloves were way too small; very dramatic.

At the Ann Bender trial, the prosecution went to great lengths to describe how John Bender was a left-handed person. Several people confirmed that fact for the judges. Dr. G certainly believed that Bender was left-handed, and showed how nearly impossible it would have been for him to have shot himself in the right inferior occipital region of his head, using his left hand. The actual gun was brought in with its own armed guard who stood by to protect and handle it. The prosecutor and Dr. G demonstrated how impossible a left-handed shot would have been. Then the defense showed a photo from *Outside Online Magazine* of John Bender wearing his pistol on his right hip. Several employees then testified that John shot well with either hand, but always wore his gun on the right side. Wow. The trial now had its own Perry Mason moment.

<<>>

Poor Ann Bender hobbled daily into court with her cane for almost one full month, having to relive the agony of the worst day of her life over, and over again. Team Ann formed a human shield brigade around her to protect her as she entered and exited the courtroom, and while she was on break. She had two security guards hovering over her throughout the trial, who were on the defense's payroll. Ann dressed in somber, flowing skirts and loose-fitting, gauzy tops, and always wore heels, which struck many people as bizarre since she was having mobility issues which required the use of a cane. Several bloggers commented on feeling that Ann's use of high heels weakened her contention that her Lyme disease had severely limited her mobility. She was holding onto her remaining dignity as best she could, and that clearly meant wearing heels to court. Ann wore her hair long and flowing, and had gone from looking like Audrey Hepburn, to looking like a Modigliani painting: elegant, thin, pale, and a little tragic.

With the arrival of the Eikelenbooms, the trial was catapulted from the 1970s to 2015. They reinforced the chasm between the elegant and highfalutin' defense and the rough-around-the-edges prosecution, their in-depth and painstakingly thorough study of all details of the case as well as on-site crime scene re-creations were eye-opening to all in attendance. Costa Rica is a simple country with few serious crimes and murders and little access to laboratories sophisticated enough to process the intricacies of crime investigation necessary to handle a crime scene as complex and detailed as John Bender's. The Eikelenbooms scrutinized every single detail of the crime scene using all the modern methods and equipment from the US investigation. They could process evidence as small as eight human cells. They knew their stuff, and thanks to all the crime scenes they had processed in the US, they had crime scene experience that forensic experts in Costa Rica could only dream about. These were the modern pros.

The Eikelenbooms began their testimony by stating that they had processed the crime scene using International Standards of Crime Scene Procedures, something the Costa Rican authorities had not used. They outlined for the court what that meant in terms of preservation of the crime scene, preservation of the evidence, collection of evidence, proper photography of the scene, and procedures for handling both the crime scene and possible witnesses. There was some difficulty with their statements throughout their presentation, because they spoke in long, careful sentences, which left the poor Tica translator frantically trying to keep up with them. Normally one says a short phrase, and then waits for the translator to translate before continuing; these two just kept right on talking until the translator would wave her hands and look at the judges for help. The prosecution tried to discredit the translator for not having been approved by the court prior to the trial. She was really very good—no one could have remembered Richard and Selma Eikelenboom's lengthy baroque statements.

Next the prosecution tried to discredit the Eikelenbooms as being unlicensed to testify and practice forensics in Costa Rica. The judges just let that challenge pass. It was pretty clear from the Eikelenbooms' reputation and international standing that their expert and professional opinion would be very helpful to everyone trying to understand what had truly happened on the night of January 8, 2010, at Bender Dome.

The Eikelenbooms had spent one month at their American Crime Farm before arriving in Costa Rica, where they went over photographs, transcripts, and evidence of the Bender crime scene sent to them by Ann's lawyer Fabio Oconitrillo. The forensics of this case were the key, everyone agreed.

They testified that the case had been both compromised and confused by the following issues: the photography was incredibly poor, very dim lighting along with bad angles, an inexperienced crime scene photographer, and the photos were taken several hours after John's death. The trace recovery had not been performed on location, but instead bundled up and taken to the forensics lab. Neither the bedding nor the pillows had been processed at the scene, another recipe for contamination of evidence. The investigators had bungled collection of both the blood residue and gun powder residue on John and Ann's hands. The gun had never been fingerprinted. The blood back-spatter on the bed, blanket, and headboard was not documented at the scene, or back at the lab. The case reeked of insufficient evidence.

There were serious problems with almost every aspect of how the crime scene had been handled. The Eikelenbooms were very gentle in how they described these problems (other than using overly long sentences), but the end result was obvious to all: Costa Rica was just not sophisticated enough to handle such a complex forensic case. The hairs on the back of the prosecutor's neck could be seen rising, as his lips curled back from his teeth. He clearly viewed the Eikelenbooms' testimony as being akin to stomping on the Costa Rican flag. He launched into a tirade about this fancy-ass forensic couple who had come to Costa Rica, feeling superior in every way, to protect an American woman who was clearly guilty as hell. He railed that they did not have nearly the years of experience as Dr. Gretchen, and did not have nearly as many autopsies during their careers as Dr. G. Prosecutor Ramírez was clearly ready to battle to the death. The judges remained silent.

Dr. G had testified that the length of Bender's left arm, combined with the length of the gun, indicated that the distance was too short—it had to have been someone firing from a little farther away—to create the wound size and blood-spatter pattern found at the scene. She suggested the distance of someone lying next to him would be about perfect. That, of course, was Ann. Dr. G testified that Ann had ample time to move the gun, as well as the bullet casing before OIJ arrived. The Eikelenbooms had performed detailed recreations of the crime scene at Boracayán, incorporating the correct time of night, breezes through the Bender bedroom, the same kind of gun and bullets, and the actual bedding and headboard in the Bender's bedroom.

They had concluded that Ann's version was much more likely to be correct than the prosecution's. They also stated that John's body had very likely been moved, and that the bullet casing was also out of its correct location, probably kicked by accident. Everyone remembered a real crowd scene in that bedroom once the OIJ arrived to investigate. Anything could have happened to that bullet casing. Some of the photographs seemed to indicate that the casing had blood on it, maybe put there with bloody fingers. It was impossible to know for certain with such poor evidence collection.

The Eikelenbooms showed the television show *48 Hours* how a struggle over the gun could have happened between John and Ann, which could have resulted in the gun accidentally firing and killing John. They declared on tape that, "Our experiments support Ann's story far more than they do the prosecution's version, especially when we recreated those few deadly seconds at Boracayán." Richard added, "Looking at the facts we have here, the scenario of the prosecution is wrong." Selma stated to *48 Hours*, "I'm pretty convinced that it was an accident." Richard opined, "I tend also to more that it's an accident than this was homicide." After months of careful scrutiny of all the details of the crime scene, those statements certainly seemed to exonerate Ann.

The couple, however, commented that their forensic review did turn up some disquieting questions about Ann's story:

They declared that there was an unusually small amount of blood found on Ann, considering she had allegedly been right at his side when he was shot, and there was an unexplained tear in the pillowcase under John's head which looked pretty much exactly like one caused by someone firing a gun from next to him, according to their re-creations of the scene. They both felt that John's body had been moved after his death, since his death was instantaneous, and dead people don't move around.

It was a relief to know that John had died instantaneously. Ann hoped at some point he would be able to rest in peace.

<<>>

To support Dr. Gretchen's testimony (Ms. Flip-Flop), the prosecution had called an esteemed semi-retired public defense lawyer by the name of Donald Montero Navarro. There was some confusion over whether Montero would in fact be attending, and when exactly he would arrive from Cartago. The defense seemed to not be in favor of his testimony, but that could have just been pro-forma trial wrangling. Montero, it was revealed, teaches criminal justice to university students two days a week and is one of the leading experts in criminal justice and crime scene analysis in Costa Rica. He came prepared for this event.

Where the Eikelenbooms had used a borrowed pointer to draw everyone's attention to a certain spot on a photograph or slide, Montero had brought his own two pointers, undoubtedly from his classroom: one telescoping, the other shorter, with a laser light. He had a manuscript of typed notes, presumably from Ann's previous trials and from his own notes taken from reviewing the evidence of the case, which he could refer to if he needed a reminder. He at least was taking this case very seriously, and didn't seem bored or disengaged. He had brought his own replica plastic gun to use when talking about trajectory of the bullet and distance from the deceased. All his hand gestures and movements back and forth to the video screen were very precise and clean. He did Costa Rica proud, and John Bender—himself obsessive-compulsive—would have appreciated Montero's presentation.

Montero had done his own extensive analysis of the Bender case, he testified, including scrutinizing more than one hundred photos of the crime scene and the autopsy. He had analyzed the weapon, the bullet casing, the bullet fragments from John's head, the blood stains, the gunshot residue—he testified to having done the most thorough and detailed study of the crime possible in Costa Rica. He was able to clarify that the bullet that killed John had never exited his head. This was important because statistically, suicide shootings to the head involve a clean through-and-through wound. It was also of note because the bullet probably jumped around in John's skull instead of exiting; meaning John had no chance of survival from that wound.

Montero stated that he had been the person to remove John's body from the evidence bag when it was delivered to the hospital for examination, and he had removed the paper bags from both of the Bender's hands. He had scraped their fingernails and collected trace evidence from both of them. He had taken the statements from both Ann and the guards at Boracayán. His entire testimony seemed to support Dr. G's, which was probably why the defense was not in favor of having it heard.

The Eikelenbooms did the cross-examination of Montero, and were able to create some doubt in his testimony in the following areas: the gun was probably moved from the right to the left after John's death, the pillow on which John reclined was probably also moved; they disputed the bloody bullet casing as being improbable. They made their points succinctly, and planted the seeds of doubt in some minds. It was at least apparent to the court now that the slam-dunk case the prosecution was presenting was not that at all.

There was still the huge question of motive. Why on earth would Ann have wanted to kill John? She certainly seemed to have the world on a string. The *Daily Mail* described their life together like this:

> "The story of John and Ann Bender's marriage reads like a pulp fiction novel packed with every trope of the genre: astounding wealth, tales of alleged diamond smuggling and bouts of madness set against the background of a tropical paradise."

Who would want that adventure to end?

Friends to the Rescue

"Think of love as a state of grace not as a means to anything...but an end in itself."

Gabriel García Márquez – *Love in the Time of Cholera*

CRAZY JUNGLE LOVE

Throughout Ann Bender's trials there was always a strong—and possibly misunderstood—overriding theme of mental illness. It hung thick like mosquito netting over all three trials. It seemed obvious to most that both John and Ann suffered from a variety of mental illnesses. They both suffered from bipolar disorder, and probably also from paranoia and obsessive-compulsive disorder. It certainly did not take a trained psychologist to conclude that their behavior was not normal. Who collects $20 million in jewels just for the heck of it? Who injects their loved one with dirty river water thinking it will cure them? Who helps their husband rehearse his suicide for months on end? Who imprisons themselves in a heavily guarded fortress, surrounded by guards patrolling with illegal automatic weapons? These were not mentally stable people, but their vast wealth insulated them from the challenges that confront other mentally ill people in Costa Rica. That is, until John's death, when the lid was pried off Pandora's Box and no stash of cash could protect them from the judicial system, the press, and internet chatter.

In Costa Rican slang, "crazy" is translated as "loco," or "*chiflado*," and to say someone is crazy as a loon or crazy as a mad hatter, one says, "ma' loco que una cabra." That means crazier than a goat, an expression easily understood if one has watched goats frolicking with absolute wild abandon in the fields of Costa Rica. Many people came away from the Bender trial feeling that the Benders were crazier than goats—but that certainly did not indicate that Ann was a murderer. Proving to the court that she wasn't was an uphill battle for Team Ann because mental illness is not well understood in much of Latin America; it's a relatively new field of medicine.

According to the WHO (World Health Organization), mental health resources in Latin America are very scarce. The recent estimated figures for mental health professionals per 100,000 citizens in Costa Rica are: 1.6 psychiatrists; 2.7 psychiatric nurses; 2.8 psychologists; and 1.9 social workers. These figures are far below statistics for Europe and the United States, where numbers of health care professionals per 100,000 are 40-60 percent higher, depending on the country or state. That being said, there seems to be much less of a stigma against those with mental health challenges in Costa Rica, and families often take care of their family members who are suffering from mental illness, or brain disorders such as dementia, by tending to them at home where they are treated extremely well and in a familiar environment. John and Ann clearly felt that they were taking care of each other in their time of illness. They just didn't seem to realize how very sick they were.

Most of the witnesses on the defense's side were able to describe in great detail the telltale signs and symptoms of the mental illnesses from which John and Ann suffered. But of course, the testimony that packed the biggest wallop was the testimony of Ann's personal psychiatrist, Dr. Arturo Lizano-Vincent, who spoke to the court on day four of Ann's trial. It's quite certain that Dr. Arturo had no idea at the time of his testimony that the gallery of onlookers who comprised his audience (seated behind him in this particular courtroom) was filled in part with people who could quite possibly have made good use of his medical services.

From the rabid reporter from *Inside Costa Rica* (who thought she was Brenda Starr), to the fellow who claimed he could communicate with Bender "in the beyond" via a pendulum, to the lady who came to the trial to find a gringo boyfriend, to the female farmer who always slept outside under the stars on her farm near Boracayán, to the dude trying to invent a balsa wood car in Costa Rica—it would have looked like someone had released all the inmates from the funny farm especially to attend this trial. Má locos que unas cabras!

Ann's psychiatrist had treated her for depression and bipolar disorder at CIMA Hospital and in his private office before John's death. He is a renowned Tico specialist in addictions. His medical title is Psychiatrist and Neuropsychopharmacist, and he has published extensively on the subject, especially about the treatment of bipolar disorder. It was never made clear if Ann had any problems with addictions, but she certainly took a wide array of drugs to try to tame her bipolar disorder. John's autopsy after his death revealed no drugs in his system. Friends reported that John was both anti-drugs and anti-doctors. Dr. Lizano-Vincent testified after the prosecutor had announced, with his usual bluster, that "both of them were bipolar and obviously had personality disorders. But in Ann's case, she knew what she was doing and planned to kill him that night." Ramírez portrayed Ann always as a conniving gold digger who planned John's murder with total malice and sangfroid.

Dr. Lizano-Vincent took the opposite view. He had admitted Ann the day after John's death, and described a woman so traumatized and debilitated by her experience that she was flirting with her own death. Randi Kaye of CNN interviewed him for *48 Hours* and asked him, "How would you describe her mental condition when you first saw her after John's death?" Dr. Lizano-Vincent answered, "Flat is the way we call it in psychiatry. A blank stare, because her psychosis was monumental." He added, "I thought they both must have been psychotic."

Psychosis is a disorder typically involving losing touch with reality, manifested by delusions and hallucinations. Delusional thinking often occurs in psychotic people; this consists of believing that people are out to harm or are plotting against them. This had been both the Benders' agony for several years. Those suffering from this disorder are often thought to be evil and nefarious, but in fact, the opposite is often the case. Wrote Scott Barry Kaufman, a *Psychology Today* researcher,

> "There are a lot of inaccurate perceptions of psychotic people as immoral people. This is simply not true. While some bad people such as serial killers sometimes have psychotic episodes, the vast majority of psychotic individuals are not immoral. In fact, many who are psychosis-prone contribute positively to society."

John and Ann had created an entire nature reserve and lab as a gift to their new country and community—a totally selfless and altruistic project.

Dr. Lizano-Vincent described Ann's emotional condition upon arrival at CIMA Hospital as being extremely apathetic, with diminished facial expressions, speaking in a monotone voice, and manifesting a severe reduction in emotional expressiveness. Ann was frozen in a condition known clinically as "blunted affect." He described that it took many months before she began to come around to a healthier demeanor. His vivid description of her diminished condition was further elaborated upon by Ann's personal physician, Dr. Hugo Villegas, also of CIMA Hospital, who at trial described Ann as arriving at the hospital after John's death weighing only sixty-six pounds (30 kilos), roughly the weight of a small ten-year-old child.

As Dr. Villegas had previously stated, "Ann was severely malnourished with pockets of pus and abscesses on her skin." Dr. Villegas' specialty is general medicine for adults. He stated privately that he had never seen anything quite like Ann's deplorable condition during his long medical career.

Dr. Villegas testified about Ann's condition upon her arrival at CIMA Hospital,

> "She was literally blank. She had no recollection of what was going on, and she basically was unable to fathom what was going to happen tomorrow. She knew why she was in the hospital but was not aware of it. She knew, *Yes, my husband died.* But that was it—with no emotion whatsoever. Finally ... she became a lot clearer about what happened and what the consequences were. Of course, that generated its own levels of anxiety and despair."

The judges seemed to pay very close attention to the two doctors' testimony, asking only for clarification of a few medical details. The entire courtroom was having trouble imagining this frail and weakened Ann Bender, suffering both mentally and physically, as the murderer prosecutor Ramírez was accusing her of being. She seemed too weak to lift a teaspoon, much less a Ruger handgun. It was really starting to seem as though the whole struggle over the gun that ended in John's death was just a shockingly tragic accident.

Also testifying about Ann's fragile mental and physical condition at the time of John's death were Ken Patton, Pete DeLisi, and Paul Meyer. It was very difficult to find people close to the Benders who could testify because their disease isolated them from the community, and Boracayán always had a "Do Not Disturb" sign hanging out front. You could count on one hand the people who had ever even been inside their home or spoken to them face to face. It seemed especially odd that Ann had no female buddies in Costa Rica; her only real friend was Celine Bouchacourt, a high school friend from Switzerland with whom she had rekindled a friendship after Ann had been accused of murder. Such an odd way to reconnect!

Apparently, Ann's only friends had been the animals she surrounded herself with at Bender Dome, and they were no help to her now. She missed them daily and always felt a dull ache in her heart when she thought of each of them. The ache she felt for both John and Greg Fischer was indescribable. Ann's family was her rock, the support team that stood by her through thick and thin, interrupting their lives to travel down to Costa Rica to stand by her side through this ordeal, which they certainly could not control, in a language they could barely understand.

<<>>

Pete DeLisi was the person who probably knew John Bender the best of those who were called to testify. John's parents were unfortunately unable to attend this third trial. DeLisi had been the best man at John and Ann's wedding. In fact, John wore a suit borrowed from Pete for the ceremony. Both men were giants, but where John's mass had been mostly muscle, DeLisi had gone soft around the middle. He looked like a gentle cartoon giant, and demonstrated incredible loyalty to John and compassion for his widow. John had worked closely with DeLisi on the Philadelphia Stock Exchange and had probably been John's best friend ever since, although they had naturally drifted apart a little after the Benders moved to Costa Rica.

DeLisi wrote about John's death on a fellow hedge fund manager's blog: *jonathankaplan.livejournal.com* on January 20, 2010, ten days after John's death, as follows:

"My name is Pete DeLisi. I knew John for

eighteen years. I spoke with him in December before he passed. John suffered from manic depression and sadly took his own life. The past ten years were difficult for him. He had a stroke, his wife was ill with an undiagnosed illness, and he had a lengthy litigation regarding the wind-down of his fund. John was buying those stones for his wife and mentioned to me that he was buying hard assets due to the global recession. He was a contrarian, so when everyone was looking to raise cash, he was buying undervalued assets at fire sale prices. Sadly, the world lost one of its brightest minds. I always felt he could have made serious contributions to the scientific and mathematical fields, but he chose to live a secluded life with his wife. He was an amazing trader and a great friend."

DeLisi's testimony to the Pérez Zeledón courtroom echoed his statement above, but with some amplification on John's career, mathematical talent, and enormous financial success. All of that information had been well-rehearsed with the lawyer who had prepped Pete for the trial, but was still a real struggle for the average Tico to understand. For instance, DeLisi testified that, "by the time John was twenty-five, I think he had amassed about $80 million."

With the whole concept of Wall Street, the stock market, hedge fund management, and international investments being completely foreign to most attending the trial, DeLisi unfortunately came off as being a spoiled, entitled rich American. The prosecutor, of course, continuously pointed those assumptions out to everyone, with thinly veiled anti-American overtones. There seemed to be no way to portray the business John was involved in and the amount of money he earned through it, in a way which didn't seem corrupt to the average José. These were sums of money one cannot even win in the huge El Gordo (The Fat One) Christmas lottery in Costa Rica.

What DeLisi did manage to make crystal clear to the court was John's fatal attraction to the idea of suicide. While on the stand, DeLisi referenced three different times when John had confessed his suicidal urges, usually motivated by his own inability to handle disappointment and failure. DeLisi seemed to feel that it had always been a matter of *when*, not *if* John would end his own life. DeLisi testified that John's suicidal urges were well known among both friends and family, but they all felt powerless to prevent the inevitable tragedy of John's death by his own hand. DeLisi delivered his statement with dignity and gravitas, even as the prosecutor sniped and sneered at him. DeLisi was now acting as Ann's spokesperson in Costa Rica. The following is how he described the Bender story in a letter which accompanied the *Petition to Free Ann* while she was being held in preventive detention in San José after the trial in which she was found guilty of pre-meditated murder in 2014.

SUBMITTED BY PETE DELISI, JOHN BENDER'S CLOSEST FRIEND, TO A NEWSPAPER IN COSTA RICA:

Following Ann's second trial in which she was convicted unanimously of murder.

I write this article with a heavy heart. During the late hours of last Tuesday (May 27, 2014), I may have possibly said goodbye to my dear friend's wife, while she sat in a holding area in a wheelchair surrounded with enough armed police to make one think she was Charles Manson.

Ann Maxine Patton went on trial for the death of her husband last January, 2013. She was acquitted. The judges were unanimous. This time the trial was over before it even started. I would like to note, I was a close personal friend of her husband. I testified at both trials, and like John Bender's parents, no one is calling for justice. John was seriously bipolar. This was well known. He suffered from serious depression, and since moving to Costa Rica, they had nothing but problems there. Her recent guilty charge, confirms that this was all about money.

In America, like most places, double jeopardy is not allowed. In Costa Rica, they do what they have to do in order to get the result they want. Before the first trial, Ann and John were no strangers to the Pérez Zeledón Police and DA. In 2001, they were kidnapped by corrupt cops, and very little or nothing was done to the cops involved.

During the first trial, Ann was very nervous that she could not get a fair trial. She was acquitted. This should have been over. Luis Oses and Edgar Ramírez stopped at nothing to get an appeal. It was granted on the basis of the previous judges not looking at the "scientific evidence." It is like getting a bad test grade back (and given an opportunity) to take it over again. The two DAs this time focused on the ballistics, the "irrefutable proof" said Ramírez. Ok, let me tell you exactly what changed from the first trial to the second and you make the call:

The medical examiner in the first trial said it

was possible that the victim committed suicide if he was ambidextrous. John was ambidextrous, this was well known. During this retrial she changed her statement and said it was "impossible," but never said how she shot him. 100% impossible. How does that sound? Does that seem ok? I should note she testified via teleconference the first time, this time she was in court.

The Prosecution witnesses all changed or enhanced their statements from the first trial. You cannot go back and look at what they said. Does that seem reasonable? You can go look at the records if you would like.

Did Ann change her statements or did any of us that testified in the first statements? Absolutely NOT!!

A new Prosecution witness testified who had a major conflict of interest and was paid $6,000 by the ex-trustee, Juan de Dios Álvarez, who was removed by the Costa Rican courts as trustee, but to date approximately $40 million is missing. Keep in mind, this report that the witness wrote, was used by the trustee to get his hands on

$15 million in life insurance money. Oses and Ramírez used his report. The judges were shown documents of the check cashed and a copy of the invoice. They not only allowed him to testify, but referred to his words in their verdict. Again, you make the call? Does this seem fishy? I would use the words, downright corrupt.

The judges did not ask me, her brother, their neighbor, or her medical doctor a single question. Does that seem fishy? Ann did say this was a suicide. One would think you would at least ask some questions.

At one point during the latter days of the retrial, Ramírez jumped out of his seat and called the judges into the back room with her attorney. As I was outside, I noticed twelve heavily armed police all of a sudden. We were later told that a "death threat" was called in, but no specifics. I found it strange that Ramírez all of a sudden found out about this. How was he told? He was in his chair. No one came in the court room. His phone did not ring. Do you let someone know about a death threat via text, email, or even better Facebook! Later that day, two

OIJ policewomen start hanging around.

On the day of the verdict, the closing arguments, they finished around 12:30. We were told to come back at 3:00 pm for a verdict. Assuming these judges had some lunch; they came back at 3:00 pm and read a one hour-long verdict. Can you write something that long and concise in two hours? The best part was Ramírez calling a press conference ten minutes before the verdict was read. Those same OIJ policewomen were now standing behind Ann before those judges came in, and myself, her brother, friends, neighbors had six OIJ surrounding us.

I think the only people in San Isidro that did not know about the verdict at this point was anyone who did not have a pulse!

Lastly, there is so much more I could go into about ballistics and forensics. These are the same experts who never fingerprinted the gun. Do you think that might be a good place to start? They sat there with their witnesses who now changed statements, proclaimed the distance to the shot, but could not show how she did it. These judges were downright disrespectful, did not pay attention for the majority of the trial, and at the end remanded her into custody like an animal. They were nice enough to knock off three years of her sentence because of her medical conditions.

Folks, I was in utter shock seeing what I saw. Please keep in mind, there was never a motive. She waited three years to go to the first trial, she was acquitted. She did not leave CR. She knew they would appeal. She waited fifteen months and sat for a second trial. This time she was not released on her own recognizance, pending an appeal. Just taken away like an animal.

I know that not all Costa Rican citizens are like this, but what I witnessed, this was a rigged game and always was. This is all about money, gems, land, and a big smash and grab job.

My name is Pete DeLisi. I was recently on the CNN piece, mentioned in the *Outside Magazine* article, testified in both trials and what I have said is nothing but the truth.

All About the Money

"And her soul brightened with the nostalgia of her lost dreams."

Gabriel García Márquez – *One Hundred Years of Solitude*

Following the detailed testimony from Pete DeLisi came the testimony from Ann Bender's brother Ken Patton. Kenneth Patton IV attended all three of Ann's trials, had been the first person Ann called after John's death, and had assumed the role of press contact in Costa Rica for the Patton family. He had monitored all Facebook postings and given live interviews with local television and print media. Ken had virtually put his own life on hold for five years to be able to assist Ann in any way he could, both emotionally and financially. Ken helped Celine Bouchacourt with the petitions to free Ann, and the *GoFundMe* page to raise money for Ann's defense. He and Greg Fischer had bonded before Greg's death in their efforts to keep Ann alive while she was in preventive detention, and Ken was the conduit between Ann and her parents, who were often panicked over the series of events which had befallen their only daughter. Ken, two years older than Ann, was super-protective of her, as any good older brother would be.

Ken's Spanish reflected a decidedly Portuguese accent, as he had learned that language first while living in Rio de Janeiro as a child with his international banker father. He was a smallish guy—all the Pattons being short in stature—with straight prep school brown hair and piercing green eyes. Those eyes would positively shoot sparks when he discussed Ann's situation with friends and family. Ken was the go-to guy if you wanted a succinct summary of exactly what Ann had endured at the hands of the Tico justice system. He did not mince words. Ken was the only one in interviews with the press who would call out the lawyer who had allegedly stolen the Bender fortune and used the nature reserve's endowment as his own private piggy bank: Juan de Dios Álvarez.

Ken made his feelings crystal clear about the prosecutor who was on a witch-hunt to convict Ann, the court which seemed to be doing nothing to protect his innocent sister, and the circumstances in which Ann had found herself after her husband's death. Ken echoed the assessment by taxi driver Randall Baldí regarding Ann's plight in Costa Rica: *chorizo*. He also added the Tico slang *pura paja*, meaning pure bullshit. Ken certainly did not feel that Costa Rica was the happiest place on earth.

Ken was forty-nine years old at the end of the trial, although people associated with Ann's nightmare should really be measured in dog years, seven years for each human year; that's how stressful and agonizing it must have been for all. He is now married to Kathy Turetzky, the author of the *Petition to Free an Innocent Woman*, Ann's petition to the Costa Rican government and people. Ken has returned to his profession as a credit and portfolio manager in the Greater Detroit, Michigan, area, and remains wonderfully close to his baby sister Ann. On his LinkedIn page, Ken describes his recent past as "spent the last three years overseas assisting in a family-related situation." Such an understatement of his role in saving his sister!

The press who had interviewed Ken during those three years chatted in the courtroom hallway on the morning of the trial saying that it was going to be a miracle if Ken could keep his cool while he testified. He performed admirably; there was very little indication of the indignation he and his family held for the entire ordeal they had been put through at the hands of the Tico court's definition of "justice."

Ken took the stand calmly, dressed in a crisp open-collared dress shirt and black dress pants—the Eikelenbooms were the only people to have worn suits to any of the trials. When in Central America, dress like the natives, it seemed. He began by describing how close he and Ann had been all of their lives. He elaborated on Ann's mental illness challenges throughout her life, and how bravely she had confronted those challenges. He described Ann's powerful love for both John Bender and the vision they had shared for the Boracayán Nature Reserve. He confirmed the fact that the whole Patton family had been aware of John's multiple threats to kill himself. He expressed profound sorrow that John had finally, as many who commit suicide eventually do, followed through on that threat. Ken expressed his concern for his sister's well-being going forward, and his absolute certainty that Juan de Dios Álvarez wanted her dead so that he could claim the entire nature reserve and the Bender trust fund as his own. Ken spoke in English in clear, short sentences which made it easy for the translator. He did not express anger, but was exceedingly direct in his evaluation of what had befallen his sister while in Costa Rica. Ann's ability to have loyal, caring, and devoted men around her—always—was remarkable.

Ken had discovered from their father that Ann had been diagnosed with bipolar disorder in 1995, when he had just completed his military service. Since that discovery, Ken testified that he had worried pretty consistently about his sister, particularly given the remoteness of where John and Ann lived in Costa Rica. He confirmed Ann's account of her phone call to him on the night of John's death, and that Ann had said, "He finally did it." Ken said his immediate concern was that Ann would also attempt to kill herself. He instantly dropped everything and got on the next plane to San José. One of the security team from Bender Dome picked him up and brought him to the private hospital in Pérez where Ann was being held. Ken said he was shocked at Ann's frail appearance; he had never seen her so skeletal.

Ken's role in the defense testimonies seemed to be to humanize and garner sympathy for Ann. He was certainly able to describe in detail the life of John and Ann as a couple, which fleshed out their puro amor, and portrayed them as a happily married couple who just happened to suffer from serious mental illnesses, and just happened to be mind-bogglingly rich. He was able to describe their lives in a way which focused much more acutely on their devotion to their pets, families, nature sanctuary, and of course, their strong bond to each other. He made them seem a little less creepy. Ken was able to downplay the Benders' incredible wealth and privilege in favor of pointing out their heroic struggles with mental illness and attacks from corrupt lawyers and justice officials. His testimony certainly helped counteract the prosecution's image of Ann spending her days counting gems and rearranging her jewelry box, while John continued to make more millions through dubious hedge fund deals executed online.

Ken stated in court at Ann's trial, "There's no chance she murdered her husband." This was his refrain throughout the four years of trials; he always described John's death as "an accident." Ken would refer to the accusation of Ann as a murderer as "a theatre of lies." He was convinced that she could beat the murder rap and go on with her life. To *48 Hours* he declared, "She's a fighter; my sister's not going to give up … and I'm behind her every step of the way."

The following is Ken's declaration which formed part of Ann's Petition on *change.org* on February 20, 2015, revealing some of his insights into Ann's incredible predicament in Costa Rica:

CRAZY JUNGLE LOVE

20 DE FEBRERO, DE 2015 —From Ann's brother, Ken Patton:

Yesterday, my sister Ann Maxine Patton was released from prison in Costa Rica after nine months of incarceration for a crime she did not commit. This is not over by a long ways yet. All we know for now is that in addition to ordering her immediate release yesterday, the Costa Rican appellate court has ordered a third trial, likely since the second trial in May 2014 in Pérez Zeledón was so clearly corrupted. That second trial resulted in her conviction for premeditated homicide and a subsequent 22-year sentence, which clearly had no legal merit as this trial was a complete theatre of lies by the Prosecution and perjury by state employees posing as "credible" Prosecution forensic experts.

This is all about money. If it wasn't for the large sum of money and assets, Ann would not even be charged. Ann is not permitted to leave Costa Rica once again, but is "free" to remain in the country while the battle continues.

Ann is an innocent person who absolutely

did not murder her husband. She could not harm a fly. Meanwhile none of Ann's assets are titled in her name and the individual primarily responsible for this abortion of justice, Juan de Dios Álvarez, has fled to Nicaragua where he remains a free man. There is no doubt he bribed several parties in this country to pave the way for Ann to be framed for murdering her husband. His intent was for her to die in prison given her health problems so he could steal all of her wealth and pay off all of his associates in and outside of Costa Rica who aided him in this smash and grab scheme.

As of today, Ann has limited funds to continue funding a legal Defense since all of the assets held for her in a Costa Rican trust remain stolen.

This is not over…

The third American to testify for Team Ann was her neighbor from Florida de Barú, Paul Meyer. Paul and his wife Judy lived on Paul's tree farm next door to the Benders. Paul echoed the testimony of both DeLisi and Patton, and indicated that he had seen John less and less as time went on, but each time John seemed to look worse and worse physically. He remembered having seen John with his hands so swollen he could not shake hands, nor fit them in his pocket to remove his keys. Paul wasn't exactly sure what was going on at Boracayán, but to him it was obvious that there were worsening mental health issues for both John and Ann. He had made a very intuitive and profound statement about the Bender situation to the show *48 Hours*. Paul Meyer had told them, "What you have here is a genius who's losing his mind. And I think, in a moment of sanity really, he took his own life so that he didn't start killing the people he loved around him." Paul made a similar statement at Ann's trial. Paul had contributed very generously to Ann's defense and to keeping the wildlife sanctuary operational. He will likely never get that money back.

Someone who lobbied very hard for Ann's freedom and the return of her fortune was a world-famous hedge fund manager named Jack Schwager, who had known John Bender extremely well, and had even interviewed him at length for his best-selling series of interviews titled "Market Wizards," about the most successful hedge fund managers in the last three decades. John Bender was one of those success stories. Jack Schwager joined Team Ann from the United States, and in 2014 wrote a short statement of support for Ann on his web page. He called it "The Death of John Bender and a Miscarriage of Justice." Here is part of what he wrote in support of Ann, which was presented in court by her defense team:

> John Bender was a math genius who ran a successful investment fund with his wife Ann and his best friend Peter DeLisi. John and Ann closed the fund, moved to Costa Rica, and dedicated their lives to saving the rainforest. They established a 5,000-acre nature reserve and put US $70 million in a trust to ensure their nature reserve would survive forever. The only two beneficiaries of this massive trust are the nature reserve and Ann Bender.
>
> Both John and Ann have documented psychiatric problems, including bipolar disorder and suicidal tendencies. On January 8, 2010 John died of a single gunshot wound to the head. Ann has always maintained John tried to kill himself and she tried to stop him. But the local district attorney opened a murder investigation against Ann and a court date was set for January 2013.
>
> John and Ann's $70 million trust was managed by a lawyer named Juan de Dios Álvarez. In 2012, Álvarez's offices were

raided by the police, and he was removed from trust management for failure of fiduciary duty. All of the trust's liquid assets—approximately $40 million—have disappeared. In addition, property titles to trust assets have been transferred to companies outside the trust umbrella. The trust's CFO testified in a CR court "Álvarez acted as though the trust was his." In a court deposition in 2012, the CFO testified he knew of at least $20 million stolen by Álvarez. Ann Bender has lodged a preliminary financial fraud court case against Álvarez to try to recover the trust's assets.

Ann was ruled innocent at her murder trial in January 2013. There is no double jeopardy statute in Costa Rica, so the DA immediately filed for appeal. Appeal was granted and the second murder trial against Ann concluded on Tuesday May 28, 2014. She was found guilty and sentenced to 22 years in prison. Ann was immediately remanded to a psychiatric hospital's suicide ward where she was under guard. When deemed healthy, she will be sent to prison.

Two of the Prosecution's witnesses

markedly changed their testimonies from the first murder trial in 2013 to the second murder trial in 2014. In 2013, the forensics doctor said suicide was possible. In 2014 the same doctor said suicide was impossible. In the 2013 trial, one of Ann's former employees said Ann was frail and unhealthy at the time of John's death but she had a loving relationship with John. In the 2014 trial, the same employee said Ann was healthy and the couple had an argument the day of John's death. His revised testimony differed materially from the testimony of four other employees who testified at the 2014 trial.

Another key Prosecution witness in 2014 was arguably ethically compromised. A ballistics expert who testified in the 2014 trial said the ballistics evidence showed homicide. In 2010, this same ballistics expert was allegedly paid by Álvarez to write a ballistics report about John's death. (The invoice of this payment was found in the police raid on Álvarez's office.) This 2010 ballistics report was allegedly used by Álvarez to claim $14 million from John's life insurance policy. The whereabouts of this

$14 million is unknown.

In early 2013, the Costa Rican government appointed an interim trust manager named Mario Gomez to manage the trust. As mentioned, the only two beneficiaries of the trust are the nature reserve and Ann. Yet Mario Gomez has not visited the nature reserve in the year since he has been appointed. He has not called either of the two employees who are managing the reserve. Nor has he paid any of the reserve employees. Mario has not disbursed any money to Ann to cover her legal or medical fees.

For the last three years, all of Ann's living expenses and all of the salaries of the nature reserve's employees have been paid by family and friends. But this nightmare has dragged on for years, and we are all tapped out.

The testimonies of DeLisi, Patton, Meyer, and Schwager should certainly have been enough to move the needle in Ann's favor. Then again, this trial was happening in its own Macondo, where anything was possible.

<<>>

Interestingly, the Costa Rican court never sought phone records from any of the people involved in Ann's life just before John's death. Nor had they obtained the travel history of Ann in the months leading up to John's death. They also seemed disinterested in all the internet chatter that had surrounded the case. Meanwhile, folks were commenting very creatively online about Ann's possible frame of mind before and during the tragedy. Ken was aware that several bloggers from both San José and the United States were convinced that Costa Rica had it right, and that Ann had indeed been the killer. This was the most popular conjecture by those posting anonymously, and some folks seemed to have a fairly good understanding of the terrain and logistics of getting to and from Boracayán, which made it difficult to totally discount their writings.

The most persistent anonymous poster reminded everyone that John Bender had suffered a stroke while on his honeymoon with Ann, which the poster felt was suspicious. Ann's boyfriend Greg Fischer had also died under mysterious circumstances. The blogger sensed a pattern there. He went on to describe a theory which had Ann returning from one of her jewel-collecting trips, when she carelessly dropped the receipts from the jewel purchase which she had taken out of her suitcase to show the customs agent, along with a ledger of previous jewel purchases. He claimed that these items had both been found alongside the road to Boracayán. He then went on to claim that when John discovered that Ann had returned home without the paperwork, he went berserk, trying to rough Ann up for leaving such a clear paper trail of their dubious dealings. He claimed that Ann had killed John in self-defense, and then tried to stage the scene to look as if John had killed himself. The anonymous poster never came forward to testify, and the entire Bender case was heavily tilted anyway—toward purely circumstantial evidence.

Another blogger claimed to have heard rumors that there were hitmen seen fleeing up and over the mountains, down to the beach road at about 1:00 am on January 9th, the day after John's death, near Bender Dome. The blogger claimed that this incident had been confirmed to them by two second-hand witnesses. Neither of these bloggers seemed to understand how incredibly fragile Ann was at the beginning of 2010, really on her last legs, and very unlikely to have pulled off something as intricate as a hired assassin or a re-created death scene intended to prove her innocence. Ann couldn't even find the strength to put herself to bed unassisted at night. As a non-driver, it was especially far-fetched that she would be driving around the mountains at night with receipts and ledgers bouncing out of car windows. People were struggling to make sense of this bizarre incident by applying imaginary bad television scripts to what had possibly taken place. It only added to what Ken Patton called the "theatre of lies."

Yet another wacky story told online was from someone who claimed to have spoken often to a security guard employed for years by the Benders, who said he was sometimes asked to escort John via helicopter down to the beach at Uvita, where he was met by a boat which whisked him away for two or three hours, by himself, then returned him to the beach where he and the escort guard were flown by helicopter back to Bender Dome. The anonymous poster said it was assumed that Bender was meeting a drug sale contact in open water for some illegal drug deal. He said Bender would wear a photographer's or fisherman's vest with lots of pockets, and return with seemingly less in the pockets. The guard reported that he considered this the least attractive part of his job because he had to be at the helicopter pad before dawn, and escort a man who never spoke to him—not once.

The *Inside Costa Rica* reporter got as far as speaking with the Bender guard by phone, but he refused to comment on the story unless *ICR* produced a subpoena, which they could not obtain. It began to seem to the *ICR* reporter that no one would ever know the truth about John Bender's life and death, even after three criminal trials.

There were also the many religious bloggers who promised to continue praying for Ann, and for John, and even for their various companion animals. Luckily, none of the Escazú witchcraft disciples seemed to be aware of what was transpiring in the Pérez Zeledón courthouse in August, 2015. That would have really stirred the conspiracy and evil-doers' kettles of malevolence.

The murder trial of Ann Maxine Bender careened forward at its own random pace.

Jungle Love

JUNGLE LOVE

Third verse - Refrain:

Jungle love, it's drivin' me mad
It's makin' me Crazy, Crazy
Jungle love, it's drivin' me mad
It's makin' me Crazy, Crazy
You treat me like I was your ocean
You swim in my blood when it's warm
My cycles of circular motion
Protect you and keep you from harm
You live in a world of illusion
Where everything's peaches and cream
We all face a scarlet conclusion
But we spend our time in a dream

Steve Miller Band, 1977

Ann's third trial went on for one full month, with a short break for the prosecutor to have some minor surgery. Costa Rica has socialized medicine, meaning there are often very long waits for surgery or procedures deemed to be non-emergency in nature. One dares not postpone the procedure, or you could have to wait another couple of years to be rescheduled. Everyone tries to deal with these waits gracefully, knowing they are lucky to have such fine medical attention at low cost as part of their rights as a citizen of Costa Rica. People in prosecutor Ramírez's income bracket usually opt to have their surgery done on their own schedule, in a private hospital or clinic, and pay out of pocket. He was conveying a strong proletariat message for the court: not everyone in this world has Bender-size billfolds to pay for extended stays at resort-hospitals. His message was clear; the Benders' tragedy was nothing but rich people's problems. At week three, the trial took a sudden and unannounced break to await Ramírez's return to the courtroom. *Así es el arroz* (that's life), as they say in Pérez Zeledón.

Ann's lawyer, Fabio Oconitrillo, was showing more white hairs in his beard, and was a bit pudgier at the waist. Ann was dressed always in dark colors, usually in flowing skirts or dresses, mostly in jersey or some other soft, stretchy fabric. She continued to wear low, open-toed heels, but her feet seemed to be bothering her quite a bit, and they looked swollen and often discolored. She continued to walk with a cane. Her Lyme disease still seemed to be taking its toll. On the morning she was sentenced to twenty-two years of preventive detention (at her second trial), Ann had been wearing a shoulderless cocktail dress with a thin evening stole around her shoulders. Her team would not let her appear like that again; this time Ann was defending her life. It had never been more important for Ann and her legal team to win. Ideally, Ann should appear in court looking a bit like a nun: Sister Boracayán.

Among the attendees of the trial were some pretty interesting characters. There were several versions of "crazy jungle love" that floated around the Bender case. They say that Americans who come to Costa Rica are either Wanted or Unwanted, meaning they are either hiding out from criminal charges back in the US (tax evasion, unpaid child support, criminal conviction, etc.), or are people who were unsuccessful socially, financially, or professionally back home. Costa Rica offers a new start for all these folks, but people often tend to bring their misfortune and troubles with them, so sometimes things don't work out a whole lot better for them in Ticolandia. For many, however, a new life allows them to flourish in new directions and enjoy new freedoms unavailable to them back in the US.

One such person was the Benders' neighbor whose land abuts the Boracayán estate, Jesse Blenn. Jesse had first come to visit Costa Rica as an eighteen-year-old on a school trip to visit Central America and to continue improving his classroom Spanish. It was love at first sight for him. He remembers arriving in San José wanting nothing more than to see a coconut tree growing in the jungle. Jesse had somehow not known that coconuts grow also in Florida—he was from Kansas—and he arrived ready to live out all his fantasies of the Tarzan books and movies he had devoured in his youth, in the wilds of Costa Rican jungles and forests.

Jesse was craving a *Son of Tarzan* experience, or at least a *Gilligan's Island* adventure. He became smitten with the amazing flora and fauna, which launched his ongoing study of native plants found in Costa Rica. He was especially captivated by fruits, and claimed to own examples of every fruit tree in the world, except for two varieties native to Borneo, all of them happily growing on his farm. It took two tries, but Jesse now has a successful and well-known fruit emporium in the south of the country. He named it Jardines Cambria (Cambria Gardens).

Jesse is now sixty-something, married to a Tica, with a second family living with him on his fruit farm across from Boracayán. Jesse had been an airplane mechanic and blimp designer in the US, and soon found himself drawn back into the transportation design field, with a burning desire to create an environmentally responsible Tico vehicle. In 2012, Jesse introduced an electric car made of balsa and aluminum, which he called CambYo Car. He wanted to manufacture and sell the CambYo in Costa Rica, thereby offering an environmentally responsible form of transportation to everyone, which would not break the bank like imported electric cars do in the local market. Importing any car to Costa Rica is an expensive undertaking due to import taxes and fees.

He now calls the car the Cambria, which boasts some snazzy features and unusual touches to set it apart from other electric cars made elsewhere—but the Cambria production will be employing people right in Costa Rica, and helping to protect the environment in the process. Jesse likes to rail against the so-called "ecovillages" that have sprung up around Costa Rica, and who transport tourists and residents around town in gas-guzzling Land Rovers and buses, which are anything but eco-friendly.

Jesse's motto is "To change the world, we have to change the car." He and his lovely wife Matilde Gutierrez co-manage the exhausting process of trying to get the Cambria into production in a country which has few investors in entrepreneurship, and tends to prefer "tried and true" to innovative business plans. In 2013 they won a Costa Rican government contest to fund innovative projects, but to date have only been awarded four months of funding. Jesse has invested his entire inheritance in the Cambria project. The couple continue working on the Cambria, showcasing it at trade shows in San José, and continuing to perfect the design.

In a Cambria, the driver sits in the middle of the car, and there is room for three other passengers comfortably. The interior features teak and pejibaye wood trim and electric door closings. The best part of this car are the gull-wing doors, which open up and out, providing room for one to open an umbrella before stepping out of the car, to avoid getting soaked by rain—perfect for Costa Rica's rainy season. He has also designed a folding electric tricycle called a Turismo, which would be ideal for all those tourists wanting to zip around their eco-villages responsibly.

As of 2016, ramping up of production on the Cambria car is on hold pending a decision by the Costa Rican government (Ley de Incentivos y Promoción para el Transporte Eléctrico, Expediente N. 19.744) as to whether or not electric cars will be tax-free to their drivers. This law would grant huge tax breaks to those purchasing electric vehicles. Imagine the effect this could have on the number of electric cars Ticos would see on the roads, and the reduction in air pollution for this tiny eco-friendly country.

Jesse's occupation as a creative designer of electric vehicles is rather tame compared to another talent Jesse claims to possess: He speaks with dead people. Jesse was observed in the courtroom hall at Ann's trial, discreetly dangling a small pendulum between his knees. What the heck was that? After the reporter from *Inside Costa Rica* had interviewed Jesse several times regarding his electric car project, it was revealed that he could communicate with dead people via a pendulum, and in fact had spoken with John Bender on various occasions. OMG! The reporter naturally wanted every single detail of the conversation, beginning with wanting to know if Jesse had ever asked John the Big Question: Did Ann kill him? Jesse described John as currently being in a noisy, chaotic place, full of turbulence and angst, but able nonetheless to answer Jesse's question, "Did Ann kill you?" to which John replied, "No, I believe I killed *her.*"

This answer could be interpreted in one of two ways. Either John was feeling tremendous guilt at the nightmare his death had thrown Ann into, or that he was perhaps still crazy in his afterlife and maybe did not even know himself precisely what had happened on the night of his death. The reporter emerged from that conversation as puzzled by the facts of John's death as ever, but convinced that Ann was completely correct in one thing—John was still not at peace. Jesse Blenn believes that John and Ann are still able to communicate with each other at will, and are still very much in love. The reporter asked if it would be possible to observe Jesse communicating with John, and Jesse agreed to that, but felt it would work better if his wife stepped in as the channeler, as she was more experienced than Jesse in these forms of communication.

The reporter had watched a video on YouTube from October 17, 2014, of Jesse using the pendulum to balance Ann Bender's chakras, followed by a series of questions Jesse was able to "ask" John about his previous and current life. Chakra is a Sanskrit word that refers to the circles of energy we have within our bodies. There are seven chakras in the human body, and they can become under-active, over-active, or open, the latter being the ideal state for balance. If there is a blockage in one of these chakras, energy cannot flow freely, and illness is likely to follow. Jesse had offered his services to Ann's family to help improve Ann's health via the pendulum, but they had politely refused. Jesse went ahead and asked permission from both John and Ann to communicate via the pendulum. He said they both agreed.

In the video, Jesse is sitting in his pajamas (fairly ratty old ones, which did not enhance his fifteen minutes of YouTube fame), and allowing the pendulum to swing between his knees. The pendulum would variously circle one way, the reverse way, change speed, or stop completely, which Jesse would interpret as having meaning. He narrated the proceedings as he asked questions and allegedly received answers. Jesse swore he was not moving the pendulum himself, and indeed he does not appear to be. The video is as odd as the whole Bender case—maybe *slightly* weirder. Jesse was apparently able to get Ann's chakras back in balance and strengthened in this session, particularly her fourth, or heart chakra, and her seventh, or crown chakra, which is responsible for spiritual energy. Both Ann's heart and crown chakras, the pendulum revealed, were almost paralyzed. Jesse freed them up.

Next Jesse asks permission to speak with John Bender. Jesse begins his interview with Bender by asking him how much money he had made in his life. The pendulum circles steadily, turning again and again, while Jesse counts the dollars by millions, until it stops at what Jesse Blenn has counted at $1.25 billion. Sounds about right. Next, John is asked how much of the money was earned illegally—the pendulum circles in reverse before it slows to a complete stop. Jesse interprets that as meaning none of John's money was earned illegally. The more detailed questions Jesse had were answered using Jesse's wife Matilde as a channeler. This was how Jesse learned how chaotic John's purgatory was.

Finally, the million-dollar question was asked regarding Ann's culpability. The answer was a backward whirling pendulum; the answer was no.

CRAZY JUNGLE LOVE

It is possible to watch his videos on YouTube, but be forewarned, Jesse is into some heavy stuff with exorcisms, aliens, and reptilians.

<<>>

Another of the candidates for the "Crazy Jungle Love Club" who was at Ann's last trial was the Benders' neighbor Amy Schrift. Neither Jesse nor Amy had ever met Ann Bender, but turned up anyway in support of a fellow expat who was having a rough time. That's what people often do in a foreign country; they circle the wagons.

Amy is a striking woman with long very curly hair, beautiful big eyes, a lovely figure, and a dancer-like way of moving. She looks way too hip for Pérez. That's probably because in her previous life, Amy was a well-respected jazz trumpeter and music teacher in New York City. She played with the Dan Carillo Sextet, among others. She went from the concrete jungle to the tropical jungle, and things went pretty Macondo for her almost immediately. She lived in total isolation for six years on a seventeen-acre fruit farm near Boracayán, living in what is called a *rancho*, which has a hardwood floor with a thatched roof and no walls or furniture. Most people in Costa Rica use their ranchos as party space. Not Amy. Amy lived for years with no radio, toilet, bed, refrigerator, oven, television, washing machine, or even lights.

Amy described her life on her farm with great gusto, including details of her fruit-only diet, her dedication to "mono meals," which means eating like the animals—only bananas, then only mangoes, then only *mamones chinos* (rambutans), etc. She said animals she observed did not combine foods in the same meal. She said she washed herself without soap in the brook at the bottom of her property, and then walked back up to her rancho naked to dry off. She avoided all chemicals. She claims she doesn't need to drink water. She said she was composting her own waste, since human waste is not malodorous if the human eats nothing but fruits and vegetables. She described being fond of sleeping at night in different places around her property, on an old air mattress, with a light cover for cool nights. Her favorite sleeping spot, however, was a small yoga platform not far from the rancho with a magnificent view of her farm and the valley it is nestled in. Rainy season required her to sleep inside the rancho most nights.

Amy described this favorite sleeping spot on a webpage she finally began called "Bare Feet with Amy." She said, "During the dry season, I sleep on a small yoga platform under the open sky, allowing cosmic radiation to freely penetrate my body." She took sun showers throughout the day and described feeling cleansed and uplifted by them. Amy is a newlywed to "the man in her life," Bill Van Horn. She and Bill call themselves "homesteaders," and they have begun work on the creation of what they are calling "a healing arts village." They are selling off portions of Amy's farm to like-minded people with the goal of "creating a healing arts village that will attract people from around the world to visit for extended stays and benefit from the services provided by the professionals in the village." They offer themselves as consultants for how to transition into Costa Rica, how to create your own piece of paradise, and how to avoid the pitfalls so many people have stumbled over as they seek their forever homes in Central America. They can also show you how to build and protect your own "Tiny Tropical Home and Little Homestead." It's the complete package. But as one person at the weekly farmers' market in Pérez Zeledón commented, "Yes, but make sure you don't drink the Kool-Aid."

Bill Van Horn is like many other expats who have resettled in the Southern Zone of Costa Rica. He subscribes to many conspiracy theories, from the mildest to the most far out, and writes about them on Facebook. One can only assume that Amy was ready for this after six years of living all alone, and in silence. Sheena, Queen of the Jungle, must have had a lot of adjusting to do as a new bride with a non-Tarzan husband. They seem to be crazy in love, and Bill has brought Amy out of the jungle and into a tiny house with a bathroom, and a kitchen, and a fridge. "Living large" in Pérez Zeledón!

Amy continues to lecture on the benefits of her raw foods and chemical-free lifestyle. She and Bill conduct workshops and seminars on this topic at the farm, but Amy also travels back to the US to lecture. Amy is very well-liked by the *campesinos* (peasants) who live and farm in the Diamante Valley near her, and a handful of them traveled all the way into Pérez for some of the Bender trial. They gathered around Amy in the hall, chatting away about what was happening at the trial, and what it might mean for the future of Boracayán. Ann Bender's bodyguards prevented the farmers from approaching Ann, who would surely have enjoyed seeing some of the folks who were part of her life with John for over a decade. The farmers looked longingly at Ann as she entered the courtroom, but she never looked up once. Too painful.

An issue not discussed at all at the Bender trial was what would happen to the area of Costa Rica that the Benders had transformed into a nature reserve, and was now virtually abandoned. This was of great concern to the Benders' neighbors, who envisioned a return to the old days when drug smugglers and illegal animal poachers had free reign over the Diamante Valley. The Bender saga was a Shakespearean tragedy which would end up touching many lives and costing many people their jobs and incomes. At

Boracayán alone thirty-seven people had lost their employment, which had a tremendously deleterious effect on their families and communities.

Some people seemed to have even lost their minds.

<<>>

Someone who seems to have found himself, as well as his happy place in Costa Rica, is a naturotherapist and expert herbalist by the name of Ed Bernhardt. Ed and his Tica wife Jessica Benavides bought a five-acre farm in the foothills of the Talamanca Mountains in the Southern Zone, and founded what they called the New Dawn Centre. Ed described his life-altering arrival in Costa Rica as follows:

"It was like I had come on a rocket ship and had landed on a completely different planet because everything was tropical. I had a lot of studying to do."

Ed's journey into Costa Rican herbalism came out of a tragic experience in 1970 in the US. Ed was at the anti-Nixon student demonstration at Kent State University in Ohio, demonstrating against Nixon's Vietnam War. The demonstration, as many remember, turned violently ugly. The National Guard fired upon students, leaving four of them dead. One of the dead students was a good friend of Ed's who he helplessly watched die right beside him. It took Ed several years to recover.

Ed came to Costa Rica thirty years ago with the intention of creating a "Sanity Centre", a place where you eat well, talk about your feelings, and look closely at the state of your mind and spirit. Had the Benders ventured out of their Dome into the community at large, they might very well have found a kindred spirit in Ed Bernhardt. The Benders owned 5,000 acres of land; Ed only owned five, but managed to create an entire food forest on his land, using his degrees in biology and botany to light the path.

Ed and Jessica continue to manage the New Dawn Centre, educating people in permaculture, Spanish, and medicinal plants. He has written three books in English while in Costa Rica, including *Medicinal Plants of Costa Rica* and *Natural Health Care Therapies for Tropical Living*. Much of the information Ed shares in his books he credits the indigenous with having taught him when he first arrived.

Why is it that Ed fell crazy in love with Costa Rica, yet managed to sanely find his soul there and create such wonderful educational programs? It seems that love, like cholera, impacts people differently. Some people succumb quite suddenly, while others fade away agonizingly slowly, and still others find themselves feeling triumphantly reborn. Some people never show any symptoms at all! Love in Costa Rica can be a mysterious and thrilling thing. Sometimes, however, it makes you totally unhinged.

A Verdict...Almost

"There are things you do only for love."

Gabriel García Márquez - *Love in the Time of Cholera*

Team Ann was informed through lawyer Fabio Oconitrillo that the trial was ready to resume. As they sat in the open-air breakfast restaurant at Hotel Zima on the morning of the trial's resumption, they were reviewing new information they had received, and their new understanding of how the Costa Rican judicial system operates. The Pattons had been venting their indignation at the unchallenged flip-flops of witnesses at the trial. According to Costa Rican law, these testimonies were not in contradiction of previous statements made under oath. Each trial is unique and self-contained in Costa Rica—tabula rasa—that is to say, at each new trial witness statements stand alone and cannot be challenged as being contradictory to those made at previous trials. That was a new concept for all people accustomed to American-style justice where one cannot be tried multiple times for the same crime. There is no prohibition against double jeopardy under Tico law. That explained a lot to Ann's family about how the trial was proceeding. It was not comforting news.

The Pattons had also gained understanding of the fierce pride Ticos have in their judicial system and officers of the court. To foreigners, it seemed clear that the Eikelenbooms, with their vast scientific background and acumen, far out-performed the testimonies of the forensic experts Costa Rica provided. That conclusion was not at all shared by Ticos in the courtroom. A Tico lawyer not involved directly with the Bender trial explained:

"In any legal proceeding involving a foreigner in Costa Rica, the local team will always win. Remember, here the legal challenge is between Ann and Costa Rica, so the full force of the country is against her, as well as all the powerful undertones of patriotism and xenophobia. I always advise foreigners who get in legal trouble here to get out of town as quickly as possible. The chances of winning are very small, and what you spend in lost time and legal fees is never worth the effort. There are always forces at play in these situations that foreigners will never understand."

Team Ann sat mulling that over as they ate their traditional Tico breakfast, while admiring their lovely surroundings. Hotel Zima has adopted a young, up-and-coming artist named Gibrán Tabash, who created the painting of an endangered jaguar that greets guests at the hotel reception desk, as well as other works found throughout the hotel. Tabash is also responsible for the iconic sculpture in the central park of a farmer plowing his fields with two oxen, which complements the enormous fresco of San Isidro on the front of the cathedral, overlooking the town's epicenter. The remarkable secret of this sculpture is that it is made entirely of recycled newspaper, which was painted and varnished to repel the rain. From a distance, the sculpture looks to be made of wood. Tabash has made himself a one-man artistic recycling plant. Even given its progressive ecological reputation, the concept of recycling has taken some time to catch on in Costa Rica. Tabash was a remarkable leader in this movement. Ann certainly felt she was in need of some gentle recycling herself.

Breakfast consisted of the famous *gallo pinto* (spotted rooster), a staple at all three meals in Costa Rica, and a dish which won a place on the *Time Magazine* "Top Ten Healthy Breakfasts of the World." Gallo pinto consists of black beans, rice, cumin, pepper, and garlic, served with fried plantains on the side. It is usually accompanied by scrambled or fried eggs, and lots of the fabulous fruit grown all over this fertile country: mango, pineapple, banana, mamón chino, mangostan, granadilla, and other exotic and mouth-watering fruit choices. This dish is always served with Salsa Lizano on the side (or mixed in when cooked), which is a mild, thin, brown sauce made of vegetables, not too spicy, and guaranteed to zest up any dish. Lots of Costa Rica's delicious coffee that has made the country famous among java connoisseurs provided the perfect finish to the meal. Ticos like to say about something which is quintessentially Costa Rican, "Mas Tico que el gallo pinto," meaning, more Tico than the spotted rooster, the traditional beans and rice breakfast dish. That is a most flattering way to be described in this proud little country!

Team Ann was also digesting the news that the lawyer they were accusing in a separate court case of stealing much of the Bender fortune and all of the Bender property had his passport recently taken away from him by the courts. Could this mean that Juan de Dios Álvarez might finally stand trial for his alleged crimes against Ann? The lawyer who had explained the self-contained aspect of multiple trials, meaning that each trial stood alone and testimonies could not be discounted for contradicting testimonies made at previous trials, was not very impressed by this development, explaining that the borders between Nicaragua (Álvarez's current home country) and Costa Rica are incredibly porous, and he felt that the confiscation of Álvarez's passport would barely slow him down. He also had information indicating that Juan de Dios was in very poor health, and was looking weak and sickly. It certainly did not help that Álvarez was a chainsmoker, now with a deep hacking cough and chest pains. The lawyer summed up his thoughts on Juan de Dios' current condition: bad karma.

Also enjoying breakfast at Zima that morning was the world-renowned CNN and CBS producer, Josh Yager. Josh is a tall, handsome journalist from Washington, DC, with salt-and-pepper hair and a winning smile. He wears those safari pants with multiple pockets, which dry quickly after rainstorms and zip off at the knees to convert into shorts for crossing rivers and streams. That outfit would seem pretentious were it not for the fact that Josh has been on assignment in dozens of dangerous and physically challenging locales, including being embedded with US forces during the invasion of Iraq in 2003, covering the tsunami in Indonesia in 2004, and reporting on the outbreak of the Ebola virus in Africa. Josh has been a producer for *48 Hours* since 1996, over twenty years of award-winning reporting. It was a supremely lucky break for Ann Bender that Josh was assigned "Paradise Lost," the *48 Hours* treatment of the Bender saga which aired originally in September 2014, and was updated in July 2015. Were it not for the efforts of Josh Yager and the *48 Hours* staff, Ann would probably not have had access to the forensics experts who stopped the momentum of the trial, and started it rolling in Ann's favor. Josh specialized in David-versus-Goliath stories.

Team Ann, producer Yager, and the translator he had hired to help understand the proceedings finally got up and began the three-minute car ride down to the courthouse for an 8:00 am gavel, which never seemed to drop until 8:30. That is Costa Rican time. By now, the Americans were quite used to this method of doing business.

<<>>

Prosecutor Ramírez looked well-rested after his mystery surgery, and had a clean new haircut, making him look much like the barristers from England on Ann's team. Even Ann looked refreshed after the break, having spent some time outside by the pool at Zima in the fresh air and sunshine. Her look was completed by a nice new set of fingernails provided by Zima's manicurist, painted a discreet neutral color.

The first kerfuffle to tackle on the opening day back in court was the testimony of someone Team Ann had discovered was on Álvarez's payroll, and therefore wanted dismissed. It was classic conflict of interest to let him testify. That person was a Costa Rican ballistics expert named Donald Montero. Montero had been scheduled to testify at Ann's first trial, but it seems he never was called to appear. Oconitrillo furiously objected that Montero was a tainted witness, paid by Álvarez, and the defense would prove it. This statement caused a great uproar at both lawyer's tables, and the incriminating document showing who paid Montero was eventually produced after a great deal of arguing back and forth over how the document had been obtained, by whom the document was obtained, and the veracity of the document to be presented.

Eventually the history of Montero's document turned out to be fairly straightforward. At the time Álvarez had been removed as the trustee of the Bender Sociedad Anónima

(SA, similar to a limited liability corporation), the OIJ had found in Álvarez's files a letter between Álvarez and Montero in which Álvarez agreed to pay Montero a hefty sum of money for his testimony at trial. Oconitrillo was overruled, and Montero began his testimony. The level of stress in the entire courtroom rose palpably.

Montero reviewed for the court the details of the position in which John's body had been found, emphasizing the unlikelihood of a candidate for suicide going to bed with his earplugs in his ears, and emphasizing that in all his years in ballistics science he had never seen a man kill himself at his wife's side. He reminded everyone what a grisly scene that would have been for a wife to wake up to, especially a wife he claimed to worship and adore. He reminded the court that Ann had described suicide rehearsals with pills, never with guns, which indicated to Montero that Ann's account of that night was not credible. He described many forensic details which led him to believe it would have been impossible for John to have shot himself and end up with his body, the gun, gunpowder residue, blood-spatter, and shell casing in the positions in which they were found.

Montero also touched on a topic that had not been given close attention by either Dr. Gretchen or the Eikelenbooms, and forensic experts not associated with this case thought it was a piece of evidence that spoke volumes: the top pillow of three which supported John's body at the time of death. That pillow had not been gathered as evidence until much after that fateful night, but when it was retrieved, it showed light blood spatter, gunpowder residue, possible microscopic bullet fragments—but absolutely no smoke residue. Both Montero and the independent forensic experts felt that the condition of the pillow indicated that the shot had been taken from a distance, not at close range. That would indicate that the gun was not fired by John. Montero suggested that it was more likely that the gun had been fired by someone crouched down low beside the bed. But again, the forensic evidence was so mishandled and compromised, that no accurate conclusion could be made. No one had tested the pillow formally for these trace clues. And no one had fingerprinted the gun. The issue of the pillow hit a dead end.

It was abundantly clear why the defense had been worried. Montero summed up his testimony as follows, "I can't imagine a suicidal person shooting themselves like this." This testimony was in direct conflict with that of the Eikelenbooms, who had testified earlier that Bender's wound at the back of the head could have been self-inflicted, and that the bullet casing could probably have skidded fifteen feet from the body, on the smooth granite floor of the Bender's bedroom.

As prosecutor Ramírez told *48 Hours*, "When someone wishes to kill themselves they aim the gun into the mouth, under the chin or at the temple—not at the back of the head." Montero's testimony packed a wallop for the onlookers at Ann's trial.

People had come back to the trial with renewed optimism that things would turn out well for Ann, but were now not so sure. The US Embassy had sent two representatives as observers to the trial who were there allegedly to make sure Ann's rights were not violated. These two observers had seemed to be enjoying themselves, almost as though they were on holiday, but now looked worried. It was widely believed that should Ann be returned to prison, she would not survive. Costa Rica had confiscated Ann's passport to prevent her from leaving. Sometime after the trial's resumption, the decision was made quietly to obtain a replacement passport for Ann, in case she needed or wanted to leave. Many expats had been critical of the Embassy for not intervening on Ann's behalf throughout her ordeal, but the move to get her a new passport would have put their minds at ease. Throughout the trial Ann had always stated to the reporters watching her exit or enter the courthouse that she considered Costa Rica her home, and had no intention of leaving under any circumstances. Her sentiments were surely shifting now that she was confronted with a possible catastrophic outcome. She was forty-five years old; she had a whole lot of living yet to do. It was looking like her love for Costa Rica was far from reciprocated.

<<>>

There was a lot of administrative work left to be done publicly by the court, such as entering into record all the evidence, appropriately labeled and identified, and logging all the photos as well. All of those records were then stored in the court's archives in Heredia and were no longer available for review. Each photo and authenticated piece of evidence was viewed and approved by both the prosecution and the defense, and that was a time-consuming endeavor. CBS *48 Hours* videotaped the entire trial, and local television videotaped some of the more interesting portions. The British arm of Team Ann transcribed every word said at trial, tolerating the grimaces of the prosecutor as they did so.

The trial was moving along again, and everyone hoped it would wrap by the end of the week. Rumors circulated around the coffee stand that veteran trial watchers were anticipating a verdict by Friday. Ann had secretly received her new passport, so was ready for any outcome. Her brother Ken was itching to go back to his new bride and successful career. The Patton parents were ready to go home and sleep in their own beds. Pete DeLisi had taken way too much time away from managing his hedge fund.

CRAZY JUNGLE LOVE

The British legal team had other cases awaiting them back in England.

Fabio Oconitrillo was doing his best to keep Ann's spirits up during this agonizing wait, but the truth was, any outcome was possible. The prosecutor's tunnel vision and animosity for all things Ann Bender seemed insurmountable, even to an optimist like Fabio. The three judges who would decide Ann's fate were inscrutable, giving nothing away in their faces as to which way they planned to rule. The reporter from *ICR* strolled over to the young lady operating the lobby cappuccino machine who had watched everyone's entrances and exits for one month and eavesdropped on conversations held around the coffee bar; she had seen years of exciting trials in her past. The young lady was asked which way she thought the judges would rule. The barista smiled a tiny smile while lowering her eyes, and responded:

> "This is my country, and I'm very proud of it. We do many things very well and take very good care of our citizens, usually. The one thing we have not seemed to be able to control, however, is corruption. My impression of this trial is that it is riddled with corruption. Americans seem to bring out the very worst of this behavior in us; I don't know why. I feel very sorry for the

rich American lady, but I doubt she will go free. There are too many egos and reputations on the line. Too much money at stake. She seems very frail and vulnerable, and that simply enflames this prosecutor. He obviously smells blood in the water. I'm aware of upcoming trials on the calendar with other American defendants, and wish them all well. But this lady with the cane, she should run away. She should do it as soon as possible, or she will be back for a fourth trial or back in jail."

Barista wisdom at its best!

The time arrived for closing statements.

<<>>

As with American criminal trials, in Costa Rica the prosecutor makes his closing statements first, followed by the defense and a final statement by the accused, if desired. These statements for the third murder trial of Ann Bender began on Friday, September 4, 2015, once again in the Pérez Zeledón courthouse. The spectator crowd had grown to an almost full house, which caused parking problems out front and traffic snarls on the highway. Of course, the proceedings began late.

The *ICR* reporter arrived early as always to chat up other reporters, and see if anyone had inside information. She greeted the barista with a wave, and the barista shook her head gloomily. There was tension throughout the hall. Jesse Blenn and his pendulum were absent. The reporter for *perezzeledon.net* seemed to feel there was a good chance there would be a verdict rendered that day, which made no sense, because the judges had not heard final arguments nor deliberated among themselves. Was the trial really rigged after all, and had everyone wasted their time in court over the last month? The Pattons had complained at the second trial that a document with Ann's verdict had appeared all printed up only minutes after the court had adjourned—in a country where everything takes days and weeks to complete. It seemed suspicious.

Everyone rose as the three judges took their places at the front dais, and the AV tech fussed over them briefly. The chief judge welcomed everyone to the closing arguments of Ann Bender's trial, and once again cautioned everyone that there were to be no outbursts or exclamations from the spectators. And with that, Edgar Ramírez stood to make his final case against the widow he so obviously despised.

There were only a handful of Americans in the courtroom for this. Some, like Ann's family, having lived through her criminal trials previously and knowing what to expect, others thinking, *Here we go, we have to listen to the blowhard prosecutor do his schtick again and hope we get out of here before dinner.* The newbies were completely wrong—Ramírez was completely organized, prepared, and succinct.

Ramírez recounted the details of the "homicide" of John Felix Bender, combining the abbreviated testimonies of the first Ticos to arrive on scene: the Red Cross, the Fuerza Pública, the OIJ, the head of security for the Benders, and he spent much time reviewing the testimony of Dr. Gretchen Flores. He was, of course, bursting with confidence as he described the crime scene as being unequivocally the scene of the murder of Mr. Bender, not possibly the suicide of that poor man. Ramírez indicated that he thought Ann had premeditated the whole incident, probably in an effort to get the entire jewel collection, and called her a cold-blooded murderer. Ann sat looking down at her hands in her lap.

All things considered, this was probably Ramírez's best performance to date in the trial. He was cool and composed, and remained on topic rather than going off on anti-American rants. He was mercifully brief.

After a very short break, the defense took its turn to give closing statements. Oconitrillo was smoother than ever, unwavering in the facts of the case as he saw them: Ann had no motive to kill her beloved husband, had tried valiantly to prevent a suicidal man from killing himself, all forensic evidence by the best experts in the world confirmed that fact, and now unlucky Ann Bender must be set free to rebuild her life as best she could, while honoring her husband and the great nature reserve they had built. She had paid enough for this tragedy; Costa Rica should let her move on and express their gratitude for the reserve she and John had built, not lock her back up to die in prison. Oconitrillo was very moving in his summary—and very persuasive.

Next, Ann was called to the stand, but was allowed to make her statement from where she was sitting at Oconitrillo's table, to avoid the awkward hobble to the witness box. She said, "I have faith that finally justice will be served." She expressed her confidence in the judicial system of Costa Rica, and added, "This is my opportunity to finally, hopefully, get true justice." She seemed sincere. She explained that she had lost her husband, her property, her belongings, her pets, her jewels, and all her money. She asked the court to please not take the only thing she had left—her freedom. She declared, "I did not kill my husband." Several eyes in the courtroom were tearing.

The chief judge closed his notebook with a tidy snap, and declared that the court would announce its decision after the weekend, on Monday, September 7, 2015, and with that, the court was adjourned early, leaving everyone shaking their heads and wondering what the verdict would be. Poor Ann had another agonizing wait. But at least she would finally know her fate, after five years of torment. Oconitrillo kindly did not remind her that even after another possible acquittal, she could still be brought back for a fourth trial. Macondo.

Free at Last

"There is bound to be someone driven mad by love who will give you the chance one of these days."

Gabriel García Márquez – *Love in the Time of Cholera*

September 7, 2015

Ann hardly slept the night before her verdict was to be read by Judge López Cambronero in the Pérez Zeledón courtroom. How could she? This would be the trial that determined the rest of her life. Ann had suffered from bipolar disorder all of her adult life, with many bouts of suicidal fantasies, but today she was in full warrior mode, ready to take on the world. She had packed her bags repeatedly—twice just last night—and kept feeling for her new replacement passport in her purse to make sure it was still there. She took it out to look at several times a day. That reminded her of John's obsessive-compulsive disorder, and it made her miss him even more acutely. The sight of her new passport comforted her. She still felt quite close to John Bender's spirit and sometimes felt guilty that she was hoping to head away from Costa Rica and leave the life they had shared together in paradise. It felt a little like a betrayal of him. John would be at her side in court, gently cradling her elbow as he used to do when she was unsteady on her feet. John was still her rock.

Hotel Zima had prepared Ann's final invoice several times throughout her stay with them. This time it was the real deal. Zima owners Santiago and Ana were at the reception desk as Ann passed by on her way to the breakfast area. Ken Patton insisted that Ann at least try to get a little something in her stomach before heading down to court.

Ana Fernández stepped out from under the jaguar painting to give Ann a hug of encouragement and luck. They had become good friends during Ann's lengthy stay at Zima, and the entire staff at Zima would miss Ann and her family. They had been easy guests to serve, up until very recently when the press had discovered where they were staying. Then everyone had been put on protection detail, with Ann's two guards watching the front entrance.

The Patton group was seated at their favorite table, up one small level from the other tables, a little closer to both the Zima office and the kitchen. Staff from the kitchen were watching them from the pass-through between the dining area and the cooking area. The waiter kept bringing out small samples, called *bocas*, of Ann's favorite fruits or baked goods. The overall feeling was that this was their final breakfast at Zima; Ann would either be heading back to prison, or back to the US. One of the female cooks in the kitchen kept wiping away tears. Owners Ana and Santiago joined the group for a few minutes to express how sad they would be to see them go, but how hopeful they were that Ann would be allowed to leave the country at last. Santiago is a hotel developer and had rescued Zima from being a rundown motel to being one of the quietest and most enjoyable places to overnight in Pérez. Santiago at one time even expressed an interest in converting Boracayán into a luxury hotel once things had settled down. When *would* things settle down?

A joke had been circulating among expat trial-watchers at Ann's ordeal that her trial should be called a "mulligan," to reflect the unconventional sequence of events that had befallen her. A mulligan is a second chance to perform an action, usually after the first chance went wrong through bad luck or a blunder. Best known as an informal golf term, it describes a scenario whereby a player is allowed to replay a stroke—even though this is against the formal rules of golf. Costa Rica was playing a mulligan, people said, by retrying Ann again and again. A mulligan—in Macondo. To Americans, it just did not seem kosher. To taxi driver Randall Baldí, it was simply *chorizo*. Perhaps today that whole charade would come to an end. *Si Dios quiere.*

Most countries, like the United States, have laws in their constitutions which prohibit double jeopardy in criminal cases. In the US, the Constitution's Fifth Amendment says "nor shall any person be subject for the same offense to be twice put in jeopardy of life or limb...." This amendment is the source of the double jeopardy doctrine which prevents authorities from trying a person twice for the same crime. A similar double jeopardy doctrine is also included in the constitutions of Canada, Mexico, India, and Israel. There are only a handful of countries where this is not the law. The biggest example of a country that does not abide by this law is China. Even in Uganda you cannot be tried twice for the same crime. Costa Rica has recently seen some interest in overturning this policy. Online legal newsletter

"Modern Powers" wrote in 2015 about the push to overturn the double jeopardy laws in Costa Rica,

> "Currently we do not have any double jeopardy laws in Costa Rica. This tends to lead to exhausting a defendant in any case by trying them over and over and over again. If this law is passed, many cases currently being filed against foreign individuals could get dropped. This law will be added to the Political Constitution of Costa Rica as an amendment if it is passed."

There are also hundreds of Ticos moldering away in preventive detention, waiting to be tried again for the same crime, over-crowding prisons, who would benefit from a new law.

The Pattons finished breakfast and returned to their rooms once more to make sure everything was in order for a seamless escape. Oh, how they had prayed for a day of justice for Ann! Ann zipped up her suitcases, put them by the door, brushed her teeth, smoothed her hair, and said a passionate prayer for her freedom. Her last quick look in the hotel mirror showed a woman who was looking older than she probably should—and simply terrified. Her passport was still where she had tucked it in her purse; it felt warm and hopeful. Ken came to get her to take her to the waiting caravan. The Zima staff was lined up in front to wish her courage and luck. They assured her that today was her day.

<<>>

There was a mob scene at the courthouse. Press had come from all over the world to hear the verdict. Osvaldo helped Ann gently out of the car, and she immediately had a dozen microphones stuck in her face by reporters wanting to know how she felt, now that her big day in court was upon her. She gathered herself to answer in that short-sentence, hesitant way she spoke, with lots of head bobbing. She said, "My gut has been telling me all along that this third time I would actually be heard and that the evidence would be evaluated correctly." Reporters continued to yell questions at her, but she moved toward the courthouse door, clearly wanting to save her energy for what awaited her inside.

A photographer from the *Daily Mail* (UK) snapped a close-up photo of Ann as she entered the court. They captioned it "Bad Romance." Her pupils were immense, and she had loose, curly tendrils of fine hair framing her face. When the photo was published, several people commented that she looked just like Michael Jackson. She certainly was thin and pale enough to resemble him. On this morning, to the ordinary Tico, she was just as famous as Jackson.

Oconitrillo met Ann just inside the security check and gave her a warm hug. He whispered something in her ear, and she nodded and whispered back. The crowd in the hall opened a tunnel to allow Team Ann to make their way into the courtroom and down the treacherous stairs to the front. Ann was looking nervous, but the translator patted her hand, and the legal assistant to Oconitrillo whispered something encouraging in her ear. No one could really predict how long the proceedings would last today. There was a sense of immense drama and expectation in the courtroom. There were almost no empty seats to be had. If she were found guilty of murder again this morning, would she fall apart and faint like at her second trial? Would her family cry out in protest and grief? Would Ann end up back at CIMA on suicide watch? Would her brother Ken finally explode in anger? As always, the trial could go in many directions.

The chief judge called the court to order. Once again, he welcomed people back, and encouraged them to respect the court by not calling out or causing a scene after the verdict was read. The accusation against Ann for the murder of her husband John Felix Bender was read by one of the judges. She was accused of pre-meditated, first-degree murder (*homicidio calificado*), of John Bender on January 8, 2010, in their home in Florida de Barú, Pérez Zeledón. Homicidio calificado is the highest degree of homicide in Costa Rican law. The description in legalese of her alleged transgression was read in its entirety. Onlookers in the back of the hall could be heard fidgeting and shifting in their seats. Onlookers at the front, including the Team Ann members from Great Britain and Ann's friends and family, were like statues—not daring to move a muscle or even breathe. At last, it was time for the verdict.

On September 7, 2015, at 9:15 am, Ann Maxine Patton was absolved of all guilt and responsibility in the death of John Felix Bender, based on the rule of *in dubio pro reo*. This means that a defendant may not be convicted by the court when doubts about her guilt remain. The ruling was unanimous. Ann was FREE, effective immediately. Her household effects and guns were to be returned to her. There was no mention of return of the jewels, as that was part of another of Ann's legal cases yet to be resolved. Under Costa Rican law, both the prosecution and the defense may make final statements after the verdict is read.

Edgar Ramírez spoke directly and succinctly, saying "We do not share the opinion of the judges. This was not a suicide, there is no doubt. The only one who could be responsible is Ann Maxim (sic) Patton." Throughout the trial, Ramírez had mangled Ann's full name; today was no exception. He strongly declared his intention to appeal the verdict and seek a fourth trial.

Fabio Oconitrillo said about the prosecution, "After a third time of being told they're wrong, they need to move on. But it's also clear that this is a personal case for the prosecution, and they're going to exhaust all the resources they can."

Ann began to weep the minute the verdict exonerating her was read. She was experiencing five years of pent-up frustration and anger—it just washed over her in a flood. Following Oconitrillo's statement, the British lawyers surrounded her to congratulate her, joined by members of her own family. The crowd had restrained themselves, as per the judges' orders, and now swirled around the defense table, wanting to congratulate everyone. Innocent! Finally, justice was served. TV camera crews were filming constantly while newspaper photographers snapped photos for the front page on Tuesday. Ann looked weak but unmistakably relieved. Her face had some color to it, and there was a new light in her eyes. She just wanted to be alone with her family to process what she had just been through.

Team Ann decided to go ahead and check out of Hotel Zima and get on the road back to San José. They had an interview with a San José newspaper to complete later that afternoon and could eat lunch at one of the homey rest stops that cater to travelers to and from San José. Ann didn't feel hungry; there were too many more pressing sensations. Back in San José they would book a flight out of the country first thing Tuesday morning. Ann would be free!

Ann and her family had no way of knowing that on the next day, Tuesday, Ann would approach the airline ticket counter at Juan Santamaría Airport, and be refused a boarding pass. She had been placed on a No-Fly list, placed there by the Costa Rican courts....

When would it ever end?

Sentencing Document No 679-2015 for Ann Patton Bender

EXPEDIENTE: 10-000049-0064-PE
CONTRA: ANN MAXINE PATTON
OFENDIDO/A: FELIX BENDER JOHN
DELITO: Homicidio Calificado

SENTENCIA N° 679-2015

TRIBUNAL DE LA ZONA SUR, SEDE PÉREZ ZELEDÓN.- San Isidro de El General, a las nueve horas con del siete de setiembre del dos mil quince De conformidad con lo que dispone el artículo 364 párrafo cuarto del Código Procesal Penal, se dicta parte dispositiva de la sentencia en este acto, señalándose las dieciséis horas del catorce de setiembre de dos mil quince , para lectura integral de la sentencia que se redactará por escrito. La parte dispositiva de la sentencia es la siguiente.

POR TANTO:

De conformidad con lo expuesto y con base en los artículos 39 y 41 de la Constitución Política; 1, 11, 30, 45, 111 Y 112 inciso 1) del Código Penal; y 1, 8, 9, 141, 142, 265 a 267, 341 a 366 del Código Procesal Penal, por unanimidad **se ABSUELVE DE TODA PENA Y RESPONSABILIDAD a ANN MAXINE PATTON** en aplicación del Principio Universal **IN DUBIO PRO REO** por un delito delito de **HOMICIDIO CALIFICADO** en perjuicio de **JOHN FELIX BENDER** que le venía atribuyendo el Ministerio Público. Se ordena dejar sin efecto las medidas cautelares que se hubieren impuesto a la acusada. Se ordena el comiso en favor del Estado de dos armas de fuego AK-47 y sus municiones, que fueron decomisadas en el proceso. En cuanto al arma Ruger P95, C9mm, se ordena su devolución una vez firme esta sentencia a quien demuestre ser propietario de las mismas, y aporte los respectivos permisos y matrículas. Son los gastos del proceso al cargo del Estado. (f)

ERICKA CORDERO MARROQUIN

ESTEBAN LÓPEZ CAMBRONERO   MANUEL MORALES VÁSQUEZ

JUECES DEL TRIBUNAL DE JUICIO

latencio

EXP: 10-000049-0064-PE

CAROL BLAIR VAUGHN

3L7TM2MAZJK61

ERICKA ISABEL CORDERO
MARROQUÍN - JUEZ/A DECISOR/A

FDNQXWUVKLM61

ESTEBAN ANTONIO LÓPEZ
CAMBRONERO - JUEZ/A DECISOR/A

GW47HBQB5WQG61

MANUEL MORALES VÁSQUEZ -
JUEZ/A DECISOR/A

EXP: 10-000049-0064-PE

I Circuito Judicial Zona Sur, Edificio Tribunales de Justicia, 3er Piso, Pérez Zeledón, 150 metros sureste de McDonalds, sobre Carretera Interamericana Teléfonos: 2785-0324 ó 0325 ó 0326. Fax: 2785-0430 ó 2771-3281. Correo electrónico: pze-tribp2@Poder-Judicial.go.cr

Almost Got Away

"She was a ghost in a strange house that overnight had become immense and solitary and through which she wandered without purpose, asking herself in anguish which one of them was deader: the man who had died or the woman he had left behind."

Gabriel García Márquez – *Love in the Time of Cholera*

By December 31, 2016, there were thirty-four US Citizens incarcerated or on parole in Costa Rica, according to a Justice Ministry spokesman. Ann Bender was not one of them. For that, Ann was incredibly grateful.

The two-car caravan came back up and over the Cerro de La Muerte, carrying Ann, her family and entourage back to San José. They would have the final interview with *The Tico Times*, and a brief meeting with Fabio Oconitrillo to discuss plans going forward. Everyone still felt numb and not yet ready to allow themselves to feel joy and elation. Anything could still happen. Amazingly, in fact, it did.

The Pattons were quiet as they drove up and over the mountain, enjoying for perhaps the last time the beautiful scenery along the road. It reminded everyone of Jurassic Park—plants with immense leaves called "poor man's umbrellas" (*Gunnera insignis*), wild orchids, and bromeliads hanging from moss-covered trees, wild flowers of every bright color sprouting alongside the road, tiny waterfalls emerging from between boulders, tall palm trees mixed among shorter, leafier shrubs and trees. It *was* fifty shades of green.

Ann would miss Costa Rica when she went back to the US; there was no doubt in her mind about that. In her final statement for the press, standing in front of the courthouse, Ann had said about the possibility of a fourth trial, "My hope is that the verdict will be strong enough so that an appeal cannot be written or won't be accepted, and that it can end now, and John can finally rest." From her lips to God's ears, as the saying goes.

The group stopped for lunch at La Georgina, one of the best-known rest-stops on the highway, near the top of the mountain. Georgina features rows of hummingbird feeders outside the huge picture windows, designed to entertain travelers while they eat. There are some fifty-four different species of hummingbirds in Costa Rica, and Georgina is considered a must-visit for the many birders who visit the country. The coolness and abundant flowers of the Georgina neighborhood are perfect for happy hummingbirds. Food is served cafeteria-style, cooked by one of the owner's family members, and people usually rave about the cost, quality, and selection of food. It turned out that the Pattons had gotten quite hungry since breakfast; they felt relaxed enough to have a wholesome meal while savoring Ann's new freedom. Ann was smiling.

They set off again, fairly sure they could make it to San José and off the highway before dusk. The sun goes down in Costa Rica at 5:30 every day, in every season, and most Americans try to be off the road before then. Accidents on the road at night can be extremely dangerous and frustrating; there are almost no pull-off areas, and visibility at night is dicey, David Boddiger, for her final interview.

David had stayed on top of all the twists and turns of Ann's convoluted legal case and had done his best to make sure the case got accurate and fair coverage in his newspaper. Ann wanted to begin her thank-you tour with David Boddiger and would continue it thereafter from the safety of the US. Only *The Costa Rica Star* had done a thorough and fair coverage of Ann Bender's case. She was grateful to both news outlets. It was exceedingly difficult at this point for Ann to put her thoughts about her ordeal into words. Once safely in Boddiger's office, Ann was able to relax a little and compose herself.

Ann told Boddiger, "I'm not yet feeling the relief. It takes some time to assimilate what the news was. My gut has been telling me all along that this third time I would actually be heard and that evidence would be evaluated correctly. It's impossible to say that I'm happy after five years of this, but yes, I'm relieved. There's a lot left to do, but at least the question mark over my head is halfway erased." She went on to say that she knew there was a possibility that the Prosecutor's Office would file an appeal, but she was confident that the three judges had managed to craft a ruling strong enough to survive it. She said that it was still very difficult for her to find the correct words to describe the nightmare she had endured. She certainly could not find the appropriate words to comment on prosecutor Ramírez's final words to the court which were, "The Costa Rican court system is extremely fair." In her own mind she probably thought, *not exactly*. Ramírez had filed his appeal for a fourth trial before Ann was even out of the country.

<<>>

Among the many issues left to be resolved for Ann was how to get back her nature reserve, now in the hands of lawyer Juan de Dios Álvarez in Nicaragua, and what to do with it once she had it back. Since John's death she had often thought that she would like to create a retreat for humans on the 5,000-acre Boracayán Reserve. She had heard that in the five years since she left her home, an interesting group of individuals had moved into the Diamante Verde Valley, the area at the foot of Diamante Waterfall, right beside the Bender property. The most visionary and "conscious" person seemed to be someone John had met prior to his death and had mentioned to Ann. That person was Jonathan Chapman, who claimed to own the caves at the top of Diamante Falls that were called "La Casa de Piedra" (The Stone House). This claim was heavily disputed among other residents of Diamante Valley, most especially by Jon's ex-wife, and some of his family, who also claimed ownership of the caves. Jon's extended family leads tours up to Diamante Falls and they have a new website for information on these tours: *www.pacificjourneyscr.com*.

In an interview with *Inside Costa Rica*, Chapman claimed that the caves were probably going to become more important as a tourist site than Machu Picchu in Peru. He explained that the caves were a portal that people could use to arrive at a higher consciousness, something he and others had achieved. He spoke of becoming fifth dimensional, a level of consciousness that makes it easier for a person to live a better, more conscious life. He explained that Costa Rica is known as the "heart chakra of Central America," and explained that Diamante Valley would become the world's epicenter of wellness and consciousness. He even claimed that a new back route had been found to the top of Diamante Falls, one much easier to navigate, and less physically taxing—more accessible to all. He mentioned that his name—Jonathan Chapman—was the same as Johnny Appleseed's given name, and he was seeding consciousness throughout Diamante Valley. Chapman was a very interesting character.

Chapman's description of his one meeting with the Benders was fascinating. He said that John was a mountain of a man, very powerfully built and muscular, the kind of man Chapman with his slender frame and body built for long meditations was usually intimidated by. In this case, Chapman described that Bender radiated fear and timidity, not at all what one would have expected from someone built like a Mack truck. They discussed Bender's desire to purchase Chapman's property along with the Casa de

Piedra. Chapman said he had no problem telling Bender a flat out *no*; the caves were not for sale. Meanwhile, Ann looked on from a distance; Chapman said she had a nice white light around her—no fear at all.

Now there is a new organization in Diamante Valley called the Diamante Valley Solution Center, which has a mission statement saying they are "committed to co-creating a regenerative future for ALL life." They are in their start-up phase, and are focused on creating a wellness and education center that builds a regenerative society. One of their first programs was what they called a "Liberate Your Inner Great Ape Retreat," in 2017. There are, of course, no great apes in Costa Rica, but the retreat includes ape yoga, tree climbing, wild foraging, social grooming, and non-lingual communication, among other ape-like topics. Many international twenty-somethings are drawn to this part of the country, and an adult trapeze camp has attracted quite a following. There has recently been a large influx of young Israelis to the valley, all seemingly wanting to achieve their own Fifth Dimension. There have been no more hedge fund managers or Wall Street tycoon types relocating to the valley.

A group that had begun to take up residence in Diamante Valley, just before the time of John's death, were the survivalists and preppers who had been drawn there before the time of the "end" of the Maya calendar in 2012, and

351

even before that, during the anticipated Y2K collapse. The terms survivalist and prepper are often used interchangeably. Both groups share an End Times way of thinking, believing that some apocalyptic event—either natural or man-made—will put an end to life as we know it, and catapult us back to a way of life similar to the 1850s. This includes a shortage of food and water, collapse of the world financial system and electric grid, and a possible war between the haves and the have-nots of the world. Both groups feel that it is necessary for everyone to prepare responsibly for this catastrophe.

According to *The Prepper Journal,* "Survivalists and Preppers both have a deep desire to live—not a fear of dying, but rather a strong yearning for life on their own terms. You will find tenacity in both Preppers and Survivalists to see the options they have before them. If you give up easily or become defeated too quickly you probably don't deserve to call yourself a member of either team just yet." Ann Bender was unknowingly playing on both teams for most of her Costa Rican journey.

Whether you consider yourself a prepper or survivalist, it basically comes down to wanting to provide for yourself and your family without having to rely on some government bureaucracy to keep you safe. That was certainly John's outlook on life. He probably would have been considered a survivalist, as of the two groups, they tend to be lone wolves, shunning group efforts and the pooling of resources and information for survival, in favor of going it alone. He was forever preparing to survive the anarchy of a breakdown of society. Sadly for the Benders, the apocalyptic breakdown came between the two of them, no need for an asteroid strike or coronal mass ejection to finish the job.

It wasn't clear how Ann's imagined retreat would sync up with these other groups in the valley, but at least there seemed to be an acceptance of alternative lifestyles and creative solutions to human challenges. Any number of people would undoubtedly be interested in working with Ann on her vision, especially if she would underwrite the dream. It was not widely understood by the public that Ann had been left penniless after John's death; even her property was in someone else's hands. Rumors were rampant that Ann's family was going to return to Costa Rica with suitcases of cash and start again. There was a lot for Ann to do on the legal front, many battles to wage. But on September 7, Ann was just fixated on getting back to the US, and back to the grandmother. Ann Esworthy was waiting for her to return.

The newspaper interview ended, and Ann was exhausted. She and her family went to the San José hotel they usually stayed at when traveling to or from the United States, or when on one of their jewel-buying expeditions. They checked in and crashed. Ann felt she had never been so exhausted. She took a shower and went to bed, leaving her brother Ken to make the plane reservations to fly back home the next morning. Ann slept well that night for the first time in a month. It would take her a while to adjust, but she felt that she would get over her drama, and begin to move on with her life. Possibly the new residents of Diamante Valley would accept her as a neighbor, and she could start over with the help of kind, like-minded people. Perhaps she could find the cure for her Lyme disease as John had foreseen, right in that Garden of Eden at the foot of Catarata Diamante.

<<>>

The morning of Tuesday, September 8, dawned exceptionally sunny in San José. September is smack in the middle of the rainy season, but this day was sparkling and bright. Ann had slept well the night before, but for some reason she awoke nervous again, nervous like she had to go back to court. Of course, she did not; that hideous month in court was behind her now. She would try not to think about that courtroom ever again. She had chills just reliving the ugly green walls and constant cold air-conditioning. The Pattons would have a good breakfast, and then head out to the airport to fly home. Ken had booked Ann and her parents on a direct flight to Florida to see Ann's grandmother and have some down-time before Ann had to dive back into the fray of legal worries and financial nightmares. Ken would go his own way and return to his bride and business in Michigan. Things were going to be just fine.

The group had breakfast together in the hotel dining room and discussed the timing for getting to the airport nice and early. The Pattons moved slowly: Ann because of her cane, and her parents because they were elderly. They decided against ordering a wheelchair for Ann, but decided to allow lots of time for slow movement through the airport. They had to allow time to pay the exit tax—always a long line for that. They had been so focused on the trial that they found themselves with no little souvenirs or knick-knacks to take back as small gifts for friends and family. Those could be found at the shops in the airport's main terminal. They made a quick list of who they wanted to shop for. Small bags of Costa Rican coffee were always a hit; maybe some indigenous trinkets would be nice as well.

Juan Santamaría International Airport is 20 km (12 miles) west of downtown San José, in an area called Alajuela. The airport was named after a Costa Rican hero, a courageous drummer boy who died in 1856 defending Costa Rica against the notorious American filibuster William Walker.

Walker was an American who came to Costa Rica hoping to establish an English-speaking, private slave-holding empire. He was defeated, and Santamaría became a national hero. It was a relatively new airport, with a freshly paved access road, and there wasn't much traffic at all that morning. Ann commented that she still felt stressed, and the driver mentioned that the airport had a massage salon that would help her feel better. Ann just wanted to pay the exit fee, shop a little, and get the heck out of Dodge.

The Pattons, including Ken, waited in line, paid the $29 per person exit fee, and headed for the check-in counters in the main terminal to get their boarding passes. It was at the check-in counter that Ann discovered why she had been feeling so uneasy that morning. To her amazement and horror, Costa Rica had put Ann on the *impedimentos de salida* (No-Fly) list. She was not going to be able to fly out; her family was free to go without her. The guards separated her from her family and escorted her to a private office so as not to make a public scene. She began to weep. They would not give her many details, but apparently Ann was still listed as someone awaiting criminal trial, and therefore not permitted to leave Costa Rica. It was a clerical error. One guard suggested that she could probably leave over land if she wanted; the No-Fly list did not prohibit American citizens from returning to the United States by land. There were buses, he said. Ann felt right back in Macondo, swirling in the immigration riptides yet again. She just could not believe her never-ending bad luck. She had arrived in Costa Rica with $600 million, and was now being told she should leave on the bus. She called Fabio Oconitrillo for help. Then she called her contact at the United States Embassy and said, "Help me. Please."

Oconitrillo got right back to Ann, and briefly explained that to resolve this *impedimento* Ann would have to appear in court in person, Oconitrillo right by her side, with the appropriate documents showing that Ann had been found not guilty and could not be prevented from leaving Costa Rica. He explained to Ann that like everything in that country, this might take some time to arrange. He would petition SOAP, Sistema de Obligados Alimentarios y Penal, which governs the No-Fly list, and get the earliest available appointment. Ann's heart sank.

This was a huge surprise to the Pattons, who had no idea that this action by the Costa Rican authorities was even possible. They knew of Americans whose identities had been stolen, or confused, or whose names sounded Muslim, and so were hassled when traveling by air. This situation, given all Ann Bender had been through, well, it broke their hearts. They had seen the *60 Minutes* show in 2007 which interviewed twelve individuals who shared the names of people on the No-Fly list, and described how they were stopped each and every time they flew. Some of them were still trying to get off that list, at a terrible cost in time and money to have themselves removed. They could only imagine how complicated it was going to be to remove Ann's name from the overly bureaucratic Costa Rican list. Another guard suggested that the Pattons might consider chartering a plane to return back to the United States, thereby circumventing the commercial No-Fly restriction. Ann and Ken walked their parents to their departure gate, and sat glumly watching them take off without them. How would Ann ever thank Ken enough for his unending loyalty and kindness? Eventually, they gathered themselves and went to check back into the same hotel they had just left to await Oconitrillo's phone call.

At 7:15 that night, the attorney called to inform Ann that he had wrangled an appointment for her at SOAP for the next Monday, six days from then, and that he would have all the paperwork with him which would prove her innocence—yet again. She should not worry; this was just a small detour on her road to freedom. Ann was reminded of an Iranian proverb her father used to quote: It's not the length of the journey; it's the pebble in your shoe.

Sunshine Syndrome

"Everything that belonged to her husband made her weep again: his tasseled slippers, his pajamas under the pillow, the space of his absence in the dressing room mirror, his own odor on her skin. A vague thought made her shudder: The people one loves should take their things with them when they die."

Gabriel García Márquez – *Love in the Time of Cholera*

It took six more days to get Ann's legal paperwork straightened out and have her removed from the commercial airlines' No-Fly list. Oconitrillo stuck with Ann throughout this process, and the two said their sad farewells afterward, in front of the SOAP building. Both Ann and Fabio were feeling nostalgic already. They couldn't say for sure if they would ever see each other again. Fabio held Ann at arm's length, and tried to absorb the difference he was seeing in her since they had first met in 2011. Fabio had met Ann at a social event in San José, then was contacted by her as a potential client, saying she was not satisfied with the legal counsel she was receiving from the law firm of Juan de Dios Álvarez. The Álvarez lawyers had apparently never really considered Ann innocent, and Ann believed they had made sure she served prison time for the alleged murder of her husband. The fight for her freedom and the struggle for her rightful ownership of Boracayán had taken a toll on Ann's ingénue looks.

Ann did look older, Fabio no doubt thought, but she was still an elegant, exotic beauty and a kind and gentle spirit. Fabio could only wonder what she would look like had she not had such incredible health challenges, lost all her riches, lost two adoring alpha male companions, and sometimes even lost her will to live. She had entrusted Costa Rica with her everything —and lost. Fabio's heart had broken several times as he watched all that Ann had managed to endure. She was the most fearless survivor he had met in his career.

His office called her *"La Valienta,"* or Braveheart. It might never again be safe for Ann to return to Costa Rica, with prosecutor Ramírez still pursuing her. Pete DeLisi had agreed to take over handling Ann's Tico affairs and be the spokesman in Costa Rica for Ann and her family. There was a possibility Ann would never again return to her Costa Rican dream and home.

The mandatory wait for the removal of Ann's name from the No-Fly list gave her a chance to continue her thank-you tour. So many people to thank! She had checked in at least weekly with the two remaining staff members at Boracayán while the trial inched forward. Both Osvaldo and Marco seemed to be doing well, and said they were supremely proud of her for having been acquitted. Such nice men! It was a blessing that the evil force of Álvarez was counter-balanced by the loving support of these two men, as well as other employees with whom Ann had remained in touch. The one employee who Oconitrillo suspected had been collaborating with the prosecution, Ann simply chose to ignore. She was especially fortunate to have been able to again see the two Boracayán workers who had been in charge of the orchid collection on the reserve. They had attended the third trial, brought into town by the Bender's ex-neighbor, Amy Schrift.

These men had maintained the massive orchid collection, which was placed around the Bender Dome on specially built trellises, nursing them through the dry season, and eventually taking them to their own homes in twos and threes, to avoid watching them wither and die. The orchid-tenders are simple country farmers, and at the trial they offered to let the reporter from *ICR* visit the orchids to make sure they were still flourishing while awaiting doña Ana's return. No one had the heart to tell the old codgers that it might be a very long wait.

Imagine how much more research and discovery could have been achieved had John Bender lived, and Ann Bender not had to spend all her time, energy, and money fighting legal battles. A retired expat accountant claimed he was going to tally up the financial losses to Costa Rica due to their frivolous lawsuits against Ann in the Costa Rican courts: thirty-seven jobs lost at Boracayán, the loss of the benefits to the community of having a thriving nature reserve in its midst with visitors—both scientific and touristic—the cost of three full criminal trials against Ann and salaries for all concerned, the terrible press in international forums, and the loss of tourist dollars and investor dollars from people who now felt that Costa Rica was not a welcoming country for Americans. The losses were truly epic, and the accountant thought they were an embarrassment to this tiny Central American country. He never had the heart to do a final dollar total.

CRAZY JUNGLE LOVE

<<>>

Ann's thank-you tour continued, both in person and online, but equally pressing were the two biggest unresolved issues for her: the return of her jewels and the reclaiming of Boracayán. These would be battles she would have to continue back in the States. Nothing ever seemed to happen quickly in Central America, especially when it involved high-value objects.

Ann Bender was not the only foreign national to have faced theft of property, even by lawyers, in Costa Rica. Probably the best known case was that of Sheldon Haseltine (UK), who had been waging a seventeen-year legal battle to recover his land near Los Sueños Resort in Herradura Beach. His case had been covered in *Forbes Magazine*, and Haseltine had become the face against crooked land deals in Costa Rica. He decided in 2016 to form a group of other foreigners who had been cheated, and to petition the US government for help. "The incoming US administration has been made aware of the property abuses many expats (and locals too) have been subjected to. I personally have been contacted by over a dozen folks who have suffered these fraudulent thefts of their properties, often after the death of a spouse." This was exactly Ann's situation.

Haseltine went on to say, "We have been asked to assemble a list of US citizens who are currently being subjected to this unpleasant racket of piracy, extortion, and theft. The idea is to assemble a list and to again urge the new administration to withhold all further financial aid until such time these abuses are attended to in a timely manner as provided for by Costa Rican law." Poor Ann certainly would not have been thrilled by the thought of a seventeen-year legal battle. But at least she was not alone in her predicament, and there was some forward motion by an organized group of citizens. That was hopeful.

Less hopeful was the ongoing legal struggle with the former trustee of the entire Bender estate, Juan de Dios Álvarez, who was reportedly living high on the hog in Nicaragua, well out of reach of both the United States and Costa Rica. Ann had accused him of stealing millions of dollars in assets from the Benders and, much harder to prove, of possibly being behind all the shenanigans Ann had been put through in the Costa Rican court system. Ann could not get back those lost years of anguish, but hoped to be able to recover some of her money—that which had not been allegedly squandered by Álvarez on his mansion, Arabian horses, and decadent lifestyle. On paper, the Boracayán estate belonged 100% to Álvarez, reportedly transferred into his portfolio just weeks after John's death.

The recovery of Ann's jewels was an equally tricky issue. Pete DeLisi, speaking on behalf of Ann, said he was under the impression that the case of the jewels had been resolved by the ruling of a judge who had acquitted Ann of both money laundering and smuggling charges earlier in 2016. DeLisi stated that Ann had already agreed to pay $1.5 million in back taxes and import duties to recover the gems. Neither he nor Ann believed she owed that money, but payment of the taxes seemed to be the only way to persuade Costa Rica to return the jewels to her.

The agreement to pay the $1.5 million had been made with the Director of the Customs Office, but she had left her job on January 15, and her responsibilities had been taken over by the amazingly named Guiselle Joya. *Joya* means jewel in Spanish. Meanwhile, the jewels remain in the custody of the Banco de Costa Rica. According to *A.M. Costa Rica*, neither Pete DeLisi nor Fabio Oconitrillo has had any luck in getting a good answer regarding when the jewels might be released, nor what seems to be holding up the transfer. There was a clear paper trail describing this transaction, signed and agreed to by all parties concerned. Macondo.

Finally, there was the threat by prosecutor Edgar Ramírez to drag Ann back in for a fourth trial. Only hours after the court had acquitted Ann for the second time for the murder of her husband John Bender, even before the official acquittal documents had become part of the public record,

Ramírez announced that the government would appeal the verdict—yet again. If the appeal was successful, Ann would get a fourth trial for the exact same crime.

Declared Deputy District Attorney for Pérez Zeledón, Edgar Ramírez, "This isn't over."

Many legal experts in Costa Rica agree that a fourth trial is highly unlikely. They cite a 2014 ruling by Costa Rica's Sala IV (Constitutional Chamber of the Supreme Court) which precludes another trial for Ann because she had been found not guilty at two different trials, before two different panels of judges. According to criminal attorney Javier Llobet, a law professor at the University of Costa Rica,

> "Although Costa Rica has no prohibition against double jeopardy, there *are* limits on the state's ability to continue appealing a case. In 2006, there was a reform to the criminal code, including an article prohibiting the Prosecutor's Office from appealing a second acquittal. In 2010, that reform was reversed. Then in 2014, Sala IV ruled that the 2010 law was unconstitutional. Sala IV finally declared that there must be a 'reasonable limit' on the state's ability to continue pursuing appeals with which it disagrees."

The judges declared that without these limits, defendants would be left in perpetual legal limbo which would undoubtedly become disproportionately expensive. The judges concluded, "The state cannot act as a persecutor ad infinitum." They certainly had succeeded in the previous five years with Ann's legal cases. Team Ann truly hoped it had come to an end.

Many other Americans have run into problems in Costa Rica, and the former editor-in-chief of a local newspaper, David Boddiger, explains why this happens so often and with such grave consequences:

> "In many ways, John Bender and Ann Patton are the ultimate victims of what some of us here in Costa Rica refer to as the 'Sunshine Syndrome.' As outsiders raised under a different set of social structures and norms, we tend to falsely transpose those principles onto our new places of residence. We witness the same phenomenon time and time again. In the early 2000s it was a series of Ponzi schemes—'The Brothers' 'The Cubans' et al.—whose victims primarily, although not entirely, were foreigners who falsely believed that Costa Rica's laws and justice system would protect them from

those who sought to do harm.

"The truth is that the Costa Rican justice system is loosely controlled, significantly underfinanced, and—especially for foreigners—only selectively applied. John and Ann, with their extreme wealth and noble, yet sadly naïve, ecological ideas and blind trust in the goodness of humans, were targets the minute they stepped foot in Costa Rica. In cases like these, the wheels of justice turn dreadfully slowly, and there is no guarantee that any resolution will come of all of it. There is even less chance that the case will prompt any meaningful structural change to put a stop to the preying upon of an endless stream of dreamer-vacationers who fall in love with this natural paradise only to wind up as the latest victims of this malady we call the Sunshine Syndrome."

Ann Bender and her brother Ken Patton finally flew undisturbed out of Costa Rica and into the arms of their grandmother Ann Esworthy.

<<>>

The Bender suicide/murder was a very complicated case, one which was challenging for everyone to understand, even those with a criminal justice background. A retired FBI profiler now living in Costa Rica, who wishes to comment anonymously because of lack of firsthand information, stated:

> "We will probably never know what really happened between that troubled couple on the night of January 8, 2010. They themselves might not have known what was happening, given their severe mental health challenges. It was a very dark night, Ann was half asleep, and John was tremendously depressed. The evidence was all circumstantial. The trail of evidence was very likely contaminated by inept forensic scientists operating at the scene. Everyone was operating above their skill level, and distracted by the incredible Bender wealth, lots of it just left out for the taking in the Bender bedroom. It's very hard for poorly trained officials to keep a cool head in that situation; I understand that.

> "What is however indisputable, is that there was a hidden agenda in play involving that poor lady [Ann]. One would have to hire a

private financial forensic examiner to get to the bottom of this story, one who would trace the money that disappeared, and document each pocket it dropped into eventually, and then trace what relationship those people had to the case. I would guess that there was one or more persons being paid off. It would be a hard trace, but not impossible.

"Of course, I look at this case through the eyes of an American-trained investigator, and from that angle, this case and the judicial results were a travesty. I have taken both my adult sons aside and explained to them very carefully that when they visit us here in Costa Rica, it's a whole new ballgame. They have to really stay on their toes and not break any laws nor piss off the wrong person, particularly an authority figure. I don't want my sons to mistrust Ticos, who are some of the friendliest people on the planet, but to be aware that rules are different here, and you are really *not* innocent until proven guilty."

This assessment of the disputed criminal case in the death of John Bender was shared by various other people who commented both on and off the record. The people with the most detailed scientific information on the case, the Eikelenbooms, continued to feel that Bender's death was in all likelihood a suicide. Of course, that conclusion was not nearly as sexy and provocative as the headlines that screamed "Black Widow targets billionaire in the jungles of Central America, leaving him dead and her with enough jewels to live on to the end of her days!!" or "Ann Bender, Central America's most captivating accused murderess!!"

The person who probably best understood what happened between these two bipolar lovers was the journalist who wrote the first article on the Bender case for *Outside Magazine*, himself a bipolar sufferer, Ned Zeman. In 2011 Zeman published *The Rules of the Tunnel: My Brief Period of Madness*, in which he described his own battle with bipolar disorder; including dozens of doctors, hospitals, psychiatric meds, and finally, the BIG SOLUTION, electroconvulsive therapy, or shock treatment. Ann's brother Ken Patton had reached out to Zeman, also from Michigan, and interested him in writing about the Bender saga for *Vanity Fair*.

Zeman was a former *Sports Illustrated* writer with years of experience writing about precisely the same sort of people as John and Ann: fearless adventurers, sparkly, half-mad, charismatic people who flew just a little too close to the sun. Zeman called non-bipolar sufferers "civilians" in his book, with a certain amount of disdain. He had written about Timothy Treadwell, "Grizzly Man," the adventurer who claimed grizzlies were misunderstood, then one killed and ate him. He also wrote about Bruno Zehnder, the eccentric penguin photographer who froze to death in 1997 while crazily chasing his models in the snow. Zeman was definitely a charter member of the bipolar disorder club, and not the least bit ashamed of it. He was especially eloquent and sympathetic after Robin Williams, probably a bipolar sufferer, hanged himself. He said, "For those of us with mental illness, Robin Williams' death brings a visceral pain." He called Williams "one of the half-mad charismatics, who burned brightly, then like Williams, died lonely, violent deaths." Zeman knew exactly what Bender life was like, in all its madness and mayhem.

Someone else who would have also been sympathetic and understanding of the Benders, was the late Carrie Fisher, Princess Leia of *Star Wars*, herself a bipolar sufferer, who wrote in her advice column in *The Guardian* in November 2016, to a young sufferer of bipolar disorder,

"We have been given a challenging illness, and there is no other option than to meet those challenges. Think of it as an opportunity to be heroic—not 'I survived living in Mosul during an attack' heroic, but an emotional survival. An opportunity to be a good example to others who might share our disorder. That's why it's important to find a community—however small—of other bipolar people to share experiences and find comfort and similarities."

That is exactly the kind of community Ann had proposed she would like to build at Boracayán for those suffering from bipolar disorder and other mental illnesses.

Carrie Fisher humorously described her vision of celebrating bipolar disorder in her book *Wishful Drinking*.

"I thought I would inaugurate a Bipolar Pride day. You know, with floats and parades and stuff! On the floats we would get the depressives, and they wouldn't even have to leave their beds—we'd just roll their beds out of their houses, and they would continue staring off miserably into space. And for the manics, we'd have the manic marching band, with manics laughing and talking and shopping and fucking and making bad judgment calls."

One thing is for sure about the Bender legend. Law professors will be using it as a tutorial for novice law students to teach the challenges of practicing law in the international spotlight, with the immense pressure of journalists hounding them and misunderstanding the Tico legal system. Relocation experts will use it as a cautionary tale for those wishing to relocate to paradise. Farmers in the Diamante Valley will pass down the story of when the rich gringos came and tried to tame both the jungle and the legal system, unsuccessfully. The story will live on like the legend of the rualdo bird, for eternity.

As Ann Bender said to Ned Zeman of *Vanity Fair*, "The story is far from over. Nothing is over. Nothing."

Love Story for the Ages

"… and in the space that he had occupied in her memory, she allowed a field of poppies to bloom."

Gabriel García Márquez - *Love in the Time of Cholera*

In 2006 an erotic thriller movie was filmed in Costa Rica titled *Tropix*. The plot involves a tropical vacation that goes sordid, as the main character learns that her husband is a crook who has plundered his parents. The scenery is fantastic, the acting average, the music (by Tico musician Walter Flores) is amazing, and there are wonderful scenes of Guápiles, Playa Escondida, Parque Este, and San José. The most poignant reminder of the Bender saga in this film is the tagline,

> Come to Costa Rica.
> See endangered species.
> Become one.
> More than paradise will be lost!!!

The Benders had arrived in Costa Rica in 1998, filled with a sense of adventure and commitment to make a new start and enjoy their recent passion for each other in an ecological wonderland. They shared two very profound loves: a love for all animals, and a love for solitude. Unfortunately, they also shared bipolar disorder and clinical depression. The deck was perhaps stacked against them for achieving happiness in this peaceful country. Things went terribly wrong for them soon after they arrived and continued to worsen as the years went by. It was tragic for them, their families, and their employees. Those who met them during their years at Boracayán were divided as to whether or not they thought Ann Bender had killed her husband, or he had committed suicide as she claimed.

CRAZY JUNGLE LOVE

Susan Spencer, the *48 Hours* correspondent for CBS News, commented about the time she had spent with Ann Bender while filming "Paradise Lost: Investigating the death of John Bender" for *48 Hours*, in 2014.

> "You can usually get a sense of who's telling the truth. I didn't come away after talking to Ann Bender with any sense of that. I defy anyone who looks at all the facts in this story to say definitely 'This is what happened.'"

The reporter for *Inside Costa Rica* claimed that interviews with key players in this drama resulted only in confusion. One day it looked like Ann was innocent and abused, the next day like Ann was guilty of justifiable homicide. The truth remains unknowable. The mystery will last forever, discussed around punch bowls at gringo gatherings and Fourth of July picnic table fiestas. Everyone seems to have their own theory of what really happened, which keeps the story alive, despite Ann having moved back to the United States, probably never to return to Boracayán or Costa Rica ever again.

Today, the death of multi-millionaire John Bender rounds out the top three most mysterious events to have ever occurred in Costa Rica.

First on the list, is the mystery of the Esferas de Piedra (Stone Spheres) of the Diquis Delta. Some three hundred almost perfectly shaped spheres were discovered in the 1940s by agricultural workers of the United Fruit Company. They range in size from ping pong balls to the size of an automobile. The biggest ball weighs sixteen tons. They are made of granodiorite, a very hard stone which comes from a quarry fifty miles away from where the spheres were found. They are probably about 12,000 years old, archaeologists estimate.

Were they brought there by aliens? The product of an earlier race of super-humans? How could they have been so perfectly formed by supposedly primitive indigenous people of that area? Who moved them there, how, and why? The 1968 movie *Chariots of the Gods* mentioned them, and they have appeared in pseudo-scientific articles galore. The best archaeologists' minds have pondered their origins with no definitive answers. The Spheres are both a beloved Tico mystery and a very popular tourist attraction.

Second on the list is the mystery of the Great Treasure of Lima, Peru, estimated to be worth $208 million in today's money, and allegedly buried on the Costa Rican Island of Cocos.

In 1820, Lima found itself in the midst of the Peruvian War of Independence from Spain, and on the edge of revolt, causing the Spanish Viceroy of Lima to send the huge fortune amassed by the Catholic Church to Mexico for safekeeping. The treasure trove included 113 solid gold religious statues, 200 chests of jewels, 273 jewel-encrusted swords, 1,000 diamonds, several solid gold crowns, and hundreds of gold and silver bars.

Captain William Thompson was charged with transporting the fortune on his ship the *Mary Dear.* Thompson and his crew succumbed to temptation almost immediately and turned pirate. They cut the throats of the treasure guards and priests and threw them to the sharks. Thompson and pirates headed for Cocos Island to bury the loot, planning to then split up temporarily, and later return to divvy up the spoils. After burying the treasure, the *Mary Dear* was captured, the crew convicted of piracy and hanged, while Thompson and his first mate saved themselves by promising to take their captors to Cocos to find the treasure.

Once on the island, the pair managed to escape their captors, disappear into the jungle, and were never seen again.

To this day Cocos Island attracts dozens of treasure hunters yearly. Alas, no one has yet hit the jackpot, despite fake treasure maps and vague old rumors of people claiming to have seen Thompson back in his native Newfoundland in the mid-1800s. Sophisticated expeditions of treasure hunters with the most modern equipment for finding buried metals, have returned from Cocos empty-handed. Where is the Great Treasure of Lima today? Has it already been found and removed? Who owns it now? Is it still buried on Cocos?

Yet another beloved Tico legend and mystery.

Finally, there's the third mystery, what really happened to John Bender on the night of his death in Costa Rica in 2010. Was he murdered? Did he kill himself? Was it an accidental homicide? Will Ann ever get back her fortune and the nature reserve? Ticos say *solo Dios sabe*, which means only God knows. Some of the best forensic and legal minds have addressed this conundrum and come up as empty-handed as the historians of the Stone Spheres and the treasure hunters of The Great Treasure of Lima.

We are left in Macondo, that Twilight Zone where answers are never revealed, and residents quickly learn to live with not knowing. Ann Bender might know what happened to John, but maybe she doesn't. We are left to draw our own conclusions with the limited information we have. It all becomes part of the mysterious concept of *pura vida*. It remains a crazy love story for the ages, in a country loaded with mystery, corruption and intrigue.

But hey, it's one hell of a story.

EPILOGUE

The gift that keeps on giving.

On June 23, 2017, *The Costa Rica Star* reported that the prosecution from Ann Patton Bender's third trial was ordering a fourth trial with the goal of overturning Ann's acquittal from the September, 2015, trial, in which she was acquitted of all charges in the death of her husband, John Felix Bender. The trial would be held before a new panel of three judges, and would be Ann's fourth murder trial in seven years.

Experts agree that it is very unlikely that Ann will return for another trial, and equally unlikely that Costa Rica will attempt to extradite her. Her jewels and property remain in legal limbo.

A week before this announcement, it was reported that José Fabio Pizarro, the former head of security for the Benders, was arrested while escorting a convoy of alleged cocaine smugglers on the way to Mexico with 237 kilograms of cocaine in a false-bottomed truck. He was arrested near Alajuela with three other accomplices. Prior to Pizarro's employment with the Benders, he was the head of Costa Rica's Fuerza Pública, and then worked for the border patrol. He had intimate knowledge of the backroads and escape routes throughout Costa Rica, and of course had access and knowledge of the Boracayán estate. He has yet to be brought to trial, and remains in preventive detention.

GRATITUDE

It Takes a Pueblo

There were ninety-four people interviewed for this book, and each one deserves a huge thanks for their time and efforts. Bob Brashears was the first person I shared the Crazy Jungle Love story with, and I thank him for his support and editing input. What incredible patience this man has!

I will be forever grateful to Dr. Naima Prevots, my thesis advisor, who helped me hone my writing skills back in the day. I owe a big debt of gratitude to Peter Majerle, who jumped in to save the day with the final editing process.

Thank you Tomás Sutton for guiding me through my computer challenges and for patiently helping me over the hurdles of writing in the jungle; with all its power failures and crashes. You sure know your Tico geography and history!

Thanks to my sister Kathryn Vaughn Tolstoy for encouraging me in this project, and being a sounding-board and critical reader. There is no better sister on the planet.

Thank you David Boddiger, Ned Zeman, Steven Ferris, Benjamin Marrero, Jr., and Bryan Fabio Herrera for helping me understand various crucial facets of this story.

I am deeply grateful to The Costa Rica Star for all their support in this project – you are my super heroes – Rafael Alvarez who designed the stunning book cover and amazing map of Costa Rica, Yuri Delgado for her overwhelming patience while structuring CJL, and Andrew Pike, who took on this challenging project, and always reminded me to "Breathe!"

Osvaldo Aguilar of Boracayán was my touch stone and opened windows and doors for me to understand life at Bender Dome; mil gracias, Osvaldo.

The world is worse off without Greg Fischer, who died far too young, but gave me much insight into his great love for Ann and Costa Rica before he passed. RIP.

Thank you also to the many people who were willing to share their time and knowledge of the Costa Rican legal system, prison conditions, flora and fauna, stupid gringo stories, intimate details of life in the Zona Sur, and much, much more.

Thank you all!

Author's Note

I moved to Costa Rica in 2012, two years after John Bender's death. As a volunteer Warden of the United States Embassy for Pérez Zeledón, I became familiar with the struggles of Ann Bender and began taking note of the cultural implications of my own future in this dear country. While covering Ann Bender's trials as a journalist for *Inside Costa Rica* and then for *The Costa Rica Star*, I was given the opportunity to interview many of the characters mentioned here and document their memories of what happened before, during, and after John's death. The details given are only as accurate as the memories of those who generously shared their recollections of these events. As I began to write this book, it became overwhelmingly clear to me that the story of John and Ann Bender in Costa Rica was unfolding in the style of Magical Realism, which is described as what happens when a highly detailed, realistic setting is invaded by something too strange to be believed. Gabriel García Márquez writes in this style, and each chapter is introduced with a quote from him.

At one point in my investigation I began receiving death threats on my home phone. On the advice of a wise Tico friend, I elected to not report those threats to the authorities, as no one could be sure that it was not the authorities themselves making the calls. For reasons of security, the names of all Ann's fellow prisoners at Buen Pastor were changed. Otherwise, this book remains as true to the Bender story as possible. Not everyone involved was willing to speak with me, which I regret but well understand their concerns for their own safety. I have described the incredible and tragic love story of the Benders to the best of my knowledge, but as one of the translators at Ann's first trial commented, "Accept that you can only know so much."

INDEX OF CHARACTERS,

CRAZY JUNGLE LOVE

Oscar Arias and family: One of 85 Tico millionaires and former president and Nobel Peace Prize winner.

Audrey Hepburn: American beloved ingénue movie star of *Breakfast at Tiffany's* and other films.

Bill Van Horn: Husband of Amy Schrift and fellow homesteader.

Boracayán: Bender Dome, nature reserve and compound created by the Benders in Florida de Barú, Southern Zone of Costa Rica, and as of 2017, its ownership is hotly disputed.

Brad Glassman: Bender family attorney, now deceased.

Brian Fischer: Ann's boyfriend Greg's brother.

Bruce Holst: One of researchers from Selby Gardens who visited Boracayán in 2003.

Bruno Zehnder: Eccentric penguin photographer who froze to death while chasing penguins through the ice and snow to capture them with his camera.

Calvin Ayre: Canadian who founded an online gambling operation in 1996 and was featured in *Forbes Magazine Billionaire's Edition*, owner of large property near San José.

Caroline Kennedy: American author, attorney, diplomat, and only surviving child of President John F. Kennedy, who visited El Buen Pastor Prison and blogged about it.

Carrie Fischer: American actress and comedian, Princess Leia of Star Wars movies, author of *Wishful Drinking* and other autobiographical books, bipolar sufferer.

Casey Anthony: Victim in infamous US murder trial where her mother was accused of her murder, the Eikelenbooms testified, and the mother was found innocent.

Celine Bouchacourt Martenot: Ann's prep school best friend who reunited with Ann to lend support during her three murder trials and created the *Free Ann Petition*.

Charles Brewer: Atlanta Internet millionaire, partner in building Las Catalinas Resort and Hotel.

Chepe: Nickname for San José, capital of Costa Rica.

Cristian Calvo: One of three judges who unanimously convicted Ann of murder at her second trial.

Christopher Hoare: Greenpeace *Rainbow Warrior* boat employee, boyfriend of Kimberley Blackwell who left her to return to Australia, after which she was murdered.

Cody Dial: Son of National Geographic explorer Roman Dial, disappeared on his last solo expedition in Corcovado

National Park before going off to college, found at last by indigenous, probably killed by a falling tree.

David Boddiger: Former Editor-in-Chief of *The Tico Times* who covered all three of Ann's trials and associated local news stories.

David Rains Wallace: Conservationist and environmentalist, author of *The Quetzal and the Macaw.*

Dean Barrows: Former Belizean Prime Minister and commentator on John McAfee's lifestyle and ladies.

Donald Montero Navarro: Retired defense attorney, professor of criminal justice, testified for the prosecution at Ann's trial.

Dr. Adrian Solano: Distinguished veterinarian of Pérez Zeledón, owner of Corral Del Sol Clinic, treated numerous Bender animals, both wild and domesticated.

Dr. Arturo Lizano-Vincent: Ann's San José psychiatrist who testified at all three of Ann's trials.

Dr. Franklin Chang-Diaz: Former NASA astronaut and founder and owner of Ad Astra Rocket Company.

Dr. Gretchen Flores: Renowned Tica pathologist who changed her testimony at Ann's various trials.

Dr. Husseini Manji: Researcher working on bipolar disorder at the Brain and Behavior Research Foundation (USA).

Dr. Robert Dressler: World renowned orchidologist who visited Boracayán in 2003.

Ed Bernhardt: American author, farmer, founder of the New Dawn Centre.

Edgar Ramírez: Prosecution attorney largely responsible for Ann's murder conviction at her second trial, and subsequent nine-month imprisonment.

Edward Sides: American who invested in Jacó in 1966, and needed 350 police officers to evict squatters who had illegally taken over his property, featured in *Forbes Magazine* article about Costa Rica investing.

Enilda Ramírez: Manager of the Customs Office during the time Ann made a deal with Costa Rica to get back her $7-20 million in jewels allegedly being held at Banco de Costa Rica.

Ericka Cordero Marroquín: Judge at Ann's third trial where she was once again acquitted.

Esteban López Cambronero: Chief judge at Ann's third trial where she was once again acquitted.

Fabianne Ferande and Marc Bauer: French couple who attempted to buy a hotel in La Fortuna de San Carlos, and through attorney fraud lost $475,000.

Fabio Oconitrillo: Ann Bender's lawyer and friend through all her legal challenges and heroic efforts to regain both her property and freedom.

Figueres family: One of 85 Tico millionaires, former president of Costa Rica and Civil War hero.

Francisco Sánchez: Judge who read final verdict at Ann's first trial at which she was acquitted.

Gabriel García Márquez: Colombian Nobel Literature prize-winning author and creator of "Magical Realism" style of writing which made him internationally famous and revered.

Garland Baker: Naturalized Costa Rican citizen who offers legal advice to foreigners in Costa Rica.

Gary Johnson: Libertarian Party nominee who beat McAfee for party nomination in 2016 US primaries.

Gary Pons: Barrister from Great Britain who assisted Fabio Oconitrillo at Ann's third trial.

George Jung: Former cocaine baron alleged to be writing *No Domain*, the John McAfee formal biography, if it ever is completed.

George Soros: Hungarian billionaire whose hedge fund investments John Bender once managed.

Gibran Tabash: Pérez Zeledón artist and sculptor, creator of the largest statue in Costa Rica made entirely of recycled material, i.e., newspapers.

Gigi Patton: Ann and her brother Ken's mother, and Kenneth's wife.

Greg Faull: American found dead of a gunshot wound to the back of his head in his house next door to John McAfee's in Belize. McAfee accused of his murder.

Gregory David Fischer: Ann's boyfriend, professional personal trainer, loyal supporter of Ann during and after her months in jail, died mysteriously while in bed alone while Ann was in prison.

Guiselle Joya: Director of Customs Office which is holding Ann's jewels.

Hugo Villegas: Ann's personal physician who treated her before and during her sojourn at CIMA Hospital, offered gripping testimony of Ann's condition after John's death.

Hugo Wessberg: German father of Olle Wessberg, founder of Costa Rican National Park Service.

Iliana: Protagonist of the Legend of the rualdo bird of Poás Volcano. Greg sometimes called Ann "Iliana" to remind her of how much he loved her—loved her enough to give up his song for her.

Jack Schwager: Renowned interviewer of successful hedge fund managers for his book, *Market Wizards*.

Janice Dyson: McAfee's wife and former call girl now living with him in Kentucky.

Jesse Blenn: Bender neighbor at Boracayán, designer of electric car and bicycle, fruit farmer, allegedly able to speak to those who have passed over by using a pendulum.

Jessica Benavides: Wife of Ed Bernhardt, Spanish teacher, co-founder of New Dawn Centre.

Joel Silverman: John Bender's former business partner in offshore investment hedge fund Amber Arbitrage, who sued him for $90 million and sent goons to collect the money from him in Costa Rica.

Johanna (last name withheld): Prison friend of Ann Bender while she was in Preventive Detention.

John Felix Bender: Multi-millionaire American hedge fund manager, creator of both Boracayán and Refugio Silvestre de Boracayán, died mysteriously of a single gunshot wound to the back of his head.

John McAfee: Founder of the anti-virus software company which bears his name, legendary eccentric millionaire, unsuccessful candidate for Libertarian Party for US Presidency in 2016.

Jonah Ogles: *Outside Online* reporter who covered Bender saga, working often with Susan Spencer.

Jonathan Chapman: One-time owner of Casa de Piedra cave at the top of Diamante Waterfalls and spiritual leader of alternative-living residents of that valley.

Jonathan Kaplan: Famous hedge fund manager and blogger on that topic, supporter of Ann at trial.

JonBenét Ramsey: Victim in an infamous US murder trial where family member was accused of her murder, the Eikelenbooms testified at the trial.

José Leon Sánchez: Famous Costa Rican author and survivor of 30 years in prison on San Lucas Island.

José Luis Delgado: Chief judge at Ann's first murder trial.

José Pizarro: Head of security for Imperial Park Security, charged with protecting both John and Ann.

Josh Yager: Renowned CNN and CBS producer, creator of the first *48 Hours* show which drew international attention to the John and Ann Bender drama.

Juan de Cavallón: Spanish explorer who discovered Escazú in 1561.

Juan de Dios Álvarez: Bender attorney, now accused of embezzling millions of Bender's fortune, and living the high life in Nicaragua, far from the Costa Rican long arm of the law.

Juan Santamaría: Drummer boy hero during William Walker's attempt to establish a private empire in Costa Rica, who died in battle in 1856. Airport in Alajuela is named after him.

Julian Assange: Australian Editor-in-Chief of *WikiLeaks*, who was arrested for sexual assault and hid in the London Ecuadorian Embassy to escape arrest

Karen Morgenson: Wife of "Olle," Nils Olaf Wessberg, and raw foods and holistic medicine advocate.

Kathy Turetzky: Girlfriend, now wife of Ann Bender's brother Ken, creator of *Free Ann Bender Petition*.

Kenneth Patton III: Ann's Chase Manhattan Bank executive father and loyal supporter of Ann.

Kenneth Patton IV: Ann's older brother and staunch supporter of her throughout her ordeal, now married to Kathy Turetzky and working anew as a credit portfolio manager in Michigan.

Kimberley Ann Blackwell: Canadian homesteader on Osa Peninsula, girlfriend of Australian Christopher Hoare, killed probably by animal poachers angry at her opposition of their using her farm for hunting.

Laura Chinchilla: Costa Rica's first female president, wildly unpopular, and unhelpful to Ann.

Laurie Birch: One of researchers from Selby Gardens who visited Boracayán in 2003.

Linda Silverman: Joel Silverman's wife from whom Joel divorced with huge financial consequences.

Liner Zúñiga Herrera: One of three judges who unanimously convicted Ann of murder at her second trial.

Lisa Artz: American resident manager of Casa Tres Palmas eco-lodge near Corcovado Park, who died under mysterious circumstances, like several others in or near Corcovado.

Luis Aguilar: Investigator who testified for the prosecution at Ann's trials.

Luis Oses: Prosecutor at Ann's first trial at which she was acquitted of all charges.

Manuel Morales Vásquez: Judge at Ann's third trial where she was once again acquitted.

Manuel Noriega: Panamanian military dictator from 1983-1989, removed from power by US during the Invasion of Panama in 1989 and imprisoned under a 30-year sentence for drug trafficking and money laundering. Noriega died May 29, 2017, in Panama City.

Marco Vargas: One of the two remaining staff members at Boracayán, in charge of preventing the surrounding jungle from reclaiming Boracayán as its own.

Margaret and Michael: Famous 19th Century French couple who suffered from folie à deux.

Margie Bender: John Bender's adoring mother, wife of Paul Bender.

Marissel Descalzo: Lawyer who conducted witness preparation at Ann's third trial.

Mark Meadows: Blogger who lives on Osa Peninsula, blogs under "Eco-Tourists and Gold Miners."

Marlon Brando: American actor and star of the movie *The Ugly American*, 1963.

Matilde Gutierrez: Jesse Blenn's wife and co-manager of his electric car and bike project, allegedly able to channel the dead, including John Bender.

Mel Gibson: Celebrity actor who purchased real estate at Playa Barrigona in Nicoya, Guanacaste, Costa Rica, currently on sale for $30 million.

Michael Jackson: Famous American pop music star who attracted press in US in the same way Ann Bender did in Costa Rica.

Millie: Ann's cherished German shepherd service dog, now deceased.

Moisés Calderón: Guard on duty at Boracayán on the night of John's death, first person into the Bender bedroom after John's death, responding to a call on walkie-talkie from Ann for help.

Ña Matea: Witch who was rumored to be able to relieve you of the curse of the Evil Eye.

Ned Zeman: Writer for *Outside Online* and *Vanity Fair* who wrote detailed article on the Bender's life at Boracayán and the aftermath of Ann's first trial and acquittal; also suffered from bipolar disorder.

Nils Olaf Wessberg (Olle): Founder of the Costa Rican National Park Service, beginning with the oldest park, Reserva Natural Absoluta Cabo Blanco, and finishing up with Corcovado National Park.

Norlico Ratón: Infamous witch of Escazú rumored to possess amazing magical powers.

O.J. Simpson: Famous American football player accused of killing his wife Nicole Brown Simpson and a male friend of hers, one of the most memorable trials in American history.

Osvaldo Aguilar: Guard, chauffeur, property manager, grounds maintenance man, and Ann's guardian angel when she needed him most after John's death.

Osvaldo Rojas: Bender majordomo for 13 years, only person allowed into family quarters at Bender Dome, in charge of shopping, animal care, trusted household manager, now working as a vet tech in Pérez Zeledón.

Otzi the Iceman: 5,300-year-old mummy found in Europe, who had Lyme disease bacteria in his body.

Paul Bender: John Bender's father and distinguished law professor at Penn State University.

Paul Meyer: American tree farmer and nextdoor neighbor of the Benders at Boracayán.

Paul Watson: Founder of the Sea Shepherd Conservation Society, known to some as an "eco-terrorist."

Perry Mason: Television show about a trial lawyer, very popular during the mid-twentieth century as a television series incorporating cleverly solved criminal court cases.

Pete DeLisi: John Bender's best friend and fellow hedge fund manager, now in charge of remaining Bender holdings in Costa Rica, loyal friend to Ann in her time of need.

President Barack Obama: American president during most of Ann's trials, and all her months in prison.

Randall Baldí: Well-known taxi driver of Pérez Zeledón and commentator on PZ life and culture.

Randi Kaye: CNN journalist, creator of "Inside the Mystery: Love and Death in Paradise," about the Benders.

Renee Ellory: Deception and credibility expert who blogged about Bender case.

Richard Eikelenboom: Dutch forensic expert in Touch DNA who testified at Ann's trial after having done many thorough recreations of the crime scene with his wife, both in Colorado and at Boracayán.

Rob Lasco: Friend of Gregory Fischer who spoke warmly of Greg online after his death.

Robert Sprague: American who invested in Escazú in 1982 and became the victim of a notorious land swindle, described in *Forbes Magazine* in an article about investing in Costa Rica.

Robin Williams: American actor, movie and television star, comedian, and probable bipolar disorder sufferer who committed suicide in 2016.

Roger Peterson: Well-known lawyer at *CostaRicaLaw.com*, who specializes in land disputes.

Roman Dial: National Geographic explorer, father of Cody Dial and creator of documentary describing efforts to find his lost son in the wilds of Corcovado National Park.

Rosemary Sylvester Bradley: British microbiologist and chocolatier who sold Benders seeds for Boracayán, and helped when they were arrested on the Quebradas Road.

San Isidro del Labrador: Patron Saint of Agriculture after whom town of San Isidro was named.

Santiago and Ana: Owners of Zima Hotel (Best Western), and good friends of Ann Bender.

Sara (last name withheld): Prison friend of Ann Bender while she was in Preventive Detention, San José.

Scott Barry Kaufman: *Psychology Today* researcher, expert in psychotic behavior.

Selma Eikelenboom: Dutch forensic expert, wife of Richard, founder of the Crime Farm, testified at Ann's third trial where she was acquitted—yet again.

Sheldon Haseltine: US/UK citizen who became the poster boy for Costa Rican land fraud battles.

Sonia Escobio O'Donnell: Bilingual American lawyer who assisted at Ann's third trial, and had previously worked at the trial of Panamanian dictator Manuel Noriega.

Stanley Victor Paskavich: Author of *Genius by Birth, Bipolar by Design*, an often-funny description of life as a person living with bipolar disorder.

Stephen Baker: Barrister of Seven Bedford Row from Great Britain who assisted Fabio Oconitrillo with Ann Bender's defense at her third trial which resulted in her acquittal.

Steven Ferris: Legal consultant to Tico Times newspaper throughout Ann's three trials.

Susan Spencer: Award-winning *48 Hours* correspondent for CBS who documented Ann's saga in "Paradise Lost: Investigating the Death of John Bender."

Timothy Masters: First touch-DNA exoneration case in the US, which found Masters not guilty in murder of Peggy Hettrick in 1987, based on crime scene DNA analysis.

Timothy Treadwell: Grizzly Man, adventurer who died while chasing grizzly bears and, along with his girlfriend, was eaten by the bears.

Tom Claugus: Atlanta hedge fund billionaire who partnered in building Las Catalinas Resort and Hotel.

Walter Hibbard Esworthy: Ann's grandfather, husband of Ann Esworthy, responsible for introducing the Selby Gardens research team to Boracayán.

William Walker: American who attempted to establish a private slave-holding empire in Costa Rica, but was defeated; famous often-told legend of Tico history.

Willy Burgdorfer, PhD: Researcher who identified the bacteria which causes Lyme disea.

About Carol

Carol Blair Vaughn was raised in Latin America. She is the daughter of Jack Hood Vaughn, a former US Ambassador, Director of the Peace Corps, and Assistant Secretary of State for Latin American Affairs. She holds a Master's Degree in Performing Arts and retired from a career as a college professor of Dance and Theatre in Washington, DC.

She has written for *Inside Costa Rica*, *El Residente* and *The Costa Rica Star*. Carol has lived in the south of Costa Rica in the town of Quebradas, not far from Boracayán, for the last five years. This is Carol's first book, but she plans to write several more, all exploring the marvels and mysteries of her new home in Costa Rica. Carol volunteers as a Warden of the United States Embassy, helping Americans in distress.